USING ENGLISH
GRAMMAR AND WRITING SKILLS

**THIRD
COURSE**

Aᴅʀɪᴀɴ B. Sᴀɴꜰᴏʀᴅ

 CENTER FOR THE STUDY OF INSTRUCTION
San Francisco

 HARCOURT BRACE JOVANOVICH
New York   Chicago   San Francisco   Atlanta   Dallas   *and*   London

THE AUTHOR

ADRIAN B. SANFORD has taught English for more than a quarter of a century. He has also written materials for English instruction and conducted workshops for educators.

CONSULTING EDUCATORS AND TEACHERS

ENNO KLAMMER
Eastern Oregon State College
La Grande, Oregon

CYNTHIA BAKER
Starr King Intermediate
Carmichael, California

MARIAN O. JENKINS
Coral Springs High School
Coral Springs, Florida

JACK STRANGE
Arcade Intermediate
Carmichael, California

JO ANN STEWART
Lowell High School
San Francisco, California

BARBARA S. DEAN
Will Rogers School
Fair Oaks, California

ROBERT LEON
Palo Alto High School
Palo Alto, California

SYBILLE IRWIN
Winston Churchill Intermediate
Carmichael, California

KEITH CALDWELL
Kennedy High School
Fremont, California

JUDY A. KANTER
Howe Avenue Intermediate
Sacramento, California

KEITH WILL
San Juan Unified School District
Carmichael, California

BARBARA COULTER
Louis Pasteur School
Orangeville, California

ACKNOWLEDGMENTS

The publisher gratefully acknowledges the contributions of Jo Ann Stewart and Charlotte Herbert to the preparation of the Review Exercises for the series.

For permission to reprint copyrighted material, grateful acknowledgment is made to the following sources:

Harcourt Brace Jovanovich, Inc.: Excerpts from *The HBJ School Dictionary.* Copyright © 1977 by Harcourt Brace Jovanovich, Inc.

Oxford University Press: From a reprinting of *Mulcaster's Elementarie* edited by E. T. Campagnac.

The H. W. Wilson Company: Excerpt from *Reader's Guide to Periodical Literature.* Copyright © 1977 by The H. W. Wilson Company.

Brandt & Brandt: Excerpt from *Master of Morgana* by Allen Campbell McLean. Copyright © 1959 by Allen Campbell McLean.

DIANA WHITELEY
Project Editor

PATRICIA HOSLEY
Editor

SALLY THOMPSON
Text Designer

Printed in the United States of America

ISBN 0-15-311702-8

TO THE STUDENT

As you begin using this book, take time to become familiar with its special features. Notice the organization of sections and chapters of the book as shown in the Contents. Look within a chapter to see how the rules and definitions are printed. Note the use of color and special type to highlight important points.

An alphabetized index in the back of the book lists all the important topics in the textbook, with their page numbers. The colored tabs at the corners of the pages allow you to find any topic by its chapter number. The glossary in the back of the book gives an alphabetical listing of special terms in English. Each is followed by a definition. Many of the terms have examples to illustrate their meaning or use.

On certain pages you can see cross references printed in the margins. These refer you to other parts of the text where you can find additional information.

These features—and more—have been built into the book to aid you.

From this textbook you can learn a great deal about how to improve your use of English. Improvement, however, requires that you apply yourself to studying the book and to using what you can learn from it. As either a textbook assigned by your teacher or a reference tool in which you find what you need, this book offers you the opportunity to grow stronger in using English.

A.B.S.

CONTENTS

Preface   **iii**

UNIT ONE: GRAMMAR AND STRUCTURE

1 Parts of Speech   **3**
Nouns, Pronouns, Adjectives

*Nouns, Common Nouns and Proper
Nouns, Singular Nouns and Plural
Nouns, Possessive Nouns, Compound
Nouns, Pronouns, Personal Pronouns,
Relative Pronouns, Interrogative
Pronouns, Indefinite Pronouns,
Adjectives, Comparison of Adjectives,
Irregular Adjectives*

2 Parts of Speech   **27**
Verbs, Adverbs, Prepositions,
Conjunctions, Interjections

*Verbs, Action Verbs, Transitive and
Intransitive Verbs, Linking Verbs,
Helping Verbs, Tense, Regular Verbs,
Irregular Verbs, Adverbs, Irregular
Adverbs, Prepositions, Object of the
Preposition, Conjunctions, Coordinating
Conjunctions, Subordinating
Conjunctions, Interjections, Words as
Different Parts of Speech*

3 Phrases   **59**
Noun Phrases, Prepositional
Phrases, Verb Phrases

*Kinds of Phrases, Noun Phrases, Verb
Phrases, Prepositional Phrases*

4 Clauses   **73**
Independent Clauses, Dependent
Clauses

*The Parts of a Clause, Kinds of Clauses,
Independent Clauses, Dependent
Clauses, Kinds of Dependent Clauses*

5 Sentences   **89**
The Sentence, Sentence Problems

*The Sentence, The Subject, The
Predicate, Compound Subject and
Compound Predicate, Types of
Sentences, Purposes of Sentences,
Completers, The Patterns of Sentences,
Sentence Problems, Sentence
Fragments, Run-on Sentences*

UNIT TWO: COMPOSITION

6 Paragraphs   **126**
Developing Paragraphs

7 Guidelines for Writing   **147**
*Choosing Your Topic and Your
Audience, Organizing Your Writing,
Choosing Your Words, Revising Your
Writing*

8 Letter Writing   171

*Preparing the Letter, The Business
Letter, A Request Letter, An Order
Letter, A Letter of Complaint or
Adjustment, Mailing Your Letter*

9 Using Parts of Speech   184

*Agreement of Subjects and Verbs,
Special Verb Problems, Active Verbs
and Passive Verbs, Irregular Verbs,
Special Pronoun Problems, Personal
Pronouns,* Who *and* Whom, *Problems
with Adjectives and Adverbs, The
Double Negative*

10 Common Confusions   216

Alphabetical Listing

UNIT FOUR: MECHANICS

11 Capitalization   238

Capital Letters

12 Punctuation   249
End Punctuation, Commas

*End Punctuation, The Period, The
Question Mark, The Exclamation Mark,
Inside Punctuation, The Comma*

13 Punctuation 267

Semicolons, Colons, Hyphens, Apostrophes, Quotation Marks, Italics, Parentheses

Inside Punctuation, the Semicolon, The Colon, The Hyphen, The Apostrophe, Italics (the Underline), Enclosing Punctuation, Quotation Marks, Parentheses

UNIT FIVE: AIDS AND ENRICHMENT

14 Speaking and Listening 286

Informal Conversation, Introductions, The Telephone, Giving Directions, Formal Speaking and Listening, Outlining, Delivering Your talk

15 Spelling 307

Rules for Good Spelling, Prefixes, Suffixes, Sounds of Letters, Homonyms

16 Sources of Information 328

Textbooks, The Dictionary, The Library, Other Sources of Information

17 Using Words 351

The Meaning of Words

Glossary 366

Index 386

Tab Key Index 397

UNIT ONE

GRAMMAR AND STRUCTURE

Parts of Speech
Phrases
Sentences

1

PARTS OF SPEECH

Nouns, Pronouns, Adjectives

The words you use every day are divided into eight *parts of speech*. *Nouns* and *pronouns* are two parts of speech that name persons or things. You use nouns and pronouns often when you write or speak.

You also use *adjectives* often. Adjectives help describe, or modify, nouns and pronouns.

This chapter presents various kinds of nouns, pronouns, and adjectives you can use. It shows their forms and their uses. It will give you practice in making good use of these three parts of speech.

NOUNS

1a A noun is a word or a group of words used to name someone or something.

Nouns may name living things, such as people, animals, or plants.

EXAMPLES   Joe Wilkins, goalie, Lassie, petunias

Nouns may name nonliving things, such as earth, water, air, manufactured items, places, and even ideas.

EXAMPLES   rocks, river, gas, locomotive, cities, envy

A word used to name any person or thing you can think of is called a noun.

EXERCISE 1 The following sentences contain nouns. Number a sheet of paper 1–8. Next to each number, write the nouns that appear in each sentence.

EXAMPLE   Horses were useful to humans in ancient days.

horses, humans, days

1. Horses have been used by people for many years.
2. Horses were once a favorite food of the tribes of Asia and Europe.
3. Then it was discovered that the strength and speed of the horse could transport people and goods over distances.
4. The Egyptians and the Greeks used horses for work and for sport.
5. Some countries trained horses to carry soldiers into war.
6. The Spaniards first brought horses to America.

7. Until automobiles were invented, the horse was widely used in Europe, North America, and other parts of the world.
8. Horses are still used by farmers, police, and ranchers.

Common Nouns and Proper Nouns

(1) A common noun names a kind of person, place, or thing. A proper noun names a particular person, place, or thing.

Here are some examples.

COMMON NOUNS	PROPER NOUNS
house	White House
country	Egypt
man	Roosevelt
woman	Billie Jean
party	Republicans

Hint: A proper noun always begins with a capital letter.

If a proper noun is made up of more than one word, each important word begins with a capital letter.

EXAMPLES Lucille Jarvis, Griffith Park, Bank of the Midwest, Old Testament

EXERCISE 2 Write two headings at the top of a sheet of paper: *Common, Proper.* List the nouns at the top of the next page under the correct heading. Capitalize all the proper nouns.

twig, susanne walton, balcony, wheel, africa,
paris, greed, datsun, television, washington,
troy, summer, smoke, buick, michigan, cloud,
world, sugar, argentina, people

Singular Nouns and Plural Nouns

1b A noun may be singular or plural.

A noun that names only one person or thing is
singular. A noun that names more than one is
plural.

EXAMPLES	SINGULAR NOUNS	PLURAL NOUNS
	home	homes
	pond	ponds
	idea	ideas

See Spelling, pp. 310–312 Most singular nouns add the letter **s** to form
the plural. Other singular nouns that end in **s**, **x**,
ch, **sh**, or **z** usually form the plural by adding **es**.

EXAMPLES gas/gas**es**, hex/hex**es**,
match/match**es**, sash/sash**es**,
quiz/qui**zz**es
[Note that some nouns double the **z**
before adding **es.**]

Singular nouns that end in **y** with a consonant
before it form the plural this way: The **y** changes to
i and **es** is added.

EXAMPLES city, cit**ies**
country, countr**ies**

n

A few irregular nouns form the plural from the singular in different ways or do not change at all.

SINGULAR	PLURAL
goose	geese
ox	oxen
deer	deer
salmon	salmon

EXERCISE 3 Some of the following nouns are singular; others are plural. Number a sheet of paper 1-10 and rewrite each noun. Make the singular nouns plural and the plural nouns singular.

EXAMPLE tray

trays

1. pickle
2. army
3. ponies
4. playground
5. ax

6. branches
7. flies
8. buses
9. blouses
10. lady

Possessive Nouns

1c A noun can show that something else belongs to it or is related to it.

EXAMPLES the cat's paw, Marie's purse, Joe's classmate

When a noun shows this relationship, it is in the *possessive case*. The possessive case of most nouns is formed by adding an apostrophe (') and an **s**.

See Case, p. 368

EXAMPLES girl's shoe, winter's storms, car's exhaust

Most plural nouns already end in **s.** They do not need another **s** to show possession. Only the apostrophe is needed.

EXAMPLES rabbits' tails, musicians' union, states' highways

Plural nouns that do not end in **s** form the possessive by adding the apostrophe and the **s.**

EXAMPLES women's clothes, children's toys

If two or more people own something together, put the possessive on the last name only.

EXAMPLE Tom and Jack's store

EXERCISE 4 The following sentences need a possessive case of the noun to fill the blanks. After each sentence is a noun in parentheses. Number a sheet of paper 1-10. After each number, write the correct possessive case of the noun to fill the blank.

EXAMPLE _____ science class has been studying the ocean. (Carla and Monte)

Carla and Monte's

1. They learned that the _____ gravity causes tides in the ocean. (moon)
2. Life along the shoreline is affected by the _____ actions. (tides)
3. A _____ food, for example, is brought up by the high tide. (barnacle)

4. Many _____ lives depend upon the tides. (creatures)

5. _____ project was to study life in tide pools. (Monte and Carla)

6. Carla borrowed her _____ car to drive to the shore. (mother)

7. Carla and Monte searched for pools along the _____ edge. (water)

8. While they were jumping along the rocks, _____ feet slipped on some seaweed. (Monte)

9. It was _____ quick help that saved him from falling into the ocean. (Carla)

10. The _____ trip brought them knowledge and adventure. (day)

Compound Nouns

A *compound noun* is two or more words used together as a single noun.

> EXAMPLES baseball, footpaths, highway, great-grandmother

Some compound nouns are written as one word.

> EXAMPLE footstep

Other compound nouns are written with hyphens.

> EXAMPLE trade-ins

Still others are written as separate words.

> EXAMPLE Chamber of Commerce

If you are not sure how to write a compound noun, look it up in a dictionary.

PRONOUNS

1d A pronoun is a word used to take the place of a noun or a noun word group.

Here are some common pronouns and the nouns for which they can stand.

PRONOUNS	NOUNS
I	(the person speaking or writing)
you	(the person[s] you are talking or writing to)
he	a man or boy
she	a woman or girl
it	a thing, such as a table, a seashell, a cloud, or an animal
we	a group of people including yourself

EXERCISE 5 Each of the following sentences has one or more pronouns in it. Number a sheet of paper 1–6. After each number, write the pronouns in the sentence.

EXAMPLE In the olden days, pirates buried treasure after they stole it.

they, it

1. I heard that Long Nose Nick buried gold bars on this island.
2. Before Long Nose Nick died, he drew this map.
3. Grandma found it when she was cleaning the attic.
4. You and I are standing near the place where Long Nose Nick buried the treasure.

5. We need to dig under that tree, for the map says that it marks the spot.
6. Since Grandma found the map, we should share the treasure with her.

Personal Pronouns

1e **A personal pronoun stands for a noun or noun word group that names a particular person, place, or thing.**

EXAMPLE The women at the club gave Jeff a trophy.
They gave *him* a trophy.

The pronoun *they* stands for the noun word group *the women at the club*. The pronoun *him* stands for *Jeff*.

PERSONAL PRONOUNS

Singular	Plural
I, me, my, mine	we, us, our, ours
you, your, yours	you, your, yours
he, him, his	
she, her, hers	they, them, their, theirs
it, its	

The use of a pronoun in a sentence determines its form. This is called its *case*. Some personal pronouns change case depending on how they are used. For example, the pronoun *I* changes to *me* if it receives the action of a sentence.

EXAMPLES *I* chase Prince around the yard.
[*I* shows who the actor is who chases Prince.]

Then Prince chases *me*.
[The word *me* shows who receives
the action. *Prince* does the chasing.]

(1) The *subjective case* of the personal pronoun
shows who is the actor of a sentence.

He eats a full meal each day.
I like to see Prince happy.

(2) The *objective case* of the personal pronoun
shows the object or result of the sentence
action.

EXAMPLES   I feed *him* daily.
He makes *me* happy.

Here are subjective and objective case forms of
personal pronouns.

SUBJECTIVE CASE	OBJECTIVE CASE
	Singular
I	me
you	you
he	him
she	her
it	it
	Plural
we	us
you	you
they	them

EXERCISE 6   Each of these sentences is followed
by a personal pronoun in parentheses. Rewrite each
sentence. Take out the noun or noun word group
that is underlined. Put in the personal pronoun in
the objective case.

EXAMPLE When people heard Bella's dream story, they did not believe *Bella*. (she)

When people heard Bella's dream story, they did not believe her.

1. She claimed that she would invade the earth and conquer the earth. (it)
2. Bella said strange soldiers from another planet were backing Bella. (she)
3. Bella had agreed to lead the soldiers. (they)
4. "Where are you going to lead the soldiers?" asked Bella's father. (they)
5. Bella said to her father that after another dream, she would tell her father. (he)

(3) The *possessive* case of the personal pronoun shows that something belongs to someone or something.

EXAMPLES *My* idea is as good as *yours*.
But, *their* plan is better than *ours*.

Some possessive pronouns modify nouns. When they do, they are often thought of as adjectives.

See Adjectives, pp. 16–17

EXAMPLES *my* idea, *their* house

POSSESSIVE PRONOUNS

Singular	Plural
my, mine	our, ours
your, yours	your, yours
his	
her, hers	their, theirs
it, its	

EXERCISE 7   Each of the following sentences has a blank in it and a personal pronoun in parentheses following it. Rewrite each sentence, putting in the possessive case of the pronoun.

EXAMPLE   The bank teller saw the gun in _____ coat. (I)

The bank teller saw the gun in my coat.

1. She pressed the alarm button next to _____ chair. (she)
2. Several police officers came out of _____ hiding places. (they)
3. They told me to put _____ hands in the air. (I)
4. A detective showed me _____ I.D. card and said I was under arrest. (he)
5. He told the teller, "_____ quick thinking saved the day." (You)
6. When he saw _____ I.D. card, the detective almost fell down. (I)
7. _____ words and numbers showed that I was a police officer, too. (it)
8. "_____ quick thinking might have ruined the day," I said. (She)
9. "_____ suspects left the bank while you were arresting me," I added. (We)
10. "_____ next robbery will not be at this bank," I said. (They)
11. The detective looked embarrassed as _____ face turned bright red. (he)
12. Then the three of _____ started laughing out loud at the big mix-up. (we)

Relative, Interrogative, and Indefinite Pronouns

Other kinds of pronouns are also used in speech and writing. Three main kinds are *relative pronouns, interrogative pronouns,* and *indefinite pronouns.*

Relative pronouns relate back to persons or things referred to earlier. Relative pronouns include *that, which, who, whom,* and *whose.*

EXAMPLES   We saw the photo *that* won the prize.
The women *whose* car horn was stuck became angry.

Interrogative pronouns usually begin a question. Interrogative pronouns include *what, which, who, whom,* and *whose.*

EXAMPLES   *What* do you want?
Which will fit?

Indefinite pronouns are used to name living or nonliving things. Indefinite pronouns include the following words:

all	more	each
another	most	either
any	nobody	much
anybody	none	neither
anyone	no one	some
anything	one	somebody
everybody	other	someone
everything	others	something
few	several	
many	both	

EXAMPLES   *Much* needs to be done.
              Nobody can do it.

EXERCISE 8   Each of the following sentences has one or more pronouns. Number a sheet of paper 1–8. Next to each number, write all the pronouns in the sentence.

EXAMPLE   What is the most anybody can pay?

what, most, anybody

1. Mavis entered the gate which the others went through.
2. Everyone had something to say.
3. A few wanted to ride the loop-the-loop, which cost fifty cents.
4. "What does Mavis want to ride?" someone asked.
5. Mavis said that everybody should go on the same ride.
6. Some wanted to go on another.
7. No one could agree with what others wanted to do.
8. Who would decide on something for everybody?

ADJECTIVES

1f   **An adjective is a word used to modify or describe a noun or a pronoun.**

An adjective tells *what kind, which one, how much,* or *how many.*

EXAMPLES

what kind	a *wild* dog	a *broken* axle
which one	a *thin* man	the *oldest* tree
how much or how many	*high* water	*some* icebergs

The words *a, an,* and *the* are special adjectives. They are called *articles*.

EXERCISE 9 Copy the following sentences. Circle the nouns, then underline the adjectives. Draw an arrow from each adjective to the noun it describes. Do not underline the articles *a, an,* and *the*.

EXAMPLE   I, Reginald, heard the noise of tiny feet in the darkness.

I, (Reginald), heard the (noise) of tiny (feet) in the (darkness).

1. Then there was a small squeak.
2. So the fancy traps had not worked after all!
3. A little thief was still sneaking around the quiet house.
4. Then I saw a small shadow race across the bright hallway.
5. The nasty mouse darted under the large clock and hid there.
6. But my sharp eyes had seen it.
7. The mouse could never make the long run to the kitchen.
8. And I now stood between it and the dark room.

9. When the mouse moved, I would catch it with my strong paws.
10. The little mouse would take the place of stale, old cat food.

See Sentences,
pp. 104–107

Most adjectives come in front of the nouns they modify. However, some adjectives are placed after the noun. These adjectives complete the description of a noun and are called *adjective completers*.

EXAMPLE Marianne is *honest*.

Comparison of Adjectives

1g An adjective may change form to show how one thing compares with another.

When comparing two things, most adjectives change from the *positive form* to the *comparative form*.

EXAMPLE
POSITIVE FORM This light bulb is *bright*.
COMPARATIVE FORM That bulb is *brighter*.

Most adjectives add **er** to show the comparative.

EXAMPLES	POSITIVE	COMPARATIVE
	bold	bold**er**
	small	small**er**
	young	young**er**
	soft	soft**er**

To compare three or more things, most adjectives change form again. They add **est,** as in *bold, bolder, boldest*. The **est** form is called the *superlative form*.

EXAMPLES

POSITIVE	COMPARATIVE	SUPERLATIVE
tough	tough**er**	tough**est**
short	short**er**	short**est**
wild	wild**er**	wild**est**

EXERCISE 10 Each of the following sentences is followed by an adjective in parentheses. Number a sheet of paper 1–10. Next to each number, write the positive, comparative, or superlative form of the adjective that belongs in the blank.

EXAMPLE   Cecelia has the _____ hair of any girl in school. (long)

longest

1. An alligator has _____ skin. (rough)
2. New York has the _____ buildings I have ever seen. (tall)
3. Wyoming has the _____ skies of any state in this country. (blue)
4. She had the _____ eyes of any girl I have met. (green)
5. Godzilla was a _____ monster than Frankenstein. (large)
6. Her hair was _____ than other hair I had seen. (thin)
7. That game of checkers was the _____ game we ever played. (long)
8. The eclipse in November was a _____ one than the eclipse in December. (dark)
9. This computer is the _____ machine our company has ever designed. (smart)
10. Our computer, made in the shape of a pumpkin, is still a _____ calculator. (fast)

If an adjective is a long word, it usually does not add **er** and **est** in the comparative and superlative forms. Instead, the words *more* and *most* are used in front of the positive form.

EXAMPLES

POSITIVE	COMPARATIVE	SUPERLATIVE
desirable	more desirable	most desirable
dependable	more dependable	most dependable
exciting	more exciting	most exciting

Irregular Adjectives

A few adjectives do not form the comparative and superlative forms in either of the ways shown. These adjectives are called *irregular adjectives.* Here are forms of common irregular adjectives.

POSITIVE	COMPARATIVE	SUPERLATIVE
bad	worse	worst
good	better	best
many much	more	most

EXERCISE 11 Each of the following sentences is followed by an adjective in parentheses. Number a sheet of paper 1–10. After each number write the correct form of the adjective in the blank.

EXAMPLE The floorboards in the haunted house made the _____ noise I had ever heard. (frightening)

most frightening

1. Next, the lights went out, leaving it _____ than it had been before. (dark)
2. Then the _____ thing of all happened. (unusual)
3. A voice spoke to me in the _____ whisper possible. (quiet)
4. "It's _____ than you think," the voice seemed to whisper right in my ear. (late)
5. "It will get _____ for you every minute." (bad)
6. "Certainly you are _____ than this poor fool!" (intelligent)
7. Suddenly there was a flash and the _____ crash of thunder I have ever heard. (loud)
8. Hanging in the _____ part of the room was a skeleton. (high)
9. I have never been _____ than at that moment. (terrified)
10. The haunted house at the carnival was the _____ way to spend a quarter that I have ever found. (good)

REVIEW EXERCISE A Common and Proper Nouns

Number a sheet of paper 1–10. After each number write the common nouns in that sentence. Then rewrite the sentence, substituting a proper noun for each common noun.

EXAMPLE   When I last saw her, that woman was riding on a motorcycle.

woman, motorcycle When I last saw her, Mabel was riding on a Honda.

1. I was surprised to see the woman driving a huge car.
2. She drove right up to my school.
3. She got out of the car and munched on some fruit.
4. When a dog came by, she gave him some food that she had bought in a store.
5. Having fed herself and the dog, she got back in her car and drove off toward the ocean.
6. She stopped at the beach and looked out at a point of land.
7. Then she took out a magazine and began to read an article.
8. She and the author had gone to college together.
9. They had belonged to a club together.
10. As the woman drove down the street, she felt that she had had a busy day.

REVIEW EXERCISE B   Singular and Plural Nouns

Number a sheet of paper 1–15. Rewrite each of the following nouns. Make the singular nouns plural and the plural nouns singular. You may want to use a dictionary.

EXAMPLE   dictionary

dictionaries

1. herb	6. soprano	11. vertebrae
2. physiques	7. auras	12. plateau
3. calves	8. obituaries	13. tomato
4. diagnoses	9. lullaby	14. alleys
5. knife	10. octopuses	15. parodies

REVIEW EXERCISE C Possessive Case of Nouns

Number a sheet of paper 1–10. After each number write the correct possessive case of the noun to fill in the blank.

EXAMPLE A _____ liver is an important source of oil. shark

shark's

1. Marine specialists at the University of _____ Sea Grant College think people should learn to eat sharks. California
2. In _____ bulletin, one specialist, John Torres, even gave a recipe for oven-fried shark. February
3. A _____ meat, he says, is nutritional and economical. shark
4. Dr. _____ recipe uses salt, milk, and breadcrumbs on shark fillets. Torres
5. He says that what _____ menus sometimes call grayfish is really shark. restaurants
6. He tried an experiment to test _____ prejudices against shark meat. people
7. He invited fifty members of a neighboring _____ 4-H Club to a cookout. town
8. The club members ate the _____ catch of shark meat. day
9. The _____ reactions pleased Dr. Torres. members
10. Not knowing what they were eating, they enjoyed the _____ tender goodness. meat

REVIEW EXERCISE D Pronouns

Number a sheet of paper 1–10. After each number write the pronouns in that sentence.

EXAMPLE   Has anyone told you about the curse of King Tut's tomb?

anyone, you

1. King Tutankhamun, who died in Egypt about 3,000 years ago, was buried with great wealth.
2. He became king when he was a child.
3. All of the wealth buried with him was his to use after death.
4. In 1923, an archeologist who had been searching for King Tut's tomb for several years found it.
5. When he looked into the tomb, he saw riches that had been buried for 3,000 years.
6. They included furniture, jewelry, and images of animals that the king had hunted.
7. The goddess Selk stretched her arms toward the dead king to guide him.
8. For 3,000 years she did the job given to her.
9. After the discovery a rumor spread that the tomb had a curse on it.
10. No one with good sense believed it, though.

REVIEW EXERCISE E Adjectives

The adjectives in the following sentences are underlined. Number a sheet of paper 1–10. Copy each adjective. Then write the word or words that it modifies.

EXAMPLE Ramon saw an <u>ugly</u> dog in the <u>empty</u> lot.

empty, lot   ugly, dog

1. On a <u>pleasant May</u> morning in 1850, a wagon train <u>from</u> Salt Lake City stopped for a <u>few</u> minutes in the <u>cool</u> shade by the Carson River.
2. A <u>small</u> stream was flowing there from a range of <u>high</u> hills.
3. A <u>young</u> man felt bored in the <u>quiet</u> morning.
4. He took a <u>small</u> pan down to the <u>little</u> stream.
5. When he had washed away the <u>worthless</u> sand and gravel, he found <u>glittering</u> gold in his pan.
6. That <u>young</u> miner never became <u>rich.</u>
7. In <u>later</u> years, though, <u>many</u> miners made <u>huge</u> fortunes by that stream.
8. The <u>rich Nevada</u> soil was mined first by <u>local</u> miners.
9. <u>One</u> miner gave an <u>old blind</u> horse as payment for a <u>small</u> piece of land.
10. In the <u>first</u> day after he had bought the land, he found $5,000 in <u>valuable</u> gold and silver.

REVIEW EXERCISE F Pronoun or Adjective

Number a sheet of paper 1–5. After each number write the underlined word or words in that sentence. Tell whether each word is used as a pronoun or as an adjective.

EXAMPLE <u>Some</u> miners lost <u>their</u> claims.

Some, adjective
their, adjective

1. <u>Both</u> Snowshoe Thompson and James Jinney were early miners in Nevada.
2. <u>Neither</u> became rich, but <u>both</u> enjoyed the satisfaction of finding gold.
3. Snowshoe crossed the Sierra Nevada <u>many</u> times on snowshoes.
4. Using <u>this</u> method he could cross the snow carrying eighty pounds of mail.
5. <u>Few</u> people could stand the cold <u>that</u> he could stand.

2

PARTS OF SPEECH

Verbs, Adverbs, Prepositions, Conjunctions, Interjections

In Chapter 1 you saw how three of the eight parts of speech work. This chapter presents the other five parts of speech: *verbs, adverbs, prepositions, conjunctions,* and *interjections.* Each of these parts of speech works within sentences by relating to other parts of sentences.

As you study the parts of speech, you will become better at using English sentences.

VERBS

2a   A verb is a word used to help tell what happens or what exists.

EXAMPLES   A dog *growls.*   It *is* curious.
It *wags* its tail.   *Are* you happy?

Verbs are of two kinds: *action verbs* and *linking verbs.*

Action Verbs

(1) **An action verb tells what someone or something does.**

EXAMPLES   Alva *studies* hard every night.
[*Studies* tells what Alva does.]

She *writes* notes from her reading.
[*Writes* also tells what she does.]

EXERCISE 1   Number a sheet of paper 1–10. Next to each number write the action verb in the sentence.

EXAMPLE   The sun shines somewhere every day.

shines

1. Brad saw the sun early in the morning through his window.
2. He shouted happily to his sister in the next room.
3. She rushed into his room.
4. Sunlight streamed across his bed.
5. It brightened the whole room.
6. The rays blazed like gold through the blue and white curtains.
7. Brad and his sister called excitedly to their mother.
8. Their mother came upstairs.
9. Together they admired the light and color.
10. They smiled with joy at the first sunlight of the year in northern Alaska.

Transitive and Intransitive Verbs

**(2) An action verb is transitive if its action is
received by someone or something.**

The word transitive means "crossing over." The
action of the verb "crosses over" to some receiver.

EXAMPLES The bullet *hit* the tree.
[*Hit* is the transitive action verb.
The action crosses over to *tree,*
which receives the action.]

Wesley *baked* the cake.
[*Baked* is the transitive action
verb. The action crosses over to
cake. It receives the action.]

The receiver of the action is called the *object*.
For example, *cake* is the object of the sentence *Wesley baked the cake.*

**(3) If there is no receiver of the action of a verb,
the verb is intransitive.**

Intransitive means "not crossing over." The
verb's action does not cross over, or pass, to a receiver, or object.

EXAMPLES Joanie *slept*.
[*Slept* is an intransitive action
verb. No person or thing receives
the action.]

Marie *fell* from the roof.
[*Fell* is the intransitive action verb.
No person or thing receives the
action.]

EXERCISE 2 Five of the following sentences have transitive verbs. The other sentences have intransitive verbs. Number a sheet of paper 1–10. Next to each number, write the verb in the sentence. Next to the verb, write *T* if it is transitive and *I* if it is intransitive.

EXAMPLE Angelina stayed alone in the house.

stayed, I

1. First Angelina washed her hair.
2. Her comb was missing from her drawer.
3. She found it.
4. She combed her wet hair straight.
5. Then she sat under the dryer.
6. She waited twenty minutes.
7. Her hair dried.
8. She found her book bag in the closet.
9. She slung it over her shoulder.
10. She raced down the walk toward the bus stop.

Linking Verbs

(4) A linking verb joins someone or something with words that describe or rename that person, place, or thing.

Usually a linking verb cannot complete the thought of a sentence all by itself. It needs to be followed by other words.

EXAMPLES We were late to school.
[*Were* is the linking verb that is followed by *late,* a word that tells something about *we.*]

The road *was* snowy.
[*Was* is the linking verb that joins
snowy with *road*, the word it is
describing.]

We *are* cold.
[*Are* is the linking verb that joins
cold to *we*, the word it is
describing.]

The most common linking verbs are *am, are,
is, appear, seem, look,* and similar words. Linking
verbs are few in number. There are many more action verbs than linking verbs.

EXERCISE 3 Number a sheet of paper 1–8. Write
the linking verb in each sentence next to its
number.

EXAMPLE   Yesterday I was ill.

was

1. The day became dark and dreary.
2. The littlest sound seemed too loud.
3. My friends looked like strangers.
4. Their words sounded odd.
5. "What is wrong with you?"
6. "Are you all right?"
7. Yesterday I was not all right.
8. I became someone I did not like.

A linking verb is always followed by a noun, a
pronoun, an adjective, or an adverb. These words
are called *subject completers*.

See Sentences,
pp. 104–107

EXAMPLES Angus is a *man*.
[*Man* is a noun that renames what Angus is.]

Angus was *proud*.
[*Proud* is an adjective that describes Angus.]

Hint: Remember that a linking verb joins with another word or words to describe a person, place, or thing. An action verb helps tell of something that happens or has happened.

Helping Verbs

(5) A helping verb helps the main verb tell what happens or what exists.

EXAMPLES Jeannie *will come* tonight.
[The helping verb *will* helps the main verb *come*.]

She *has promised* us a surprise.
[The helping verb *has* helps the main verb *promised*.]

In the following list, you will find the most common helping verbs.

am	have	can	might
are	has	may	must
is	had	should	do
was	shall	would	does
were	will	could	did

Sometimes other words come between the helping verb and the main verb.

EXAMPLE She *was* already *pouring* the milk.
[*Already* comes between the helping verb *was* and the main verb *pouring.*]

EXERCISE 4 Number a sheet of paper 1–8. Next to each number write the helping verb and the main verb in each sentence. Draw a line under each helping verb.

EXAMPLE Part of the Atlantic Ocean is called by some the "Bermuda Triangle."

is called

1. Many strange things have happened there.
2. Over one hundred ships and planes have disappeared in the Bermuda Triangle.
3. More than one thousand people were lost in those waters.
4. No trace of people, ships, or planes was ever found.
5. No one can explain these mysteries.
6. How could jets and giant ships disappear completely?
7. One day we may know the answer.
8. Until then, the mystery of the Bermuda Triangle will remain one of the world's great secrets.

Tense

2b Most verbs change form to show a change in time, or *tense*.

EXAMPLES

PRESENT You *brush* your hair. You *are*
                brushing your hair.

PAST You *brushed* your hair.

FUTURE You *will brush* your hair.

Tense, or time, is shown in most verbs in simple ways. To show *present tense,* verbs use the base form called the *infinitive*.

EXAMPLES SINGULAR

I smile
you smile
he, she, it smiles

PLURAL

you smile
we smile
they smile

Note that only the third person singular *(he, she, it)* adds **s** to the infinitive.

Another way to show present tense is to use a helping verb and add **ing** to the infinitive. The **ing** form of the verb is called the *present participle*.

EXAMPLES SINGULAR

I *am smiling*
you *are smiling*
he, she, it *is smiling*

PLURAL

we *are smiling*
you *are smiling*
they *are smiling*

The helping verb changes form according to the number of the person, place, or thing it helps to tell about.

Regular verbs show *past tense* by adding **d** or **ed** to the infinitive. Irregular verbs do not show past tense by adding **ed**. Instead, irregular verbs have special forms for the past tense.

Another form of past tense called the *present perfect* uses the *past participle* and a helping verb to show that an action has been completed in the past.

EXAMPLES   SINGULAR

I *have written*
you *have written*
he, she, it *has written*

PLURAL

we *have written*
you *have written*
they *have written*

English verbs have several forms to show *future tense*. The most common forms use the helping verbs *shall* and *will* with the infinitive of the main verb.

EXAMPLES   I *shall go* there tomorrow.
We *will drive* in the car.

Other forms show future tense. These are not so common, however.

EXAMPLES   We *may try* tomorrow.
She *is going to swim* in the afternoon.

Regular Verbs

2c   Regular verbs add *ed* or *d* to the infinitive to show the past tense.

EXAMPLES

INFINITIVE	SIMPLE PAST	PRESENT PERFECT
scrub	scrubbed	have scrubbed
open	opened	have opened
race	raced	have raced

Irregular Verbs

2d Irregular verbs may change form to show past tense, but they do not add _ed_ or _d_.

EXAMPLES

INFINITIVE	SIMPLE PAST
swim	swam
run	ran
sing	sang

Note that many irregular verbs change the infinitive again to form the present perfect.

EXAMPLES

INFINITIVE	SIMPLE PAST	PRESENT PERFECT
swim	swam	have swum
sing	sang	have sung
write	wrote	have written
bite	bit	have bitten

EXERCISE 5 In one of the rows next to each number, a word is missing. Number a sheet of paper 1–8. Next to each number, write the missing word. After each word you write, put _R_ if it is a regular verb and _I_ if it is irregular.

EXAMPLE

INFINITIVE	SIMPLE PAST	PRESENT PERFECT
bring	brought	_____

have brought, I

	INFINITIVE	SIMPLE PAST	PRESENT PERFECT
1.	run	_____	have run
2.	walk	_____	have walked
3.	_____	wrote	have written
4.	spill	spilled	have _____
5.	_____	broke	have broken
6.	slide	_____	have slid
7.	_____	rode	have ridden
8.	_____	hopped	have hopped

ADVERBS

2e   An adverb is a word used to modify an action verb, an adjective, another adverb, or a group of words.

When an adverb modifies an action verb, it tells *when, where, how, how much,* or *how often* the action happens.

An adverb can tell *when* an action happens.

EXAMPLE   Alex left the gym *early.*
[When did Alex leave the gym?
Answer: *early.*]

EXERCISE 6 Copy the following sentences on a sheet of paper. Underline each adverb. Draw an arrow from the adverb to the verb it modifies.

EXAMPLE   The Cranshaw brothers regularly go to dances.

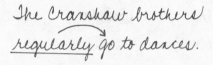

The Cranshaw brothers regularly go to dances.

1. Calvin Cranshaw dances constantly.
2. He arrives at parties early.
3. He starts immediately with the music.
4. He waltzes occasionally.
5. Calvin learned the Bump yesterday.
6. Who knows what he will do tomorrow?

An adverb can tell where something happened.

EXAMPLE   We stayed *inside* during the storm. [Where did we stay during the storm? Answer: *inside.*]

EXERCISE 7   Copy the following sentences on a sheet of paper. In each sentence, underline the adverb that tells where something happened. Draw an arrow from the adverb to the verb it modifies.

EXAMPLE   Mr. Phogg put his glasses down.

Mr. Phogg put his glasses down.

1. "I know I put them somewhere," said Mr. Phogg.
2. "Yes, I placed them there," he said and pointed to the desk.
3. "I've looked everywhere!" he said.
4. "But I can't find them anywhere!" he cried.
5. "Oh, I find them here," he said, touching the glasses on his nose.

An adverb can also tell *how, how much,* or *how often* something happens.

EXAMPLES Wilfreda Bowens calmly chopped the liver.
[How did Wilfreda chop? Answer: *calmly.*]

Juanita De Hoog eats chopped liver daily.
[How often does Juanita eat chopped liver? Answer: *daily.*]

EXERCISE 8 Copy the following sentences on a sheet of paper. Draw a line under each adverb that tells how or how often. Draw an arrow from the adverb to the verb it modifies.

EXAMPLE Some singers sing well.

Some singers sing well.

1. My neighbor sings loudly.
2. He sings daily.
3. He also sings badly, like a lonely coyote.
4. I talked to him politely.
5. But he shut the door angrily.
6. I talked to him again.
7. In fact, I begged him repeatedly.
8. He sang quietly only after another neighbor called the dog pound.

Some adverbs modify adjectives.

EXAMPLES Melva Crook walks with *surprisingly* long strides.
[The adverb *surprisingly* modifies the adjective *long.*]

Sam Wright likes to swim in *very* cold water.
[The adverb *very* modifies the adjective *cold*.]

Certain adverbs modify other adverbs.

EXAMPLE Mona Zillinger jumped *quite* suddenly.
[The adverb *quite* modifies the adverb *suddenly*.]

EXERCISE 9 Copy the following sentences on a sheet of paper. Underline each adverb. Draw an arrow from the adverb to the adjective or adverb it modifies.

EXAMPLE The cheetah runs unusually fast.

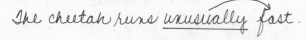

1. Cheetahs are very unusual animals.
2. They are exceedingly fast cats.
3. There are few animals who can escape the cheetah's almost unbelievable speed.
4. They change direction amazingly quickly.
5. Cheetahs are also incredibly graceful animals.
6. They leap from trees extraordinarily quietly.
7. Only much larger animals are safe when the cheetah is hungry.
8. Walk very carefully when you see a wild cheetah.

An adverb can do more than modify one other word. Adverbs can modify groups of words. The word *nearly* is an adverb that can modify either one word or a group of words.

EXAMPLES

MODIFIER OF ONE WORD   She was *nearly* late.
                            [*Nearly* modifies *late.*]

MODIFIER OF A GROUP   She was *nearly* in the
OF WORDS   chair.
                            [*Nearly* modifies *in the chair.*]

The words *not* and *never* are special adverbs. They change the meaning of a verb or an adjective to make its meaning opposite.

EXAMPLES   Jake does like to swim.
                 Jake does *not* like to swim.

                 Emmy is happy.
                 Emmy is *not* happy.

                 Planes land on this field.
                 Planes *never* land on this field.

                 Shareen is late in the morning.
                 Shareen is *never* late in the morning.

2f   Adverbs help compare actions of verbs.

Most adverbs show comparison by adding **er** or **est**.

EXAMPLES   Fern Erdman can run *fast*.
                 Bettie Wilcox can run *faster* than Fern.
                 Tati Hack can run *fastest* of all three.

If an adverb ends in **ly**, it takes the words *more* or *most* to show comparison. It does not add **er** or **est**.

EXAMPLES
helpfully   more helpfully   most helpfully
sadly   more sadly   most sadly

EXERCISE 10 Number a sheet of paper 1–8. After each number write the correct form of the adverb that belongs in the blank.

EXAMPLE No animal moves _____ than a snake! (smoothly)

more smoothly

1. The python moves _____ than most snakes. (slowly)
2. It coils itself _____ around its victims. (firmly)
3. It squeezes _____ than any other snake. (tightly)
4. Of all the animals I've seen, dolphins swim the _____. (gracefully)
5. They also seem to act the _____. (playfully)
6. Of course, sharks and whales swim _____ than dolphins. (powerfully)
7. And some say the manta ray moves _____ than any sea animal. (beautifully)
8. Nothing walks _____ than a sea turtle on land. (clumsily)

Irregular Adverbs

Some adverbs show their comparisons in irregular ways.

EXAMPLES   well   better   best
            badly   worse   worst

EXERCISE 11 Number a sheet of paper 1–5. Write the correct form of the adverb that belongs in each blank.

EXAMPLE   Cory studies history _____ than anyone in the class. (well)

better

1. The ancient Romans built roads _____ than anyone before them. (well)
2. They also did _____ at building houses and aqueducts than anyone before them. (well)
3. However, the Romans did _____ of all at putting together laws for society. (well)
4. In spite of that, their civilization collapsed and people after them lived _____ than before. (badly)
5. Some believe we modern people live _____ of all. (well)

PREPOSITIONS

2g   A preposition is a word used to connect the noun or pronoun that follows it to some other word in the sentence.

EXAMPLES   The mother lion began her hunt *at* dawn.
[The preposition *at* relates the noun *dawn* to the verb *began*. Like an adverb, the words *at dawn* help tell when an action occurred.]

Slowly, the spider crept *along* the wall.
[The preposition *along* relates the noun *wall* to the verb *crept*. Like an adverb, the words *along the wall* help tell where an action occurred.]

There was a shower *of* sparks and the machine stopped.
[The preposition *of* relates the noun *sparks* to the noun *shower.* The words *of sparks* act like an adjective to help tell something about a noun.]

Most prepositions help show relationships of time, place, manner, or kind.

TIME   *at* dawn
PLACE *along* the wall
KIND   *of* sparks

Here are some commonly used prepositions.

TIME	PLACE	MANNER OR KIND
after	above	into	by
before	across	inside	except
during	along	near	for
since	behind	on	of
until	below	through	with
	between	to	
	down	toward	
	for	under	

Some prepositions are made of two and three words. They are called compound prepositions. Here are some common compound prepositions.

according to   instead of
because of   on account of
in spite of   out of

EXERCISE 12 Number a sheet of paper 1–10. After each number, write the preposition in that sentence. Some sentences have more than one preposition.

EXAMPLE   A bright light shot through the nighttime sky.

through

1. Juan watched the light speed toward him like a ball of fire.
2. It seemed to pass over his head.
3. Suddenly the light fell from the sky.
4. It disappeared behind some trees.
5. After that, Juan wondered whether he had seen a flying saucer in the sky.
6. Juan decided that it must have landed near the pond.
7. At the pond, Juan found that all of the birds were singing noisily.
8. The birds had been greatly upset by something.
9. Finally, Juan found the answer to the mystery.
10. Under the water lay a meteor.

Object of the Preposition

The noun or pronoun that follows a preposition is called the *object* of the preposition. The preposition shows the relationship between its object and another word in the sentence.

EXAMPLES *During* the night the telephone rang.

Over the phone came a strange voice.

It sounded *like* me!

EXERCISE 13 Copy each of the following sentences on a sheet of paper. Skip a line after each sentence. Underline each preposition and draw an arrow from it to its object. Each sentence has more than one preposition.

EXAMPLE Under the sea lives the blue whale, the largest animal in the world today.

Under the sea lives the blue whale, the largest animal in the world today.

1. In prehistoric times, the largest animals that lived on the earth were dinosaurs.
2. The biggest of the dinosaurs was the brachiosaurus, which stood forty feet at its highest point.
3. From the tip of its nose to the end of its tail, the adult brachiosaurus measured seventy feet.
4. Despite its size, the brachiosaurus was actually one of the gentler dinosaurs.
5. It ate a diet of plants from the prehistoric lagoons.

6. The fiercest creature at that time was probably one of the medium-sized dinosaurs, the tyrannosaurus rex.

7. Scientists can tell by the size of its brain that the tyrannosaurus rex was also one of the smarter dinosaurs.

8. Plant eaters like the brachiosaurus were no match for the smarter, fiercer tyrannosaurus rex on land.

9. During their lives, however, brachiosauruses spent most of their time wandering through the deep lagoons.

10. In the swampy waters, these huge but peaceful dinosaurs were safe from harm.

2h A preposition may have more than one object.

EXAMPLE *Before* breakfast and lunch,
Carmen does exercises.

EXERCISE 14 Write the complete prepositional phrase in each of the following sentences. Underline the preposition. Draw arrows to both objects of each preposition.

EXAMPLE It was between midnight and one that the earthquake happened.

between midnight and one

1. Frightened people woke up and ran screaming into alleys and streets.

2. Above these men and women, tall metal and glass buildings teetered dangerously.

3. Windows popped free from the swaying sky-scrapers and bending buildings.
4. Many people were injured by the falling glass and steel.
5. Emergency instructions were broadcast over radio and TV.
6. After the first quake and its damage, there were several smaller quakes.
7. During the third quake or the fourth quake, some gas pipes broke.
8. A fire began between a restaurant and a bank.
9. Firefighters fought the blaze until four or five.
10. Then, in the ashes and the broken glass, you could see where the earthquake had been.

CONJUNCTIONS

2i   A conjunction is a word used to join other words or groups of words.

The two types of conjunctions are *coordinating conjunctions* and *subordinating conjunctions*.

Coordinating Conjunctions

Coordinating conjunctions join words or word groups that are equal in importance. *And, but, for, nor,* and *or* are the most common coordinating conjunctions.

Example of a coordinating conjunction joining words:

Smythe's *and* Braun's are department stores.

Example of a coordinating conjunction joining short word groups:

They have stores in the city *and* in the suburbs.

Example of a coordinating conjunction joining longer word groups:

Smythe's will have a sale on sheets one week, *but* Braun's will put its sheets on sale the next week.

Some conjunctions are in two parts, for example: *either . . . or, neither . . . nor, both . . . and, not only . . . but also*. These conjunctions are called *correlative conjunctions*. They work like coordinating conjunctions.

EXAMPLE *Either* you stay *or* we must stay.

EXERCISE 15 Each of the following sentences needs a coordinating conjunction to complete it. Number a sheet of paper 1–12. After each number, write the coordinating conjunction needed in the blank space in the sentence.

EXAMPLE Lori thought scuba diving would be fun, _____ she had no idea there was trouble ahead.

but

1. Lori's dad liked to explore sunken ships on weekends _____ holidays.
2. He dived into the water, _____ Lori waited on the boat.
3. It was a dangerous dive, _____ he had made more dangerous ones.

4. Soon he had been down fifteen _____ twenty minutes.

5. Lori began to worry when neither bubbles _____ a signal came from below.

6. Quickly, Lori put on her equipment _____ dived into the water.

7. Her dad was down there somewhere, _____ she had to find him.

8. She swam quickly, _____ she knew he might be in trouble.

9. She found him trapped under a heavy beam _____ almost out of air.

10. Lori was small, _____ somehow she managed to roll the beam off his leg.

11. His air tanks were empty, _____ Lori shared her air supply with him.

12. Lori's dad was proud of her, _____ she had saved his life.

Subordinating Conjunctions

Some conjunctions connect word groups that are unequal in importance. These are called subordinating conjunctions. Subordinate means "less important." The most common of the subordinating conjunctions are *although, after, because, before, as soon as, if, though, unless, until, when,* and *while.*

EXAMPLES We crept away *as soon as* it turned dark.
We had waited *until* we could not be seen.
After we were safe, we broke into a loud cheer.

The group of words that follows the subordinating conjunction is never a complete thought or idea. Another group of words is needed to make the meaning of the sentence clear.

EXERCISE 16 Each of the following sentences contains a subordinating conjunction. Number a sheet of paper 1–12. Next to each number, write the subordinating conjunction.

EXAMPLE A sultan put Glencoe in a pit
because he helped people.

because

1. "Help yourself now!" said the sultan after he trapped him.
2. "If you look, you will see two doors in the pit."
3. "Unless you choose the right one, you will not leave the pit alive."
4. "One door holds certain death for you when you open it."
5. "But you can go free if you choose the right door."
6. After the sultan was gone, Glencoe looked at the doors.
7. One was tall and wide while the other was short.
8. Because it was so big, Glencoe thought the large door might hide a terrible death.
9. He did not know which door to choose until he remembered the sultan's trickery.
10. When he had made up his mind, Glencoe acted quickly.

11. He chose the larger door because it looked so dangerous.
12. Glencoe walked free while deadly snakes still waited behind the smaller door.

INTERJECTIONS

2j   An interjection is a word or group of words used to express strong feeling.

EXAMPLES   *Hurray!* We beat the Bobcats.
            Oh! I'm sorry.

An exclamation mark (!) usually follows the interjection or the sentence that contains it. Sometimes an interjection in the middle of a sentence is set off by commas.

EXAMPLE   You had him, *doggone it,* but he got away!

WORDS AS DIFFERENT PARTS OF SPEECH

2k   Many words can be used as different parts of speech.

Some words are used as one part of speech in a sentence. In another sentence, they are used as a different part of speech.

EXAMPLE   hand
NOUN   Isabel hurt her *hand.*
VERB   Please *hand* me the paper.
ADJECTIVE   The *hand* tools are on the shelf.

EXERCISE 17 Number a sheet of paper 1–8. Then write the underlined word in each of the following sentences. After it write the part of speech it is in the sentence.

EXAMPLE The clock seems <u>slow</u>.

slow, adjective

1. Asa Waldrop will <u>paper</u> the hallway tomorrow.
2. The <u>paper</u> cutter is under the stairs.
3. Line up the rolls of <u>paper</u>.
4. Let them roll down the <u>slide</u>.
5. They can <u>slide</u> down with their weight.
6. <u>Cut</u> the roll open.
7. Make a clean <u>cut</u> at both ends.
8. Now <u>paste</u> the paper on the wall.

REVIEW EXERCISE A   Action or Linking Verbs

Number a sheet of paper 1–10. After each number write the complete verb or verbs. Then tell whether it is an action verb or a linking verb.

EXAMPLE Sheila Zells was taking a course in flying.

was taking, action verb

1. One evening Sheila sniffed the wind to test the air.
2. She decided to launch her new kite.
3. She had made it herself in her workshop.
4. Sheila climbed a hill and saw the forest below.

5. Both the kite and the evening were perfect.
6. She launched her kite in a warm breeze.
7. For a moment the kite seemed to be still.
8. Then it jumped out of Sheila's hands.
9. It became completely independent of her.
10. Sheila felt terrible because she had lost a perfect kite.

REVIEW EXERCISE B   Transitive or Intransitive Verbs

Number a sheet of paper 1–10. After each number write the complete verb or verbs in that sentence. After it, write *T* if the verb is transitive or *I* if the verb is intransitive. The last sentence has two complete verbs.

EXAMPLE   Reynard the fox has found nothing to eat.

has found, T

1. For two days he had caught neither a rabbit nor a hen.
2. He feared starvation.
3. That night he crept into a rich man's garden.
4. He noticed an absolutely delicious smell.
5. Above him he saw big ripe bunches of purple grapes.
6. He stood on his hind legs.
7. He simply could not reach the tempting grapes.
8. He tried leaping at the grapes.
9. Reynard turned away in defeat.
10. "I do not want those sour grapes, anyway," he told himself.

REVIEW EXERCISE C Linking Verbs

There are nine linking verbs in the following paragraphs. Number a sheet of paper 1–9. After each number write a linking verb and its completer. Underline the linking verb.

EXAMPLE Susan B. Anthony's teachers were afraid that the study of long division would harm her brain.

were, afraid

In the early days in America, colleges were closed to women. Home was the place for them. However, women slowly won rights in the outside world. In 1836 Mount Holyoke College became the first women's college in the United States. In the same year, Oberlin College in the state of Ohio became a school for men and women.

In 1848 Elizabeth Stanton and Lucretia Mott called the first women's rights convention. Elizabeth Stanton became a close friend of Susan B. Anthony. They thought that laws preventing women from voting were unfair. Susan B. Anthony was arrested for voting in 1872. Voting was a crime for women.

By 1900 women could vote in only four states. Many suffrage workers felt discouraged. Some women even chained themselves to a White House fence to protest. Finally in 1920 the Nineteenth Amendment became law. Women at last became voting citizens of the United States.

REVIEW EXERCISE D Adverbs

Number a sheet of paper 1–10. Copy each adverb. After it write the verb, adjective, or adverb that it modifies.

EXAMPLE   Luis Lopez frequently takes his
          family's garbage to the local
          recycling center.

frequently, takes

1. Luis is an unusually quiet boy, but he sincerely hates waste and mess.
2. He was interested when he read a notice about a recycling center newly opened at Mission High School.
3. On Saturday Luis rode his bicycle down to the school to see the recycling process.
4. There he saw the schoolyard filled with trash, all carefully sorted into piles of glass, paper, tin, and food waste.
5. Luis's friend Emily was busily sorting cans.
6. When she saw Luis, Emily smiled encouragingly.
7. "We really need your help, Luis," she said rather firmly.
8. Luis became the most honestly enthusiastic recycler in the group.
9. The Lopez family's garbage cans are nearly empty.
10. Luis is already planning to do a project on water purification when he takes a chemistry class in high school.

REVIEW EXERCISE E Prepositions

Number a sheet of paper 1–10. After each number write a preposition that will fill each blank. Then copy the object of each preposition.

EXAMPLE Why does the cat always take her nap _____ my bed?

under, bed

1. This is the six o'clock news report _____ Friday, July 29.
2. A small brush fire is burning _____ Clinton, Iowa.
3. Investigators say that the fire was started _____ an abandoned used car lot.
4. Harry Hurry, mayor of nearby Bay City, has been held _____ local police for racing his car _____ an old wooden bridge.
5. The fire department was called _____ four o'clock this morning to rescue a cat _____ the tree _____ the Meadowbrook School.
6. The cat, a gray female, has been adopted _____ the fire captain, Frank Flame.
7. In the sports news, there was a small riot last night _____ the Hawks' game _____ the Bluebirds.
8. Jane Jones set a record when she caught a fly ball _____ the fence.
9. There will be thunder storms _____ the evening _____ the coastal area.
10. That's all the news _____ Barbara and Cecil _____ this evening.

REVIEW EXERCISE F   Review of Parts of Speech

Number a sheet of paper 1–15. After each number, identify the parts of speech of the numbered word.

On July 4, 1845 Henry David Thoreau went
to Walden Pond to begin an experiment in living simply. He lived quietly in a cabin which he built with materials that cost $28.13. To Thoreau machines only complicated life. He wanted to find not only joy but also refreshment in everyday living. Thoreau loved nature and feared government. In his book, *Walden,* he spoke of the beauty and simplicity of nature and of the importance of being free.

3

PHRASES

Noun Phrases, Prepositional Phrases, Verb Phrases

A single word or a group of related words may do the work of a part of speech in the English language. These groups of words are called *phrases*. The most common kinds of phrases are *noun phrases, verb phrases,* and *prepositional phrases.*

KINDS OF PHRASES

3a A phrase is a group of related words used as a single part of speech.

EXAMPLES *The low-flying plane* hit the telephone wires.
[*The low-flying plane* names something. A noun names something. This phrase is a noun phrase.]

It *was soaring* too low.
[*Was soaring* tells of the action. A
verb tells of action. This phrase is
a verb phrase.]

It plunged *into the lake.*
[*Into the lake* tells where the plane
plunged. An adverb tells where.
This phrase is a prepositional
phrase used as an adverb.]

Noun Phrases

**3b A noun phrase contains a noun and its
modifiers.**

EXAMPLES   *Thick, powdery snow* covered *the
thin ice.*
[The noun *snow* and its modifiers
thick and *powdery* make a noun
phrase. The noun *ice* and its
modifiers *the* and *thin* make
another noun phrase.]

Just like a noun, a noun phrase can be re-
placed with a pronoun.

EXAMPLE   *The roaring fire engine* shot out of
the firehouse.
It shot out of the firehouse.
[The pronoun *it* replaces the noun
phrase *the roaring fire engine.*]

EXERCISE 1   Copy the following sentences on a
sheet of paper. Each sentence has two noun phrases.

Underline each noun phrase. Be sure to underline all the related words that belong in each noun phrase.

EXAMPLE The new cars are handsome machines.

The new cars are handsome machines.

1. Their bodies are shiny plastic.
2. Their sturdy frames are carbon steel.
3. Powerful engines drive their four wheels.
4. Beautiful chrome strips line the curved windows.
5. These modern autos will make our great highways look well used.
6. The gasoline shortage, however, is giving us the big stall.

Verb Phrases

3c A verb phrase is made up of the main verb and its helpers.

See Verbs, pp. 27–36

Either an action verb or a linking verb can be a main verb. Both can have helping verbs. A main verb and its helping verbs make up a verb phrase. The verb phrase is also called the *complete verb*.

EXAMPLES The snow *began falling* about noon. [*Falling* is the main verb. *Began* is a helping verb. The two words make up the verb phrase.]

It *has been falling* all afternoon.
[*Has been* are the two helping
verbs that go with the main verb
falling. All three words make up
the verb phrase.]

Sometimes parts of the verb phrase will be in-
terrupted by other words.

EXAMPLE The workers *had* already *begun
shoveling*.
[The verb phrase is *had begun
shoveling*. The adverb *already* splits
the phrase.]

EXERCISE 2   On a sheet of paper, write the complete verb phrases in each of the following sentences.

EXAMPLE Engineers have been searching for
an improved road surface.

have been searching

1. Not many decades ago, most roads were made of
   dirt.
2. They were often washed out in bad weather.
3. Today roads are being built of weather-resistant
   materials.
4. Roadways have been constructed to withstand
   ice and snow.
5. Engineers have already found new problems,
   however.
6. The tires of cars and trucks have been destroying road surfaces.

Prepositional Phrases

3d   A prepositional phrase begins with a preposition and usually ends with a noun or pronoun.

See
Preposition, p.
384; Noun, p.
380; Pronoun,
p. 384

EXAMPLES   *under the car*
in the front seat
in back of the bureau
above it
behind her

The last word in a prepositional phrase is usually a noun or pronoun. *Under the car,* for example, ends with the noun *car. Car* is called the *object* of the preposition. Any words that modify the object of the preposition are included in the prepositional phrase.

Hint: Do not confuse a prepositional phrase beginning with the word *to* with the infinitive form of a verb, for example, *to see.* Remember that a prepositional phrase always has an object.

EXERCISE 3   On a sheet of paper, write the prepositional phrase in each of the following sentences. Draw an arrow from the preposition to its object.

EXAMPLE   Sit in this comfortable chair, please.

in this comfortable chair

1. A car manufacturer will put soft cushions in his passenger cars.
2. Car owners will then feel at home.
3. Passengers will stay comfortable on long rides.
4. They can ride for many hours.
5. Commuters in car pools gain the benefit.
6. The rides are slow in heavy traffic.

See Adjective, p. 366 **(1) A prepositional phrase may be used as an adjective.**

A prepositional phrase that is used as an adjective modifies a noun or a pronoun. The noun or pronoun it modifies is not part of the prepositional phrase. It is another word in the same sentence. It usually comes just before the prepositional phrase.

EXAMPLES   The coffee *in the cup* is cold.
[The prepositional phrase is *in the cup*. It modifies the noun *coffee*.]

The pot *on the stove* is also cold.
[The prepositional phrase *on the stove* modifies the noun *pot*.]

Those *in the kitchen* will be disappointed.
[The phrase *in the kitchen* modifies the pronoun *those*.]

Many times a prepositional phrase has a noun phrase in it.

EXAMPLES   in the dusty box
[*the dusty box* is a noun phrase]

under a colorful tent
[*a colorful tent* is a noun phrase]

EXERCISE 4 Each of the following sentences has a prepositional phrase used as an adjective. Copy each sentence on a sheet of paper. Underline each prepositional phrase. Draw an arrow from each phrase to the noun or pronoun it modifies.

> EXAMPLE   A new car with shiny paint is a problem.
>
> *A new car with shiny paint is a problem.*

1. A car in a crowded city can be a problem.
2. Finding a parking place is a challenge of a large kind.
3. Parking meters on the street often appear to be limited.
4. Officials with tickets seem to know when meters run out.
5. Parking lots near the downtown area often are full.
6. New cars without any dents can be easily scratched.
7. The damage to a new car may be expensive to repair.
8. Why not ride public transportation and ease your worries about your car?

(2) A prepositional phrase may be used as an adverb.

See Adverb, p. 366

Most prepositional phrases that are used as adverbs modify verbs. The phrases help to answer these questions: *When? Where? How? How long? How much?*

EXAMPLES   Commuters travel to work *in the morning*.
[This phrase modifies the word *travel*. It tells *when* commuters travel.]

They drive their cars *on freeways*.
[This phrase modifies the verb *drive*. It tells *where* they drive.]

They creep along *at a snail's pace*.
[This phrase modifies the verb *creep*. It tells *how* they creep.]

Sometimes on the freeways they are imprisoned *for hours*.
[This phrase modifies the verb *are imprisoned*. It tells *how long* they are imprisoned.]

A prepositional phrase used as an adverb may also modify an adjective or another adverb.

Example of a prepositional phrase used as an adverb to modify an adjective:

Maybe the cars are too big *for the highways*.
[This phrase modifies the adjective *big*.]

Example of a prepositional phrase used as an adverb to modify another adverb:

Commuters may have to leave earlier *in the morning*.
[This phrase modifies the adverb *earlier*.]

Sometimes a prepositional phrase will end with an adverb instead of a noun or pronoun.

EXAMPLE   Rosa left her car *in there.*
[In this case, the prepositional
phrase works like an adverb. It
modifies the verb *left.* It tells *where*
the car was left.]

Hint: Remember that a prepositional
phrase works either as an adjective or as
an adverb, never as a preposition.

EXERCISE 5   Each of the following sentences has
a prepositional phrase used as an adverb. Copy
each sentence on a sheet of paper. Underline each
prepositional phrase. Draw an arrow from it to the
word it modifies.

EXAMPLE   Western civilization has advanced
through its transportation systems.

Western civilization has

advanced through its transportation

systems.

1. Horses and wagons were used before the automobile.
2. They traveled on dirt roads.
3. The wagon wheels sank deep in the mud.
4. Rainstorms and floods made wagons travel at a
   slow speed.
5. Deep ruts and holes were worn by the wagon
   wheels.

6. Sometimes travelers were delayed for hours.
7. By means of the automobile and paved roads, anyone can reach a destination in a much shorter time.
8. Horse-drawn wagons would be too slow for today's highways.
9. Then again, commuter traffic is often slow out there.
10. Maybe someone could ride a horse faster on a car-choked highway.

REVIEW EXERCISE A Noun Phrases

Number a sheet of paper 1–10. Copy each of the following sentences. Underline each noun phrase.

EXAMPLE A poor man was walking down a city street.

A poor man was walking down a city street.

1. He had only a small piece of bread.
2. The hungry man walked by a hot dog stand.
3. He saw the fat hot dogs.
4. Carried away by the smell, the starving man held his small piece of bread over the roasting hot dog grill.
5. The hot dog stand owner called a local police officer and demanded to be paid the price of a hotdog.
6. The wise police officer pulled two quarters from his pocket.

7. He held the two coins in his fist and rattled them by the owner's ear.
8. The puzzled owner listened to the rattling coins.
9. "Now you have been paid a fair price," said the police officer.
10. "The sound of money is a fair price for the smell of food."

REVIEW EXERCISE B Verb Phrases

Number a sheet of paper 1–10. After each number write the verb phrase (complete verb) or verb phrases in the sentence.

> EXAMPLE The heroism of the mountain men has been recorded by many writers.
>
> *has been recorded*

1. The mountain men were roaming the Far West long before white settlers.
2. They were admired for their courage in a perilous place.
3. At thirteen, Jedediah Smith, a famous mountain man, was working as a clerk on a Lake Erie freighter.
4. At twenty-four, Smith was asked to join a trapping expedition up the Missouri River.
5. Soon he had shown his abilities as a trapper and a leader.
6. Smith explored more of the Far West than any other white man had ever done.
7. He had pioneered the trip across the desert into California.

8. One could not find rougher or tougher men than the mountain men.

9. Jedediah Smith, however, did not swear or use tobacco.

10. His early trails have become well-established routes for pioneer settlers.

REVIEW EXERCISE C Prepositional Phrases

Number a sheet of paper 1–10. After each number write the prepositional phrase or phrases in the sentence. Draw an arrow from the preposition to its object.

> EXAMPLE Do not be a fake with borrowed feathers.
>
>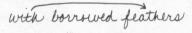
> with borrowed feathers

1. After a party a peacock hurried home without his shimmering, blue-green tail feathers.

2. A plain grey pigeon flew to the feathers.

3. "No one will mind if I borrow these for awhile," it thought.

4. It attached the feathers to its own tail with two paper clips.

5. It strutted toward its own nest.

6. Unfortunately, the shimmering, blue-green feathers dragged in the dust and looked silly on its plain, grey body.

7. The peacock tore the feathers away from the pigeon and left without a word.

8. The pigeon flew home for comfort.

9. "If you don't like being a pigeon," its friends said, "go back to the peacocks."
10. "You're much too fancy for our poor, grey flock."

REVIEW EXERCISE D Prepositional Phrases

Number a sheet of paper 1–15. After each number write the underlined prepositional phrase. Write whether it is used as an adjective or as an adverb.

EXAMPLE A Japanese boat was fishing <u>off New Zealand</u>.

off New Zealand, adverb

1. The ship's nets hauled in the two-ton carcass <u>of a mysterious creature</u>.
2. Its long, thin neck dangled <u>from its huge body</u>.
3. Some <u>of the crew</u> thought it was a whale.
4. Others thought it was a turtle <u>without a shell</u>.
5. One person thought that its four flippers were like those <u>of a shark</u>.
6. Then photographs were examined <u>by marine biologists</u>.
7. They thought that the animal was a plesiosaurus, believed <u>by most scientists</u> to be extinct.
8. A few people believe that the Loch Ness monster <u>of Scotland</u> is also a plesiosaurus.
9. The creature is too big <u>for most lakes</u>.
10. Unfortunately, the experts have no evidence <u>except the pictures</u>.

11. The crew threw the remains of the creature <u>over
    the side</u>.
12. They were afraid that the creature would spoil
    their cargo <u>of fish</u>.
13. One crew member said that he was a little
    afraid of the odd monster <u>from the sea</u>.
14. Biologists want more evidence <u>about the sea
    monster</u>.
15. Japanese fishermen have been asked not to
    throw away anything that they might find <u>on
    future voyages</u>.

REVIEW EXERCISE E   Vocabulary

Each of the following prepositional phrases has
a word that could be used to write about adventure
and mystery. On a sheet of paper write ten sentences. In each sentence use one of the following
prepositional phrases:

1. except a barbarian
2. according to the hostage
3. beneath the ocean
4. from a parachute
5. by the traitor
6. with his hammer
7. after an avalanche
8. without hypnotism
9. of her exploit
10. in a helicopter

4

CLAUSES

Independent Clauses, Dependent Clauses

A *clause* is a group of words that says something about someone or something. A clause can contain a complete thought and stand alone as a sentence. Or a clause may need some other words to complete its meaning.

THE PARTS OF A CLAUSE

4a **A clause is a group of related words that has a subject and a predicate.**

The *subject* of a clause is the person or thing being talked about. The subject contains a noun or a pronoun. These kinds of words name someone or something.

See Noun, p. 380; see Pronoun, p. 384

The *predicate* says something about the person or thing named. The predicate always contains a verb. It may also contain other words that go with the verb to tell something more about the subject.

Examples of a subject and a predicate in a clause:

> *Carlos Ortiz works with wood.*
> [*Carlos Ortiz* names someone. It is the subject. *Works with wood* tells what Carlos Ortiz does. It is the predicate.]
>
> *Maria Escobar works with numbers.*
> [*Maria Escobar* is the subject. *Works with numbers* is the predicate.]

Hint: The subject of a clause must contain a noun or a pronoun. The predicate must contain a verb.

Some groups of words may seem like clauses, but they are not. If the group lacks either a subject or a predicate, it is not a clause.

EXAMPLES Joan, the carpenter's apprentice
[This group lacks a predicate.]

Wants to become an accountant
[This group lacks a subject.]

EXERCISE 1 Seven of the following groups of words are clauses. The others are not. Write each clause on your paper. Underline the subject once. Underline the predicate twice.

EXAMPLE Charlene works on a farm.

Charlene works on a farm.

1. Cows need feed
2. The hay in the loft of the barn
3. When they give plenty of milk
4. Jersey cows with much butterfat in their milk
5. Fresh cream goes into the ice cream
6. Rich milk makes butter faster
7. A wide variety of cheeses
8. Because cottage cheese has fewer calories
9. Yogurt can taste good
10. Dairy products provide important foods

KINDS OF CLAUSES

The two kinds of clauses are *independent* and *dependent*.

Independent Clauses

4b An independent clause needs no other words to complete its thought.

EXAMPLES   *Yim is an electrician.*
Janet is a plumber.
[Both of these clauses are complete statements. Both have a subject and a predicate. They do not depend upon other words to complete their thoughts.]

An independent clause may be a *sentence* by itself. The examples above show this. An independent clause may also be a part of a sentence with another clause.

See Sentence, p. 385

EXAMPLE   *Yim is an electrician,* but *Janet prefers plumbing.*
[In this example, the independent clause *Yim is an electrician* and the independent clause *Janet prefers plumbing* are joined together in a single sentence.]

Dependent Clauses

4c   A dependent clause needs other words to complete its thought.

A dependent clause has a subject and a predicate. However, it leaves its thought unfinished. It needs other words added to it to make sense. It needs an independent clause.

EXAMPLES   *Whenever the phone rings*
[What happens whenever the phone rings? This dependent clause leaves its thought unfinished. It needs to be combined with an independent clause: *Whenever the phone rings, Madelyn leaps from her seat.*]

If you run from the room
[What happens if you run from the room? This dependent clause needs more words to complete its thought. It also needs to be combined with an independent clause: *You may trip if you run from the room.*]

EXERCISE 2 Five of the following clauses are independent. The other clauses are dependent. Number a sheet of paper 1–10. Next to each number, write *I* if the clause is independent. Write *D* if the clause is dependent.

EXAMPLE Whenever the school day begins

D

1. Red apples are usually ripe
2. When they are young
3. They start out looking green
4. If you pick them too early
5. As you smell a green apple
6. The taste is bitter
7. Sunshine helps turn them red
8. As soon as they get big
9. On the ground they turn rotten
10. When apples are sweet

Kinds of Dependent Clauses

Three kinds of dependent clauses appear in writing. They are *noun clauses, adjective clauses,* and *adverb clauses*. Each one serves a special purpose.

(1) A noun clause is a dependent clause used as a noun. See Noun, p. 380

Every noun clause depends upon other words to complete its meaning.

EXAMPLES   *What comes in the package* is all you get.
[The noun clause is *what comes in the package*. Its subject is *what*. Its predicate is *comes in the package*. The entire noun clause serves as the subject of the whole sentence.]

Subject
⌒̄̄̄̄̄̄̄̄̄̄̄̄̄̄̄̄̄̄̄̄̄̄̄̄̄̄̄̄̄̄̄̄̄̄⌒
subj.   predicate
What comes in the package
Predicate
⌒̄̄̄̄̄̄̄̄̄̄̄̄̄̄⌒
is all you get.
[A noun, such as *coupon,* or a pronoun could replace this noun clause in the whole sentence. The sentence would read: *A coupon is all you get.*]

Kimo knows *that Luis is wrong.*
[*That Luis is wrong* is the noun clause. Its subject is *Luis*. Its predicate is *is wrong*. The entire noun clause is part of the predicate of the whole sentence.]

Subj.   Predicate
⌒̄̄̄̄⌒ ⌒̄̄̄̄̄̄̄̄̄̄̄̄̄̄̄̄̄̄̄̄̄̄̄̄̄̄̄̄̄̄⌒
                     subj.   predicate
Kimo knows *that Luis is wrong.*

Whoever finds the star wins it.
[*Whoever finds the star* is the noun clause. *Whoever* is the subject of the clause. *Finds the star* is the predicate of the clause. The entire noun clause serves as the subject of the whole sentence.]

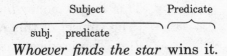

Subject   Predicate

subj.   predicate

Whoever finds the star wins it.

A noun clause usually begins with one of these words:

that	who	whom
what	whoever	whomever
whatever		

EXERCISE 3 Number a sheet of paper 1–6. Next to each number, write the noun clause from each sentence.

EXAMPLE Inez cannot find what is wrong.

what is wrong

1. A ranch in the West is what looks like a farm.
2. Whoever farms a ranch is called a "rancher."
3. Open land and livestock are what make a ranch.
4. Successful ranchers know what will grow on their land.
5. What grows well in rich valleys may not survive on mountain slopes.
6. Some ranchers have gone out of business trying to grow in high country what should have been planted in the lowlands.

(2) An adjective clause is a dependent clause used as an adjective.

See Adjective, p. 366

An adjective clause modifies a noun or a pronoun. The adjective clause is also called a *relative clause,* because it relates to a noun or a pronoun.

EXAMPLES This is the money *that Jim lost.*
[The subject of this clause is
Jim. The predicate is *lost.* This
adjective clause modifies the noun
money. It tells which money it is.]

Betty can see the fog *that covers
the city.*
[The subject of this clause is *that.*
The predicate is *covers the city.* This
clause modifies the noun *fog.* It
describes the fog.]

Alison and Jeff are the people *who
want to join the club.*
[The subject of this clause is *who.*
The predicate is *want to join the
club.* This clause modifies the
proper nouns *Alison* and *Jeff.*]

Anyone *who joins* must be a
full-time student.
[The subject of this clause is *who.*
The predicate is *joins.* This
adjective clause modifies the
pronoun *anyone.*]

An adjective clause comes right after the noun
or pronoun it modifies. The clause usually begins
with one of these words:

who   whose   that
whom   which

EXERCISE 4 Number a sheet of paper 1–6. Next
to each number, write the adjective clause from
each sentence.

EXAMPLE On clear days, you can see the snow
that caps the mountains.

that caps the mountains

1. Ranchers who want to succeed must cooperate
   with nature.
2. A good supply of water is the first thing that a
   rancher needs.
3. Anything that grows must have water.
4. For most of the crops which will produce a profit,
   good soil and sunshine also are important.
5. The rancher who raises only livestock can get by
   with poorer soil.
6. However, no rancher who plans to be successful
   can ignore nature.

**(3) An adverb clause is a dependent clause used
as an adverb.**

See Adverb, p.
366

An adverb clause usually modifies the action
in a main verb. The clause usually tells *when,
where, how, how much,* or *why* about the action.

EXAMPLES Jeri combed her hair *before she
dressed.*
[This adverb clause tells *when* Jeri
combed her hair.]

Tim painted the doors *where he had
sanded them.*
[This clause tells *where* Tim
painted the doors.]

José worked *as if his life were in danger.*
[This clause tells *how* José worked.]

Adverb clauses may also modify adjectives or adverbs, just as adverbs may.

EXAMPLES   Jo was angry *that Sheila was going.*
[This clause modifies the adjective *angry.* It tells *why* Jo was angry.]

Sheila left sooner *than the others did.*
[This clause modifies the adverb *sooner.* It tells *how much* sooner Sheila left.]

EXERCISE 5   Number a sheet of paper 1–6. Next to each number, write the adverb clause from each sentence.

EXAMPLE   Mr. and Mrs. Yuen were ready before the snows had come.

before the snows had come

1. Mr. Yuen brought in the young calves while Mrs. Yuen stored the feed.
2. After they had worked almost a week, everything seemed ready.
3. They both worked as though their lives depended on their success.
4. While they prepared for winter, they often looked at the Montana sky.

5. It would be too late to find the calves after the heavy snows had begun.
6. Mr. and Mrs. Yuen were happy that they had prepared for winter.

REVIEW EXERCISE A Identification of Clauses

Number a sheet of paper 1–11. Write *NC* if the group of words after each number is *not* a clause. If the group of words is a clause, copy it after the number on your paper. Then underline the complete subject of the clause once and the complete predicate twice.

EXAMPLE Rin Tin Tin was one of the most famous dogs in America.

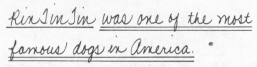

1. Lassie appeared in several films
2. Then in a television program
3. She was courageous and faithful
4. Benji is another famous dog
5. Because he follows commands
6. Sitting for a cookie
7. Would your dog go to work
8. Famous dogs and their lucky owners
9. Often dogs are named Rover or Fido
10. If the dog will eat and bark on command
11. My dog can sing

REVIEW EXERCISE B Independent and Dependent Clauses

Number a sheet of paper 1–10. After each number write *D* if the group of words is a dependent clause. Write *I* if it is an independent clause.

EXAMPLE When she returns from school

D

1. Native Americans own many of the coal fields in America
2. This is especially true of the Cheyenne
3. Who have five billion tons of coal under their reservation in Montana
4. The Hopi were the first Americans to use coal
5. Which they used to warm their homes and to fire pottery
6. Coal cannot entirely solve our energy problems today
7. It can help
8. More than 100,000 Americans have died in coal mining accidents
9. If coal mines pollute nearby streams
10. The United States has huge beds of coal

REVIEW EXERCISE C Noun Clauses

Number a sheet of paper 1–10. After each number write the noun clause in that sentence.

What Carol likes most is a tasty feast of spareribs and spaghetti.

What Carol likes most

1. Whoever planned the picnic certainly planned well.
2. Although I will eat whatever is put in front of me, I like good food.
3. The best part of this picnic was that nothing was inedible.
4. When I was greeted by the spicy odor of the cooking hamburgers, I knew that I was in for a treat.
5. What I really looked forward to was the roasted corn.
6. My brother later said that I ate the corn like a pig.
7. That a growing girl needs regular meals is well known.
8. That I had a chance to exercise afterward was a blessing.
9. The camp leader thought that all of us should take a long walk.
10. Was it wrong of me to suggest that we all walk to a store to buy more corn?

REVIEW EXERCISE D Adjective Clauses

Number a sheet of paper 1–10. Write the adjective clause in each of the following sentences.

EXAMPLE The cowboy was the man who worked on the open range.

who worked on the open range

1. Cattlemen who began to move into the Great Plains in the 1860's had to learn to handle wild cattle.

2. In Texas the herds of wild cattle that were called longhorns came from domestic cattle lost by Spanish settlers and by American wagon trains.

3. The man who handled these wild animals needed the help of a horse, a rope, and sometimes a gun.

4. Transportation of cattle to market was provided by railroads which were built in the 1860's.

5. Texas cowboys drove their cattle to the towns that grew up along the new railroads.

6. As the cattle industry grew, more people who wanted to make money began to raise cattle.

7. As the number of cattle increased, Texans who arrived in the market towns found that they could not always sell their cattle.

8. Those who could not sell their animals let them graze near town until the next spring.

9. An animal that had been eating all winter would be fat and would bring a high price in the market.

10. The rangeland that was open to all led to a cattle rush almost like the gold rush in California.

REVIEW EXERCISE E Adverb Clauses

Number a sheet of paper 1–10. After each number write the adverb clause in the sentence.

EXAMPLE   When the Cyclone opened in 1927, it was called the most fearsome roller coaster ever built.

When the Cyclone opened in 1927

1. While the last car was leaving the top of the first hill, the first car was already on a second hill.
2. A nurse stood by the Cyclone so that she could care for the fainting passengers.
3. When a rider got excited and let his elbows fly about, he might break the ribs of the poor person sitting next to him.
4. A newspaper reporter said that passengers should see a doctor before they decided to ride the Cyclone.
5. After he had ridden the Cyclone in New York, Charles Lindbergh said that it was a greater thrill than flying an airplane at top speed.
6. In Europe roller coasters are called "Russian Mountains" because the first ones were built in Russia.
7. Whenever a roller coaster loops or drops, some riders lose the contents of their pockets.
8. The operator of the roller coaster at Coney Island looked under the seat of the cars when he had time.
9. Some operators find more money under the seats than they make by selling tickets.
10. If you are brave, healthy, and a little reckless, try a ride on a roller coaster.

REVIEW EXERCISE F Review of Clauses

The following sentences contain noun clauses, adjective clauses, and adverb clauses. Choose one clause. Number a sheet of paper 1–10. After each number write the dependent clause from the sentence. Identify each dependent clause as a noun, an adjective, or an adverb clause.

EXAMPLE Arthur became king when he pulled a sword from a stone.

when he pulled a sword from a stone, adverb clause

1. The Greek hero Theseus was the only man who could find a sword that was hidden under a heavy rock.
2. When he set out for Athens, he met some interesting enemies.
3. One of these rascals was a man who would make passers-by wash his feet.
4. As they bent over to wash his feet, he would push them over a cliff.
5. Another enemy whom Theseus met was Procrustes, who was also called the Stretcher.
6. Procrustes knew that travelers to Athens by land would have to pass his den.
7. He would put whomever he captured on a stone bed.
8. If the captive did not exactly fit, Procrustes would cut off the person's feet or stretch his body.
9. Naturally, the people of Athens were grateful when Theseus killed the villain who had killed many Athenians.
10. If you read the Greek myths, you will learn how Medea tried to poison Theseus.

5

SENTENCES

The Sentence, Sentence Problems

People use more than just single words to communicate. They combine words in ways to make their meanings clear. The basic combinations of words that make meanings clear are called *sentences*.

Sentences can be written many different ways. They can also serve several purposes. Every sentence, however, must express a complete thought or statement.

Learning to write good sentences is an important part of learning the English language. Sentences are your thoughts put into words. Your language takes on a clearer meaning when you use complete sentences.

It is important to recognize what a sentence is and how its parts fit together to communicate a complete thought. An understanding of sentence structure will help you to write more effectively.

THE SENTENCE

5a   A sentence is a group of related words that expresses a complete thought.

Examples of sentences and word groups:

SENTENCES	WORD GROUPS
Bees fly.	Busy bees
Flowers are growing.	The flowers in the garden
Spring has arrived.	The noise and bustle of springtime

Each of the sentences expresses a complete thought. Each of the word groups leaves its thought incomplete. To make each word group into a complete thought, more words are needed. The words should tell what the busy bees are doing. They should tell something about the flowers in the garden or the noise and bustle of springtime.

EXAMPLE
WORD GROUP Busy bees
SENTENCE Busy bees flew around the flowers.

EXERCISE 1   Number a sheet of paper 1–10. Some of the following word groups are sentences. Some are word groups that are incomplete. Write *S* next to the number of each sentence. Add words to each incomplete word group to make it a sentence.

EXAMPLE Seeds in the ground

Seeds in the ground need water to make them grow.

1. Water dripped from the pipes
2. Water in the soil
3. The warm sun
4. Tiny green shoots poked above the ground
5. Soon the buds
6. At first only a few flowers came out
7. By midweek more than a dozen
8. In the area a mass of flowers
9. Even the smell in the air
10. Now Joan needs to pull out weeds

5b A simple sentence must contain a subject and a predicate.

The Subject

(1) The subject of a sentence is what the sentence tells about.

Usually a noun or a pronoun serves as the subject of a sentence.

See Noun, p. 380; Pronoun, p. 384

EXAMPLES Mechanics ran to the car.
[The subject is *mechanics*. They are doing the action of running.]

Cars are often hard to fix.
[*Cars* is the subject. They are being talked about in the sentence.]

Hint: You can find the subject in a sentence by asking either of these questions: *Who or what is doing the action? Who or what is being talked about?*

The *simple subject* of a sentence is the person or thing that is doing the action or being talked about. The *complete subject* is the simple subject plus all the other words directly related to the simple subject.

simple subject

EXAMPLES   Those   two   broken-down   *cars*

run poorly.   complete subject

simple subject

Evelyn's new *car* runs well.

complete subject.

Sometimes a single noun or pronoun may serve as both the complete subject and the simple subject.

EXAMPLE   *Tony* hit the ball.

EXERCISE 2   Number a sheet of paper 1–10. Write out the complete subject of each sentence. Circle the simple subject.

EXAMPLE   Newly-laid sidewalks look like flat mud beds.

Newly-laid (sidewalks)

1. Most city walkways are made of cement.
2. Cement comes from a special rock in the earth.
3. A grinding process makes it into powder.
4. The powdery cement is then heated in large ovens.
5. Special machines later mix the cement powder with sand.
6. The mixture of cement and sand can be stored many months.
7. Small stones are often mixed with the dry cement.
8. When ready for use, the dry mixture has water added.
9. This muddy mixture is poured into forms on the ground.
10. The flat mud becomes as hard as rock.

The Predicate

(2) The predicate of a sentence is the verb and related words that tell something about the subject.

See Verb, p. 387

The verb is the key word or words in the predicate. The verb tells the action of the subject. Or it tells what the subject is. Every predicate must have a complete verb in it.

The complete verb is called the *simple predicate*. The complete verb with all the related words is called the *complete predicate*.

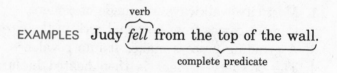

verb

EXAMPLES   Judy *fell* from the top of the wall.

complete predicate

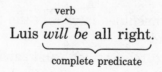

verb

Luis *will be* all right.

complete predicate

Hint: To find the simple predicate of a
sentence, look for the word or words that
tell of the action or begin a description of
the subject.

EXERCISE 3   Number a sheet of paper 1–10. Next
to each number write out the complete predicate
from each sentence. Put a box around the verb.

EXAMPLE   The wind blows seeds from grasses
and trees.

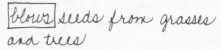

1. Seeds catch in little cracks of rocks.
2. They lodge in cracks in cement.
3. A bit of dirt will fall in the cracks.
4. The seeds grow a little in the dirt.
5. Their tiny roots catch some moisture.
6. They grow longer and stronger.
7. The roots of plants have split some rocks.

8. Patches of grass will live in cracks of a sidewalk.
9. The little roots seem stronger than cement.
10. Their search for food and water is powerful.

Hint: A sentence cannot have a subject without a predicate or a predicate without a subject.

Compound Subject and Compound Predicate

A sentence may have more than one subject or more than one predicate.

(3) A compound subject is made up of two or more complete subjects in a sentence.

The parts of a compound subject often are connected with a coordinating conjunction such as *and, or,* or *but.*

See Conjunction, p. 370

EXAMPLES *Thunder* and *lightning* descended on the valley.
All of the large power boats but *only three of the sailboats* finished the race.

EXERCISE 4 Following are five sentences with compound subjects. Write each sentence on a sheet of paper. Underline each complete subject once. Put a circle around each simple subject.

EXAMPLE   My older sister and her girl friend often study French together.

My older ⟨sister⟩ and her ⟨girl friend⟩ often study French together.

1. My mother and my father tell me not to bother them.
2. Tina, my best friend, and I try not to make noise.
3. Listening to records and popping corn can be disturbing, however.
4. French verbs and adjectives wouldn't satisfy my hunger.
5. A trip to France or a scholarship would be worthwhile.

(4)   **A compound predicate is made up of two or more complete predicates in a sentence.**

Each complete predicate is made up of the complete verb and the words that help it tell something about the subject. The parts of a compound predicate often are connected with a coordinating conjunction such as *and, or,* or *but.*

EXAMPLES   The wave *lifted the little boat* and *tipped it over.*

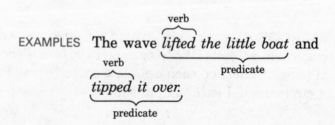

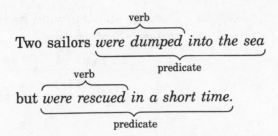

EXERCISE 5 Following are five sentences with compound predicates. Write each sentence on a sheet of paper. Underline each complete predicate twice. Put a box around each complete verb.

EXAMPLE Carlos had been seen immediately and was rescued in a few minutes.

Carlos had been seen *immediately and* was rescued *in a few minutes.*

1. Shinji was lost in the fog and could not be found.
2. A rescue boat searched for an hour but could find nothing.
3. Then the searchers heard a cry and saw Shinji in the water.
4. They steered close and saved Shinji.
5. A heavy fog will not only hide people but also will deaden sounds.

EXERCISE 6 Some of the following sentences have compound subjects. Some sentences have compound predicates. Some sentences have both a compound subject and a compound predicate. Write out each sentence on a sheet of paper. Underline each complete subject once and each complete predicate twice.

EXAMPLE The sun and the wind had been
perfect all afternoon.

*The sun and the wind
had been perfect all afternoon.*

1. Sailboats and motorboats scooted across the water.
2. The wind and the boats made wave patterns.
3. The waves slapped and bumped in little colli-
   sions.
4. The sun and wind had gone by late afternoon.
5. Low clouds and a fogbank rolled over the bay.
6. Most sailboats and motorboats had turned home-
   ward and had docked safely.
7. The fog caught a few and covered them completely.
8. A good compass and a sailor's skill would bring
   each boat home.

Types of Sentences

See Clauses, p.
73–77 **5c A simple sentence contains one
independent clause.**

A clause and a sentence are similar. Both must
have a subject and a predicate. However, not every
clause is a sentence. Only an independent clause
expresses a complete thought.

EXAMPLES Wind makes waves on water.
Some waves rise many feet high.

5d A compound sentence contains two or more independent clauses.

EXAMPLES   *Storms at sea build up towering waves,* and *those waves can do severe damage.*

              Seagoing ships try to avoid the worst weather, but *sometimes they cannot escape it.*

Note that the two independent clauses in a compound sentence are joined by a comma and a coordinating conjunction.

More than two independent clauses are sometimes combined into one compound sentence.

EXAMPLE   *The wind blew, the waves rose high,* and *the rain poured down.*

Note that when a compound sentence has three or more independent clauses, each is separated by a comma. The coordinating conjunction is used between the last two clauses.

See Punctuation, p. 253

In some compound sentences, the coordinating conjunction may be omitted. If so, the comma is changed to a semicolon (;). This usually is done only when the independent clauses are closely related.

EXAMPLES   *Our ship shuddered from the impact of each wave; I was scared.*

              The waves swept across the deck; water poured into the cabin.

EXERCISE 7   Some of the following sentences are simple sentences. Some are compound sentences. Number a sheet of paper 1–8. Next to each number write *S* if the sentence is simple. Write *C* if the sentence is compound.

EXAMPLE A hurricane can do terrible damage
to life and property.

S

1. Caribbean hurricanes usually occur in the fall,
   but sometimes they come in summer or winter
   seasons.
2. They move in a northerly direction and gather
   strength day by day.
3. They may strike the Southern states, or they
   may veer further north along the Atlantic coast.
4. Their winds can easily top 100 knots, and some
   have developed winds over 130 knots.
5. Small boats are in serious danger in a hurricane,
   and larger ships are not always safe.
6. Some hurricanes push boats right out of the
   water and onto the land.
7. Cars and trucks have been toppled along with
   houses and trees.
8. Flooding is common from high tides and torren-
   tial rains.

**5e A complex sentence is made up of one or
more dependent clauses added to an
independent clause.**

EXAMPLES The waves at sea are often large
because the wind keeps blowing for
days.
[The independent clause is *The
waves at sea are often large.* The
dependent clause is *because the
wind keeps blowing for days.*]

If the wind blows a long time on the water, the waves grow larger. [The dependent clause is *If the wind blows a long time on the water.* The independent clause is *the waves grow larger.*]

It is dangerous to steer a small boat where large waves have built up. [The independent clause is *It is dangerous to steer a small boat.* The dependent clause is *where large waves have built up.*]

EXERCISE 8 Some of the following sentences are simple sentences. Some are complex sentences. Some are compound sentences. Number a sheet of paper 1–6. Next to the number of a simple sentence write *S*. Next to the number of a compound sentence write *C*. Next to the number of a complex sentence write *Cx*.

EXAMPLE When a hurricane blows in the China Sea, it is called a typhoon.

Cx

1. The winds of a typhoon blow long and hard and kick up gigantic waves.
2. Most waves are about twenty feet high, but some have been estimated near fifty feet high.
3. If a five-story building were at the bottom of a wave, the top of the wave would splash the roof of the building.

4. In the middle the windows would be smashed by tons of water.
5. The damage that would be done is unbelievable because the force and weight of water are tremendous.
6. No one wants to be caught in a typhoon, and no one wants to be wiped out by a fifty-foot wave.

Purposes of Sentences

Sentences are used for four different purposes. Sentences that serve these purposes are called *declarative, interrogative, imperative,* and *exclamatory* sentences. Their forms and their punctuation often change to show their purpose.

5f A declarative sentence declares a fact, opinion, or feeling.

EXAMPLES The pencil rolled from the desk.
It hit the floor with a clatter.
Its point broke.

A declarative sentence usually ends with a period (.).

5g An interrogative sentence asks a question.

EXAMPLES Why did you drop your pencil?
Must I say?
Why do you interrogate me?

In an interrogative sentence, the verb and the subject often switch positions from the normal subject-verb order of the declarative sentence.

> EXAMPLES
>
> DECLARATIVE SENTENCE   You are pleased.
> INTERROGATIVE SENTENCE   Are you pleased?

An interrogative sentence always ends with a question mark (**?**).

5h   An imperative sentence requests or orders something.

> EXAMPLES   Kindly pick up your clothes.
> Then make your bed.
> Bring me the wagon.

Imperative sentences usually omit the subject *you*. When the *you* is omitted, the sentence is still complete. The subject is said to be "understood."

An imperative sentence usually ends with a period (**.**).

5i   An exclamatory sentence expresses shock or surprise.

> EXAMPLES   Look out for the hornet!
> Ow! It stung me!

Some exclamatory sentences have *you* as the subject, which is "understood" to be there.

An exclamatory sentence usually ends with an exclamation mark (**!**).

EXERCISE 9 Number a sheet of paper 1–10. After each number tell what purpose the sentence serves. Mark *D* for declarative, *I* for interrogative, *Im* for imperative, and *E* for exclamatory.

> EXAMPLE Who invented the pencil
>
> *I*

1. Several thousand years ago there were no pencils
2. What did people write with
3. They had no paper
4. That is astounding
5. Tell me how they wrote
6. They pressed stick marks into soft clay
7. How could that be writing
8. Please drop the arguments
9. Learn to read cuneiform
10. Oh, what an awful word

Completers

Often the complete predicate contains a word called a *completer.* It completes or makes clear what the subject and verb are telling about. Completers may be either *objects* or *subject completers.*

See Transitive
Verbs, pp.
29–30

5j The direct object receives the action of the verb.

> EXAMPLE Monica Robinson raised her hand.
> [*Hand* receives the action of the verb *raised*. It is the direct object of the sentence.]

Hint: Here are the steps to find the direct object of an action verb:

Find the verb. In the example above, the verb is *raised*.

Find the subject. Ask: *Who or what raised?*

Answer: Monica.

Find the direct object. Ask: *Who or what did Monica raise?*

Answer: her hand.

Hand is the direct object of the action verb *raised*.

EXERCISE 10 Number a sheet of paper 1–6. Write the direct object of the action verb in each sentence.

EXAMPLE Ms. Wollaeger nodded her head.

head

1. She opened the book on her lap.
2. She found a special page.
3. She read the page out loud.
4. Her restless dog gave a little bark.
5. It tugged her skirt.
6. She tapped the dog on the nose.

5k The subject completer follows the linking verb and completes the meaning of the sentence. See Linking Verb, p. 379

The subject completer may be a noun, a pronoun, an adjective, or an adverb.

EXAMPLES My father is a dentist.
[The noun *dentist* completes the meaning of the sentence by telling who the father is.]

That dog appears fierce.
[The adjective *fierce* completes the meaning of the sentence by telling how the dog appears.]

Ascot Beauregard is late.
[The adverb *late* tells about the time of Ascot Beauregard.]

Hint: Here are the steps to find the subject completer:
Find the linking verb. In the first example, the linking verb is *is.*
Find the subject. Ask: *Who or what is?*
Answer: my father.
Find the subject completer. Ask: *My father is who or what?*
Answer: a dentist.
Dentist is the subject completer of the subject *father* and the linking verb *is.*

EXERCISE 11 Number a sheet of paper 1–8 and copy the following sentences. Underline the completer in each sentence. Draw an arrow from the completer to the noun or pronoun it tells about.

EXAMPLE Uncle Bert looked frightened.

Uncle Bert looked frightened.

1. Jane also felt scared when she saw them.
2. Those footprints were enormous.

3. Jane was a brave girl.
4. She was an amateur detective, besides.
5. "Big Foot was hungry last night," Uncle Bert said.
6. "He was here," Bert added.
7. "I remain unafraid," Jane said.
8. She looked determined to solve the mystery.

The Patterns of Sentences

Sentences are formed in grammatical patterns, or structures. You need only a few patterns for the countless sentences you speak or write. Some of the most common sentence patterns follow.

Sentence Pattern 1: SUBJECT-VERB (S-V)

Sentence Pattern 1 is made up of a simple subject and an intransitive verb. Each may have modifiers, but the modifiers do not change the basic pattern.

See Verbs, pp. 29–30

EXAMPLES
$$\text{The little } \overset{\text{S}}{\underline{\text{baby}}} \quad \overset{\text{V}}{\underline{\text{gurgled}}}.$$

$$\text{Her } \overset{\text{S}}{\underline{\text{mother}}} \quad \overset{\text{V}}{\underline{\text{smiled}}} \text{ proudly}.$$

$$\text{Then } \overset{\text{S}}{\underline{\text{they}}} \quad \overset{\text{V}}{\underline{\text{slept}}} \text{ in silence}.$$

EXERCISE 12 Copy the following Pattern 1 sentences on your paper. Write *S* above the simple subject and *V* above the complete verb.

EXAMPLE The wind blew softly.

$$\overset{S}{\textit{The wind}} \overset{V}{\textit{blew softly.}}$$

1. The tree rocked in the wind.
2. A branch cracked at its base.
3. The sound echoed in the forest.
4. A gust of wind pushed at the branch.
5. It snapped completely off.
6. The branch tumbled to the ground.

Sentence Pattern 2:   SUBJECT-VERB-OBJECT (S-V-O)

Sentence Pattern 2 is made up of a simple subject, a transitive verb, and a direct object. The subject tells who does the action in a sentence. The verb tells what the action is. The direct object receives the action. It is the person or thing acted upon by the subject.

EXAMPLES
$$\overset{S}{\text{Workers}} \overset{V}{\text{built}} \overset{O}{\text{the dam.}}$$
$$\overset{S}{\text{They}} \overset{V}{\text{carried}} \overset{O}{\text{the dirt.}}$$

Other words may be included in the Pattern 2 sentence.

EXAMPLES
$$\text{Weary } \overset{S}{\text{workers}} \overset{V}{\text{built}} \overset{O}{\text{the dam}}$$
with their hands.
$$\overset{S}{\text{They}} \text{ reluctantly } \overset{V}{\text{carried}} \overset{O}{\text{the dirt}}$$
to fill the dam.

Sentence Pattern 2 has another form as follows:

Sentence Pattern 2a: SUBJECT-VERB-INDIRECT OBJECT-DIRECT OBJECT (S-V-IO-DO)

Sentence Pattern 2a is made up of a subject, a transitive verb, an indirect object, and a direct object. Sentence Pattern 2a is just like Pattern 2 with the addition of an indirect object. The indirect object comes after the verb but in front of the direct object.

EXAMPLES	$\overset{S}{\text{Mason}} \overset{V}{\text{paid}} \overset{IO}{\text{the clerk}} \overset{DO}{\text{the money.}}$
	$\overset{S}{\text{He}} \overset{V}{\text{brought}} \overset{IO}{\text{his wife}} \overset{DO}{\text{the present.}}$
	$\overset{S}{\text{She}} \overset{V}{\text{gave}} \overset{IO}{\text{him}} \overset{DO}{\text{a kiss.}}$

Hint: Here are the steps to find the object in a Pattern 2 sentence:

Find the verb. Ask: *What is the action?* In the first example above, the verb is *built.*

Find the subject. Ask: *Who or what does the action?*

Answer: workers.

Find the object. Ask: *Who or what receives the action?*

Answer: the dam.

Dam is the object. It receives the action of the subject *workers* and the verb *built.*

EXERCISE 13 Copy the following Pattern 2 and Pattern 2a sentences on a sheet of paper. Skip a line between each sentence. Write *S* above each subject, *V* above each verb, *DO* above each direct object, and *IO* above each indirect object.

EXAMPLE The driver of the car gave Amy a ride.

The driver of the car gave Amy a ride.

1. Heavy trucks hauled rocks to the same place.
2. The drivers dumped the rocks in large piles.
3. At noon another truck brought the workers their lunches.
4. Chefs had made the workers some sandwiches in the morning.
5. The workers eagerly ate their lunches.
6. By nightfall the boss gave the workers a rest.
7. They welcomed the end of the day.
8. Each morning the workers piled the rocks higher.
9. Finally they began pouring the concrete into wooden forms.
10. Teams of workers made the dam in a month.

Many Pattern 2 sentences and Pattern 2a sentences can be switched back and forth. Here is a Pattern 2 sentence:

S   V   O

The school gave the trophy to Throckbottom.

The prepositional phrase *to Throckbottom* can be moved between the verb and the direct object by dropping *to*.

S   V   IO   DO

The school gave Throckbottom the trophy.

Throckbottom has become the indirect object. The new sentence is a Pattern 2a sentence.

In the following example, a Pattern 2a sentence is made into a Pattern 2 sentence.

S   V   IO DO

Throckbottom brought the school fame.

S   V   O

Throckbottom brought fame to the school.

EXERCISE 14 Rewrite each of the following sentences on your paper. Make each Pattern 2 sentence into a Pattern 2a sentence. Make each Pattern 2a sentence into a Pattern 2 sentence.

EXAMPLE Manuel Sanchez gave a ring to Nan.

Manuel Sanchez gave Nan a ring.

1. He had bought her the ring with his savings.
2. He presented the ring to Nan Saturday night.
3. On Sunday she had shown her mother the present.
4. The sight of the ring brought her mother a shock.
5. Years before, Nan's father had given Nan's mother a ring just like it.
6. Nan's mother had sold the ring to a pawnbroker for cash.

Sentence Pattern 3: SUBJECT-LINKING VERB-SUBJECT COMPLETER

Sentence Pattern 3 is made up of a subject, a linking verb, and a subject completer. The completer of the subject follows the verb and completes what is being said about the subject. It may be a noun, a pronoun, an adjective, or an adverb.

EXAMPLES
$$\overset{\text{S}}{\text{Angus}} \overset{\text{LV}}{\text{became}} \overset{\text{SC}}{\text{a chief.}}$$
$$\overset{\text{S}}{\text{He}} \overset{\text{LV}}{\text{was}} \overset{\text{SC}}{\text{proud.}}$$
$$\overset{\text{S}}{\text{His clan}} \overset{\text{LV}}{\text{grew}} \overset{\text{SC}}{\text{restless.}}$$

Hint: Here are the steps to find the subject completer in a Pattern 3 sentence:
Find the linking verb. In the first example, the linking verb is *became*.
Find the subject. Ask: *Who or what became?*
Answer: Angus.
Find the subject completer. Ask: *Angus became who or what?*
Answer: chief.
Chief is the subject completer of the subject *Angus* and the linking verb *became*.

EXERCISE 15   Copy the following Pattern 3 sentences on your paper. Skip a line between each sentence. Write *S* above each subject, *LV* above each linking verb, and *SC* above each subject completer.

EXAMPLE   The countryside appeared rugged.

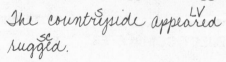

1. The land was hilly.
2. Trees seemed short in the rocky soil.
3. They were spindly.
4. The inhabitants were tough.
5. They became famous for their fighting ability.
6. They were rugged like their country.

SENTENCE PROBLEMS

A correctly written sentence must say something about its subject. The sentence must tell what the subject does, or it must tell what the subject is. In order to serve a purpose, a sentence must follow a grammatical pattern.

The following section deals with problems of groups of words that do not serve as sentences. Some are sentence fragments. Others are run-on sentences.

Sentence Fragments

5l   A sentence fragment is an incomplete sentence.

See Phrase, p. 383; Clause, p. 368

Most fragments include phrases or dependent clauses. Phrase fragments occur in the following ways:

FRAGMENT (subject missing)   *had seen the potted plant.*

COMPLETE SENTENCE (subject added)   *Marybelle* had seen the potted plant.

FRAGMENT (predicate missing)   *the sand and pieces of dirt.*

COMPLETE SENTENCE (predicate added)   The sand and the pieces of dirt *were mixed in the pot.*

FRAGMENT (subject and predicate missing) *with your fingers.*

COMPLETE SENTENCE (subject and predicate added)   *Don't eat* with your fingers.

The following examples show dependent clauses as fragments:

FRAGMENT   *as the water rushed along.*
[This dependent clause must have an independent clause joined to it to make a complete sentence.]
COMPLETE SENTENCE As the water rushed along, *it picked up sticks and leaves.*

FRAGMENT   *when it delivered the sofa.*
[This dependent clause refers to something that is missing. The missing part can be provided in an independent clause.]
COMPLETE SENTENCE *Connie recognized the truck* when it delivered the sofa.

EXERCISE 16 Some of the following groups of words are complete sentences. Some are fragments. Number a sheet of paper 1–10. Next to each number write *S* if the group of words is a sentence and *F* if it is a fragment. End punctuation has been omitted.

EXAMPLE Blossoms on the trees

F

1. Sweet blossoms attract insects
2. As the blossoms come out in the spring
3. Their smell attracts bees, for instance
4. The ever-searching bee near the nest
5. Deep in the heart of the blossom
6. Bees seek food
7. Not pollen
8. However, the pollen around the food catches on the legs and body of the bee
9. To the next blossom
10. Trees use bees to help

EXERCISE 17 Some of the following groups of words are fragments. Others are complete sentences. On your paper, rewrite each fragment. Add words to make each fragment a complete sentence.

EXAMPLE While Teresa watched

The pigeon flew back and forth while Teresa watched.

1. Higher than the birds
2. It came soaring down
3. It did quick somersaults in the air
4. As though someone had thrown it over and over
5. Before it reached the ground
6. Up it went higher again
7. In another similar flight
8. The tumbler pigeon likes its acrobatics

Run-on Sentences

5m A run-on sentence is two or more sentences incorrectly joined.

EXAMPLES The sparrow sat on the building the roof was about forty feet high.
A bread crust dropped it flew down to get it.

Both these examples are run-on sentences. Each one incorrectly combines two sentences. There are three good methods for correcting run-on sentences.

Method 1: The sentences in a run-on sentence may be divided into separate sentences.

> RUN-ON SENTENCE   The sparrow picked up the crust then it flew back to the roof.
>
> CORRECT SEPARATE SENTENCES   The sparrow picked up the crust. Then it flew back to the roof.

See
Conjunction,
p. 370 *Method 2:* The sentences in a run-on sentence may be correctly joined by adding a comma and a coordinating conjunction. Sometimes a coordinating conjunction alone will do.

> RUN-ON   Another sparrow must have seen all this he flew over to join the first sparrow on the roof.
>
> CORRECT SENTENCE   Another sparrow must have seen all this, *for* he flew over to join the first sparrow on the roof.

Method 3: Some run-on sentences may be corrected by means of punctuation.

> RUN-ON   The first sparrow pecked madly at the newcomer the crust dropped forty feet to the ground again.
>
> CORRECTED PUNCTUATION   The first sparrow pecked madly at the newcomer; the crust dropped forty feet to the ground again.

EXERCISE 18 Some of the following groups of words are run-on sentences. Rewrite each run-on sentence on a sheet of paper. Use Method 1, 2, or 3 to rewrite the sentence correctly.

EXAMPLE   Eagles can fly with heavy objects
their catches weigh several pounds.

Eagles can fly with heavy objects.
Their catches weigh several pounds.

1. An eagle can carry away a lamb the catch may weigh far more than the bird.
2. The pelican's wings are strong it flies with a heavy load sometimes.
3. It will put food in its stomach and in a pouch under its bill.
4. The combined weight of food equals what it weighs.
5. Even tiny birds like the hummingbird can fly with added weight.
6. Birds do amazing things we can find pleasure in studying their behavior.

REVIEW EXERCISE A   Subjects and Verbs

Copy the following sentences on a sheet of paper. Circle each simple subject and put a box around each verb.

EXAMPLE   Hercules was famous for his great strength.

Hercules was famous for
his great strength.

1. Hercules began his adventures in his cradle.
2. He strangled two huge snakes and threw them out of his room.

3. In Greek mythology Hercules did some amazing things.
4. He killed the ferocious Nemean lion and used its skin as a coat.
5. He cleaned some dirty stables by changing the course of a river to run through the stables.
6. Hercules caught the famous Cretan bull, showed it to his friends, and then let it go.
7. Hercules and Theseus collected an army and marched against Hippolyte, queen of the Amazons.
8. They captured her magic belt and took it back to Greece as a souvenir.
9. In the wonderful garden of the Hesperides, Hercules killed the guarding dragon and picked the golden apples.
10. Today, a very difficult job may be called a Herculean task.

REVIEW EXERCISE B   Kinds of Sentences

Number a sheet of paper 1–10. Identify each of the following sentences as simple *S*, compound *C*, or complex *Cx*.

> EXAMPLE   Henry David Thoreau, the American philosopher, spent a few days in the Concord, Massachusetts, jail.
>
> S

1. One of India's leaders was Mohandas Gandhi.
2. Gandhi believed that India should be free of Britain.
3. He believed in love and respect for others, and he fought without using violence.

4. He asked Indians not to buy the cotton cloth that the British had been selling for many years.

5. When people refuse to buy goods, they are boycotting those goods.

6. The British put a high tax on salt, but Gandhi and his followers did not buy salt.

7. He walked to the sea and taught his followers to take salt from it.

8. Of course, the British could not tax them for this salt.

9. An American reporter asked Gandhi where he had learned to fight peacefully.

10. Gandhi was surprised by the question because he had learned from the American philosopher Henry David Thoreau.

REVIEW EXERCISE C Purposes of Sentences

Number a sheet of paper 1–10. Identify each of the following by writing *D* for a declarative sentence, *I* for an interrogative sentence, *Im* for an imperative sentence, or *E* for an exclamatory sentence.

1. Peter Piper picked a peck of pickled peppers.

2. Where is the peck of pickled peppers Peter Piper picked?

3. Please pass the plate of pickled peppers, Peter.

4. There is a fire in the pickled pepper patch!

5. Peppers pickle perfectly in Persia.

6. Who was Peter Piper's papa's parent?

7. Peter's pet parakeet, Pedro, prefers potatoes to pickles.

8. Put down the pickles, Peter, and pay attention to your parakeet.

9. Peter picked the peppers punctually.
10. Does Peter provide a perfect practice?

REVIEW EXERCISE D   Sentence Patterns

Each of the following sentences is either Pattern 2, S-V-O, or Pattern 3, S-LV-SC. Number a sheet of paper 1–10. Identify the pattern of each sentence by writing its initials.

EXAMPLES   The Greeks defeated the Trojans.

S-V-O

Odysseus was a Greek warrior.

S-LV-SC

1. Homer was the author of *The Odyssey*.
2. Homer also wrote *The Iliad*.
3. Odysseus was a great Greek hero.
4. Odysseus fought the Minotaur.
5. Odysseus seemed shrewd as well as strong and brave.
6. Odysseus's heroism included shrewdness as well as bravery.
7. Odysseus's wife, Penelope, awaited his return for twenty years.
8. Odysseus's wife, Penelope, was faithful to him for twenty years.
9. Her son, Telemachus, felt depressed about his father's long absence.
10. Her son, Telemachus, missed his father during Odysseus's long absence.

REVIEW EXERCISE E Sentence Patterns

Number a sheet of paper 1–10. Identify the pattern of each sentence as S-V (Pattern 1), S-V-O (Pattern 2), S-V-IO-DO (Pattern 2a), or S-LV-SC (Pattern 3).

EXAMPLE Kino gives his dogs snacks.

S-V-IO-DO (Pattern 2a)

1. Some odd eating habits can be observed.
2. One cat named William liked canned corn.
3. His master gave William cat food and canned corn.
4. Dogs and cats should not eat sweets.
5. Helen's dog, though, ate chocolate desserts.
6. The dog became rather fat.
7. His teeth were not strong.
8. Finally, Helen became worried.
9. She gave the fat dog diet dog food.
10. Now he eats carrots and lettuce, but not candy.

REVIEW EXERCISE F Fragments

Number a sheet of paper 1–10. If the word group is a complete sentence, write *S* (sentence) after the number. If the word group is a fragment, write a complete sentence using the fragment.

EXAMPLE When he heard the news

When he heard the news, President Hayes fainted.

1. Because of the rivalry between the two players
2. Tania did a perfect somersault on the trampoline
3. An excursion into the swamps along the Atlantic coast
4. With his trophy in hand, Oscar felt fine
5. A luxurious and restful vacation
6. A buoy bounced on the tranquil bay
7. When the mosquitoes started to bite the whole team
8. My cousin was an Olympic athlete
9. If she had not worked hard all year
10. The crowd broke out in spontaneous applause

REVIEW EXERCISE G   Run-On Sentences

Number a sheet of paper 1–10. If the word group is written correctly, write *S* (sentence) after the number. If the word group is a run-on sentence, correct it. Write your correction next to the number.

EXAMPLE   Harriet was a strong, healthy girl
          she won three tennis tournaments.

Harriet was a strong, healthy girl.
She won three tennis tournaments.

1. In a magazine, Harriet read about some professional tennis players.
2. Harriet knew she was skilled she practiced every day.
3. She wanted to be a great athlete.
4. Her backhand stroke was powerful her opponents could not return her best strokes.

5. Finally the day of her first tournament arrived.

6. Harriet ran out to the courts the crowds cheered.

7. Confident of victory, she smiled at the spectators and began a perfect game.

8. Her backhands were powerful her forehand strokes were perfect.

9. Television reporters fought to be the first to interview this new tennis star.

10. Harriet smiled into the camera she said that she owed all of her success to her tennis coach.

UNIT TWO

COMPOSITION

Paragraphs
Guidelines for Writing
Letter Writing

6

PARAGRAPHS

A paragraph tells about a single idea or *topic*. Most paragraphs use several sentences to do this. The topic is often stated in the first sentence, which is indented. Then the other sentences in the paragraph give more information about the topic.

DEVELOPING PARAGRAPHS

6a A paragraph is a series of sentences that tell about a single idea, person, object, or event.

You can use a paragraph for several purposes. One purpose is to tell about something that happened—an event. Another purpose is to describe something or someone. Still another purpose is to state your opinion about some matter.

Example of a paragraph telling of an event:

The class sat in a hush after Mr. Breck asked me to give the names of the three most famous world leaders today. It was then I was sorry I had not been paying attention. I thought Mr. Breck had been explaining something about world leadership, but I had been whispering to Ace and had missed what he said. I started to admit I had not been paying attention. Just then my nose began to tickle in the worst way. A huge sneeze was growing. It came on suddenly. I just had to sneeze. Kerchoo! It crashed out. Of course the class burst out laughing. Mr. Breck never smiled. By the time I had a handkerchief out and was preparing for the next sneeze (I always seem to get sneezes in groups of three), the bell rang ending the class.

Example of a paragraph describing something:

The simple paper clip is really a clever object. It is made of nothing more than thin wire. This is wrapped in a flattened oval shape. The wire starts straight down one side of the flat oval for a half-inch. It bends back three-quarters of an inch on the other flat side of the oval. Then it bends down again, passing snugly against the first straight wire but extending another quarter of an inch beyond. There it bends back once again so as to pass along the outside of the second flat side of the oval. It comes to an end just across the flat oval from where it started. The rounded ends of the paper clip slip over and under sheets of paper, pinching them and holding them together.

There it sits, doing its important little task of pinching and looking for all the world—well, like a simple, clever paper clip.

Example of a paragraph stating an opinion:

Motorbikes are definitely dangerous vehicles. With only two wheels, they lack stability on quick turns. Driving them straight ahead is not much of a problem. But if for some reason the driver needs to turn sharply, a motorbike can easily skid or even flip over. Once the bike goes into a skid or flip, the rider has almost no protection. This means injuries occur more often than they would in a four-wheel vehicle like a car. Nor is this all, for an accident on a road with other vehicles increases the chances of multiple accidents. These are the main reasons to stay away from motorbikes.

Notice that in each of the examples the topic, or main idea, of the paragraph is stated in the first sentence. This sentence is called the *topic sentence*. The topic sentence of a paragraph is often its first sentence.

6b State the main idea of a paragraph in a topic sentence.

When you plan to write a paragraph, think carefully about your topic. Then write a sentence that puts that idea into words. This will be your topic sentence.

Following is an example of a paragraph that expresses the writer's opinion about an allowance.

Notice that the topic sentence is the first sentence.
It states exactly what the paragraph is about.

> Young adults should get allowances, no mat-
> ter how small. They need to gain experience in
> managing money. If there are no jobs avail-
> able, an allowance is the only thing that will
> make it possible to learn about spending and
> saving. If young adults will do a little work
> around the home, this is no reason for them
> not to have money. Money in the form of an
> allowance should not be denied any young
> adult.

EXERCISE 1 Each of the following paragraphs
needs a topic sentence. Following the paragraphs
are six possible topic sentences. Choose the best
topic sentence for each paragraph. Write the numbers 1, 2, and 3 on a sheet of paper. Next to each
number write the topic sentence that belongs with
the paragraph.

1.   (Topic sentence missing) This is because the airplane's high speed will not
permit mistakes to be corrected. If a pilot
must change course, the decision needs to
be made quickly. Otherwise the plane will
pass beyond the desired location before the
turn can be made. The rushing mass of
metal and fuel requires several miles of air
space to complete a turn. At such burning
speeds, planning and swift action by the
pilot make the difference between life and
death.

2.   (Topic sentence missing) Its body, about
two feet long, is covered with rounded

plates of bony material. One of these extends over part of its head. The plates are jointed at the animal's midsection, allowing it to turn or bend. When attacked by an enemy, the armadillo uses its long, sharp claws on its front feet. The claws are not for fighting, however. Instead, the armadillo digs a hole at great speed and climbs in. There, curled so that only its armor is exposed, the armadillo is safe.

3. (Topic sentence missing) Umbrella ants live in countries near the equator, where they find plenty of leaves for food. The ants cut off sections from leaves with their jaws. A section may be much larger than the ant itself. Two or three sections put together would be the size of a dollar bill. When the section is cut, the ant lifts it in its jaws and carries it back to its nest, where it will be stored for future use. Walking along the jungle floor toward its nest, an ant looks as though it were carrying a little green umbrella.

1. The armadillo is a gentle animal, well-equipped to protect itself.
2. Umbrella ants like hot weather.
3. Pilots who fly supersonic airplanes must be experienced, quick, and always alert.
4. An armadillo gave soldiers the idea for a tank.
5. In the world of the ants, the umbrella ant is one of the most unusual.
6. Supersonic airplanes are dangerous.

6c Keep every sentence in a paragraph on the topic.

Every sentence in a paragraph should deal with something about the topic. If a sentence does not tell about the topic, it should not be in the paragraph.

Example of a paragraph with a sentence not on the topic:

(1) In a country filled with automobiles, driver training is important for the safety of all. (2) Without training, drivers may get behind the wheels of cars and cause great damage. (3) These drivers may injure or kill many people. (4) Last year, more highways were constructed in the United States than in any of the previous five years. (5) By training drivers before they drive cars, we can reduce highway accidents.

You should be able to find the sentence that does not deal with the topic. It is Sentence 4. You can see that the paragraph states its topic in Sentence 1. All the other sentences, except Sentence 4, tell about that topic in some way. Sentence 4 should not be in the paragraph.

In your own writing, make each sentence in a paragraph tell about the topic.

EXERCISE 2 Number a sheet of paper 1–3. Each of the following paragraphs contains a sentence that is not on the topic. Next to each number write the sentence that does not belong in the paragraph.

1.   The common garden earthworm helps keep the soil in good condition. For one thing, earthworms bore holes in the ground. Holes allow water to seep into the soil and nourish the roots of grasses and other plants. For another thing, the dirt that earthworms eat is passed from their bodies as enriched soil. An earthworm has no backbone. The enriched soil from the earthworm aids plants in their growth.

2.   Spiders are cannibals. They begin at an early age to eat each other. A mother spider lays hundreds of tiny silver eggs in a silky bag she spins. When the baby spiders hatch a few days after birth, the stronger ones feed on their weak brothers and sisters. Only a few human cannibals are known to be living today. This is nature's way of seeing to it that a new generation will survive.

3.   Baby spiders that drop to the ground have a special way of traveling long distances. They spin out wispy strands of thread that catch in the breeze and pull them along. At first, the young spiders are blown only a short distance. They land higher up in the grass, where they can get a better take-off. From here they spin out even longer strands of thread to catch the wind. Baby spiders never go back to their nest. A breeze will lift the long strands, with the spiders holding onto the ends. Sometimes soaring spiders will drift upward hundreds of feet and be carried many miles before landing in a new homesite.

6d A paragraph may be developed with details, examples, or reasons.

You can use details, examples, or reasons to support the topic of a paragraph. Just be sure the details, examples, or reasons are closely related to your topic.

Example of a paragraph developed with details:

Chinese or Japanese brush painting requires special equipment and techniques. The painter must choose a fine bristled brush, sometimes made of fox hairs. The ink he or she uses must have a pleasant odor and at least six circles on the top of the stick to indicate its quality. The painter will also require a grinding and mixing block for the ink. Different textures of rice paper will produce different results with the brush strokes, so the painter must choose carefully. Small solid pieces of material are ground and mixed with water to make different colors of paint. Finally, the painter must sit squarely on a chair with his or her back straight and feet firmly on the ground in order to make the correct brush strokes.

Example of a paragraph developed with examples:

Several inventions of little, straight objects have made a big difference in our world. For example, think of the importance of needles. Needles had to be invented thousands of years ago for us to have clothing. And now surgeons perform medical miracles with their needles and thread. Think, too, about nails and spikes. With them, people of the world built houses, bridges, and railroads. Probably the most important little, straight invention of all is an object for writing—a pen or a pencil.

Example of a paragraph developed with reasons:

Students should be allowed to use hand calculators in General Math. One reason is that the problems in the class are studied to help students learn how to think. Calculations themselves are not the important part of work. The calculations are helpful only if the reasoning is correct. So having a calculator should not interfere with the important work in the class. Another reason is that students are going to use calculators in later life anyway. In fact, many students have their own calculators now. A class in mathematics should give students practice in correctly using calculators.

6e A paragraph may be developed through comparison or contrast.

A paragraph may develop its main idea through comparison or contrast. This means that at least *two* items are mentioned. One item is the main point, or topic. The second item is compared and contrasted with it. That is, the paragraph tells how the second item is alike and different from the first item.

Example of a paragraph developed by comparison and contrast:

A submarine-hunting warship and a hungry bat find their prey in similar ways. The warship cannot "see" a submerged submarine, but it does send out sharp pinging sounds through the water. These sounds bounce off a hard object, such as the hull of a boat. They return to the warship as echoes. The bat flying in the dusky night sends out high-pitched squeaks that echo back from objects such as insects in the air. The warship steers toward the enemy submarine to destroy it; the bat flies toward the insect to eat it.

EXERCISE 3 Choose one of the following topics. On a sheet of paper make a list of points about the two items mentioned in the topics. In your list, include points that show the comparison and contrast between the two items.

1. Shoes and slippers
2. Hats and helmets
3. Cologne and perfume
4. Sugar and starch
5. Spring and autumn
6. A newsmagazine and a newspaper
7. Iron and steel
8. Rubber and soft plastic

6f A paragraph may be developed by showing causes and effects.

The paragraph that tells of an event may show causes and effects. When something happens, it often causes something else to happen. For instance, if you walk in shoes that are too tight, they may cause blisters on your feet. If you dial a friend's telephone number, the phone will ring.

These events are closely related. They would naturally belong together in a paragraph.

Example of a paragraph developed by cause
and effect:

If you have ever inspected a burning match,
you may have wondered what caused the three
different colors in the flame. Inside the cone of
flame, next to the match stick, is a dark area.
This is made up of gas that is not burning because it has not reached the air. Surrounding
the inner dark region is a bright area where
oxygen in the air begins to combine with carbon, causing bright light and heat to be given
off. Around this area, on the outside, is a yellow flame, not as bright as the part inside it,
but hotter still. It is here that carbon dioxide is
formed because there is sufficient oxygen in
the surrounding air.

EXERCISE 4   Choose one of the following topics
and write a short paragraph. Show cause and effect
in your paragraph.

1. The rising kite
2. The wind-chill factor
3. The fire extinguisher
4. Sour milk
5. Frost on a window pane
6. The making of an iceberg

**6g Events in a paragraph may be organized
      by time.**

Related events often happen at approximately
the same time. When writing a paragraph about re-

lated events, be sure you keep in mind when those events occurred. Organize them in a time sequence your reader can easily understand.

Example of a paragraph organized by time:

There are too many buzzers and bells in my week. Each weekday morning I wake up to the buzzer on my clock radio. That really annoys me. It starts my day off with a necessary evil sound. Then, as I am getting dressed, I hear the chimes of the big old clock in the living room. That tells me I had better hurry if I want any breakfast. Bad bells continue at school. One starts every period. Another one ends every period. Even in the gym locker room there is a rasping buzzer right over my locker. It makes me jump almost out of my socks! It means I am late getting dressed again. Finally, at night the telephone starts ringing. If a friend is calling and I have more homework to do, I have to keep the call shorter than three minutes. Even the friendly telephone bell hurts, because I usually have more homework to finish. I do look forward to a bell-less weekend.

Notice how the writer of the paragraph above refers to times of the day. These references start at the beginning of a day and go in order to the end. The references help keep a time sequence in mind.

EXERCISE 5 Only the first and last sentences in the following paragraph are in the right order in time. The other sentences are out of order. On a sheet of paper, write the numbers of the sentences in the order they belong.

(1) When a customer drives into the station where you work, the first thing to do is say, "Can I help you?" (2) Then start the gas pumping into the car's tank. (3) If the oil and water and battery check out all right, then clean the windshield and the rear window. (4) When the gas is pumped, put the cap back tight on the car's tank and the nozzle back on the pumpstand. (5) While the gas is pumping, ask the driver if you should check the oil and water. (6) (No need to say, "May I," because you're not asking permission to help.) (7) Finally, report the amount of gas and the price to the driver so that you don't forget to get paid.

6h A paragraph may be organized by space.

If a paragraph describes something, its organization of the parts being described should help the reader see what the paragraph is about.

Example of a paragraph organized by space:

Some kinds of fish have been observed playing what appears to be a special jumping game. Several fish will come upon a floating stick. They will circle under it at first. Then one will dart quickly up toward the stick. With a last flick of the tail, the first fish will leap from the water directly over the stick and splash down on the other side. Other fish will then follow. Over and across the stick they jump. Sometimes they touch it. Their game seems to be who can make the slickest leap over the stick.

EXERCISE 6 Select one of the following sentences. Use it as a topic sentence. Write a paragraph of at least four or five sentences. Organize your paragraph by time or by space.

1. I saw the cleverest cartoon strip.
2. The button I sewed on works better than it did before.
3. We have found a way to reduce consumption of electricity at home.
4. Last weekend I bathed our dog.
5. The bus ride downtown went more easily than I expected.
6. I just rearranged my bedroom furniture.

6i Link the sentences of a paragraph together by connecting words.

Certain words help to link sentences together. Words like *then* and *next* help to show time relationships. Words like *in front of* or *next to* help to show space relationships. Words like *however* and *by comparison* help to show comparison or contrast. Here is a list of the most common linking words. You can use words like these to tie sentences together within a paragraph.

TIME	SPACE	COMPARISON AND CONTRAST
after that	above	however
afterward	ahead of	by comparison
before that	behind	in contrast to
next	before	
then	below	
	in front of	
	next to	

6j   Use a paragraph to show the words of a new speaker.

The words of a new speaker begin a new paragraph. If you quote the words said by someone, be sure to begin the quotation by indenting. The following example illustrates this use of paragraphs.

It is strange how you can sniff trouble on a man. Ian the Postman never said a word at first, just took off his peaked cap and passed a hand across his bald head, jammed the cap on again, cleared his throat, and spat on the grass, all common enough actions that I had seen him do a hundred times before. But this time I knew that something was wrong.

"What is it, Ian?" I asked.

"There has been . . . an . . . accident, boy," he said slowly, picking around the words as if he had a hard job putting his tongue to them. "It is Ruari. He is hurt."

"Ruari? Hurt?" I repeated stupidly. And then, "Is he hurt bad?"

"Bad enough," said Ian the Postman, his round, red face grave and set.

(A. C. McLean, *Master of Morgana*)

REVIEW EXERCISE A   Topic Sentences

The topic sentence has been left out of each of the following paragraphs. Number a sheet of paper 1–5. Choose the best topic sentence from the list before each paragraph and write it on your paper.

1. A. Meteors are part of our solar system.

   B. The lights that you see in the sky may be meteors.

   C. Few people have ever seen a meteor.

   (Topic sentence). They are small objects, somewhat like stones. As they enter the earth's atmosphere, they are heated by the friction of the air. They usually burn up before they land. As they burn, they produce a brilliant flash of falling light.

2. A. A shaman is a man or woman among the Eskimo people who is believed to have power over spirits.

   B. Many of the Eskimo people believe in powerful spirits.

   C. Among the Eskimo people are men and women called shamans.

   (Topic sentence.) This power allows the shaman to influence the weather, predict the future, and cure the sick. Eskimo people may fear the shaman, but they also respect him or her.

3. A. The Bayeux tapestry hangs in France.

   B. The Bayeux tapestry is a 900-year-old record in pictures.

   C. The Bayeux tapestry is one of many fine tapestries made in France in the eleventh century.

   (Topic sentence.) It is an embroidered linen cloth over 230 feet long and over nineteen inches high. It shows pictures of the invasion of England by William the Conqueror in 1066. Scenes include details of the Battle of Hastings in which William defeated King Harold of England.

4. A. Baby dolphins are excellent swimmers.
   B. Several scientists have been able to train dolphins.
   C. Old stories of people being saved by dolphins may be a result of the dolphin's instinct to protect its young.

(Topic sentence.) When a dolphin mother gives birth, her baby is born underwater. She must lift the baby to the surface for its first breath. She does this immediately and instinctively. A dolphin seeing someone struggling in the water might mistake the person for a young dolphin, and lift him or her to the surface of the water.

5. A. In some areas of the United States, no snow ever falls.
   B. I love snow.
   C. Snow is made up of small crystals of frozen water.

(Topic sentence.) I love the way it feels as it melts on my face. I love the quiet streets glistening with its cold whiteness. I love the smell of wet wool on snowy days. When the snow has melted as if it had never existed, I love the memory of its cold, white beauty.

REVIEW EXERCISE B   Paragraph Unity

In each of the following paragraphs, one sentence does not say something directly about the topic. Number a sheet of paper 1–3. After each number write the sentence that does not belong in the paragraph.

1.   When the storm passed, everything was a shambles. Huge oak trees had fallen over houses and lawns. These trees had been planted by the city founders in 1849. Broken glass was a danger everywhere. Some roofs were hanging dangerously from the corners of buildings. In six minutes the storm had done over a million dollars' worth of damage.

2.   My brother had a terrible time in his science class yesterday. When he started to take an important test, his only pencil broke. The pencil sharpener would not work. The company that sold those pencil sharpeners to the school should be sued. After he had borrowed a pencil, my brother discovered that he had studied the wrong chapter for the test. As he left the room, he stumbled, dropped his books, and almost fell flat on his face in front of the whole class.

3.   Some people believe that ghosts of famous people return to their favorite haunts. King Arthur's ghost is said to return to Tintagel Castle in the spring. Some people in Stratford on Avon, the birthplace of Shakespeare, see his ghost walking out to visit Anne Hathaway, his wife. They were married in 1582. On stormy nights, the figure of Ichabod Crane, a New York schoolteacher, rides along the east shore of the Hudson River.

REVIEW EXERCISE C   Paragraph Development

Each of the following paragraphs is developed by details, examples, or reasons, comparison and contrast, cause and effect, time, or space. Number a sheet of paper 1–5. Write down how each paragraph is developed.

1.   Do not make the common mistake of using the words *yogi* and *yoga* as if they were synonyms. Yoga is a science. It is the study of the nature of oneself. A yogi is a person who has mastered this science.

2.   One way to kill garden pests is to use companion planting. Beans and potatoes, for example, are ideal garden mates. The beans kill potato beetles while the potatoes protect against bean beetles. Other combinations include soybeans planted near corn and tomatoes near asparagus.

3.   Traps are also good for catching garden pests. One is the well-known honey trap. All that is needed is a shallow pan with about two inches of honey in it, set out where flies are causing damage. Unable to resist the attraction of sweets, the pests either drown in the honey or become too fat and happy to make an escape from the clever gardener.

4.   We continued down a dank corridor. As we passed through a series of low arches, the stale air grew sickening. At the end of the corridor, we entered a huge dark room lined with bones. There, in the center of that room, I met my fate.

5.   Last night, the Atlanta Sea Dragons lost the final swim meet of the season against the

Johnstown Goldfish. The Sea Dragons, who had beaten the Goldfish three times earlier this year, were obviously too tired to swim with their usual speed. Coach Diaz said the team members had had a long bus trip home from the meet against Renfrew and just did not have the energy that they needed to beat Johnstown. "If the team had been rested," said Coach Diaz, "they could easily have won the championship."

REVIEW EXERCISE D Developing Topics

Number a sheet of paper 1–6. Tell which of the following methods you might use to write a paragraph using each of the six topic sentences that are listed.

A. example
B. reason
C. comparison or contrast
D. cause and effect
E. space
F. time

1. The school band should be given new uniforms this year.
2. Our refrigerator shows that I am an important member of the household.
3. Friday is like no other day in the school week.
4. Litterbugs are a menace in and around a school.
5. I wish I could redecorate the school cafeteria.
6. The view from my dentist's chair is a familiar one to me.

REVIEW EXERCISE E   Paragraph Writing

Choose one of the suggestions in Review Exercise D as a topic sentence. Then write a paragraph of your own. Remember to use at least one method of development, as well as correct words to link the sentences.

7

GUIDELINES FOR WRITING

Often when you write about something, you choose a topic from your own experience. You may write just one sentence or a whole paragraph about that experience. Or you may find that one paragraph follows another, until you have written several pages. As you write, you find you are exploring your ideas and feelings in a new way. Your writing becomes a *composition*.

Writing down your thoughts in the form of a composition will often help you and your readers to understand ideas and events better. This is especially true if you follow the guidelines for writing that this chapter provides.

CHOOSING YOUR TOPIC AND YOUR AUDIENCE

7a   Write about what you know.

Choosing a good topic to write about is sometimes as hard as the writing itself. If you choose a poor topic, you must spend a great deal of time trying to say the right things about it. If, however, you choose a good topic, words and sentences often come easily to your mind.

You know your own thoughts and feelings better than anyone else knows them. As you start your writing, think about what you know. What you know is sometimes the best topic for your writing.

As you are thinking about a topic, ask yourself these questions: *"What has happened to me that might interest someone else?" "What words can I use?" "How can I best put these words together?"*

EXERCISE 1   Choose one of the following topics. Make a list of the things that happened to you.

1. The chance I took
2. The memory I value the most
3. The day I was in charge of things
4. The most important choice I had to make
5. What happened after I made my important choice
6. The punishment I can never forget
7. Being sick was (no) fun
8. The time I missed my big chance
9. My bad habit got me in trouble
10. My good habit saved me

EXERCISE 2 Write a composition of at least one paragraph about the experience you chose in Exercise 1. Did the event cause you or others to feel joyful? sorrowful? amused? embarrassed? friendly? angry? lonely? strange? Describe what happened and what you thought and felt.

7b Choose a topic to suit your audience.

As you begin to write a composition, think of the person to whom you are writing. That person may be an adult or someone your age. You may find it helpful to write to yourself as you would do in a diary or personal journal. Whoever is your audience, make sure your topic will interest him or her.

You might write about some topics either to a friend your age or an adult. However, you would treat the topic differently for each individual. You would, for example, include some points in one composition that you would not include in the other.

EXERCISE 3 Following is a list of topics. You might write about some of them to an adult. Other topics you might write about to a friend your age. Some topics you might write about to both an adult and a friend your age.

Choose a topic and write it on a sheet of paper. Underneath it write whether your audience is an adult or a friend. Then write at least one paragraph about the topic for that audience.

1. The time I was in the wrong
2. I used to believe that _____
3. I really hate _____

4. I really like _____
5. That movie almost gave me nightmares
6. Tests are (not) fair
7. I am still scared by _____
8. What I like most about growing up

EXERCISE 4   Rewrite the composition you wrote in Exercise 3. This time write it for a completely different audience.

ORGANIZING YOUR WRITING

In order to organize your writing, you need to organize your thoughts *before* you write. This means you *plan ahead* what you mean to say.

7c   Limit the topic you choose to write about.

Choose a topic that is neither too broad nor too limited. Too many times a topic you think of will at first be too broad.

Suppose you are interested in animals and wish to write something about them. The topic "animals" is much too broad. Just think of the many books that have been written about animals. The topic is too broad to be fully covered even by all these books. This means you must limit your topic.

You might decide to write about one kind of animal, such as cats. The topic "cats" would still be too broad. You can hardly write all about cats in a single composition. Instead, choose something about cats that you can tell about in a few pages.

For example, you might write of an experience you had with your pet cat. Maybe you have observed the actions of a certain cat in your neighborhood. In this way, you will be writing about something you know well. At the same time, you can limit your topic.

EXERCISE 5 The following list contains some topics that are too broad and some topics that are limited enough for a composition of three to five paragraphs. Make two columns on a separate sheet of paper. In the left-hand column list the topics that are too broad. In the right-hand column list the topics that are limited.

Storms I have known
Growth of professional
  sports
Safety for a jogger
The blizzard of '78
A crazy hamburger

Human rights
Popular foods
A warming-up
  exercise
How to save fuel
The finest athlete
  today

7d Organize events under major subtopics.

After you have chosen a topic, list the most important points you want to tell about it. Often several of these major points, or subtopics, will belong together. Usually you will want to write a paragraph about each subtopic or each group of subtopics.

For example, if you choose the limited topic "A warming-up exercise" from the list in Exercise 5, you may find that you can easily describe the entire exercise in a single paragraph. If you choose the limited topic "A crazy hamburger" from this same list, however, you may organize your description under three major subtopics: the bun, the hamburger, the spices. You may find you want to write a paragraph about each of these subtopics.

EXERCISE 6 For each of the following topics, think of two or three subtopics. Number a sheet of paper 1–4. Skip two or three lines between numbers. Next to each number write two or three subtopics you would include in a composition about the topic.

1. How to fool a friend
2. How to make someone laugh
3. How to prune a bush or tree
4. The care of a car's radiator

7e Relate events in the order they happened.

When you write about things that have happened, keep the events in their natural order, or *sequence*. By doing this you help your reader understand what it is you are writing about. If you have any of the events out of order, it makes it hard for your reader to follow the action.

To keep the events in order, make a list of them before you write your composition. You can study the list and be sure the events happened in that sequence. Then, as you write, you can use your list as a guide.

For example, assume you will be writing something about a cat. Following is a list of events that happened when a young cat got caught in a tree.

1. A neighbor heard the cat crying in the tree.
2. The neighbor and I went to the tree.
3. I tried to coax the cat down.
4. It climbed higher and cried louder.
5. Someone else suggested calling the fire department.
6. I volunteered to climb the tree.
7. With help from others, I reached the lower branches.
8. I climbed higher toward the cat, but with difficulty.
9. As I neared the cat, it seemed to become more frightened.
10. Before I could reach it, it scrambled across to another branch, made its way down, and ran away.
11. It took me a long time and some hard work to get back down.

As you look over this list, you can check it to be sure that each event is in order. If any event is out of order, you can rearrange it. Listing events in order before you begin your writing will save you and your readers much trouble. It will also help you decide how many paragraphs to write to cover all the events.

You can group the events from this list into sets. The first group is the *beginning*. This would be made up of events (1) and (2) from the list. These events begin the narration. They would fit into a short, opening paragraph.

Then would come events (3), (4), and (5). Perhaps you would add event (6) to these. These would fit into a second paragraph, or the *middle* of the composition.

Event (7) starts the next group of events, which is the *ending*. To (7) you would want to add events (8), (9), and probably (10). These events all would fit into a single paragraph. Or you could leave event (10) to group with (11) in a closing paragraph.

You can also see that each event is important to include. If some events are missing from a list you make up, you can add them before you write your composition.

EXERCISE 7 The following events all relate to a specific topic. Only the first and last events are in order. The other events are out of order. On your paper write these events as they probably happened.

The delivery person arrived.

Jerry must have thought the delivery person was going to throw the package at him.

The delivery person jumped back in the delivery truck and drove away.

Jerry proudly protected the package as we came out to get it.

Our dog, Jerry, barked furiously at the delivery person.

Jerry grabbed the edge of the package in his jaws.

The delivery person lifted a thin package as a protection.

Then Jerry picked up the package and brought it to us.

The package dropped to the sidewalk.

Jerry is a sort of delivery dog.

7f Tell about the setting of events.

The place where an event happens is its *setting*. By telling about the setting of events, you help your reader "see" what went on. Without the setting, your writing may leave the reader with unanswered questions.

Describe the setting of events clearly enough so that your reader can see where things happen.

EXAMPLE   The canyon narrowed to form a passageway only wide enough for the stream to rush through in a swirl of foam. After thirty feet the passageway opened out to a circular meadow surrounded by towering red rocks. Fat cattle grazed beside the stream that crossed the green grass and disappeared into the far cliff wall.

EXERCISE 8 Describe the place where you had a special experience. Tell how features of the place are situated in relation to one another. You can choose an experience from the following list. Or you might wish to choose another experience.

1. The day I visited a beautiful place
2. The time I wished I had a camera
3. I alone know this spot
4. The stage was set
5. The time I visited the ugliest place I know
6. The moon as I saw it that night
7. A visit to a special kitchen
8. Where the fight took place

7g Tie events together by causes and effects.

Many times when something happens, it causes something else to happen. For example, if you throw a ball hard against a window, it is likely to cause the window to break. Throwing the ball is the *cause;* the broken window is the *effect.*

Not all causes and effects are as clearly related as these examples. Nevertheless, wherever you find events that tie together in this way, make sure you show the relationship in your writing. By making clear the cause-and-effect ties that link events, you help to keep relationships clear in your writing.

EXERCISE 9 The first of the following lists includes causes. The second list includes effects brought about by the causes. Number a sheet of paper 1–6. Next to each number write the cause. Next to it write the related effect.

CAUSES

1. A bug lands on your face
2. An athlete wins an Olympic event
3. You eat no food for 24 hours
4. The temperature rises above 100°C
5. Spring arrives
6. A cup of milk falls on the floor

EFFECTS

You are ready to eat
Water turns to steam
You swat yourself
Flowers bloom
The liquid spills
A medal is awarded

See Conjunction, p. 370

There are a number of words or phrases that make clear how causes and effects are related. You can use these words in your writing. They are called *connectors*. Connectors are conjunctions, adverbs, or prepositions.

See Conjunction, p. 370; Adverb, p. 366; Preposition, p. 384

Examples of connectors:

because	Jill hurt her hand *because* she was careless. Cause: carelessness. Effect: hurt.
since	*Since* Pedro has heard the news already, we don't have to tell him what happened. Cause: Knowing the news. Effect: not telling.
as a result	The motor broke down; *as a result,* Miguel and Inez were delayed for an hour. Cause: motor breakdown. Effect: delayed for an hour.
therefore	No one remembered to bring the punch; *therefore,* we had to climb to the spring to get a drink. Cause: punch forgotten. Effect: climb for water.
whenever	The buzzer sounds *whenever* smoke comes in contact with the mechanism. Cause: smoke contacts mechanism. Effect: buzzer sounds.

EXERCISE 10 Following are pairs of sentences that can be combined as causes and effects. On a sheet of paper, write each pair as one sentence. Use connectors to show the relationship of cause and effect. Underline the connectors you use.

> EXAMPLE The submarine dived. Captain Juarez had seen an enemy ship.

The submarine dived <u>because</u> Captain Juarez had seen an enemy ship.

1. Jay cleaned the windshield. It was dirty.
2. The wind grew strong. The laundry fell off the line.
3. The giant balloon rose above the trees. It filled with hot air.
4. The dog snatched the bones. It was hungry.
5. Too much milk was in the glass. The table was spattered with milk.

EXERCISE 11 Write a short composition of two or three paragraphs about an event that happened to you. In your composition explain the relationship between at least one cause and its effect. Remember to use connectors to show how causes and effects are related.

CHOOSING YOUR WORDS

7h Use words and phrases that appeal to the senses.

Your reader can better understand what you tell about when you use words that appeal to the senses of sight, smell, touch, hearing, and taste. By appealing to the reader's senses, you can give life to your writing. Notice the difference in the following examples. The first one does not appeal to the senses. The second one does.

EXAMPLES
1. The old woman carried the basket of bread down the street.
2. The crippled woman, with a basket of warm, fresh-baked bread on her withered arm, darted between honking cars to reach the high curb across the street.

Nothing in the first sentence describes the woman or the setting. In the second sentence, however, the reader can begin to get a clearer picture. Words like *crippled, withered, darted,* and *high curb* appeal to the reader's sight. The *warm, fresh-baked bread* appeals to the reader's sense of touch, smell, and even taste. The word *honking* appeals to the reader's sense of hearing. These words that appeal to the senses give more life to this description of an old woman. In your writing choose words that appeal to the senses.

EXERCISE 12 Following is a list of words that appeal to the senses. Make five columns across the top of a sheet of paper. Write one of the senses as a heading for each column: *Sight, Hearing, Touch, Taste, Smell.* Under each heading write the words from the list that appeal to that sense. For example, the word *clang* goes under *Hearing* because it ap-

peals to the ear. Some words appeal to more than
one sense. You may put them under either heading.

slapping	trickle	spattering
sweet	bent	acid
green	bump	velvet
spicy	painted	peppermint
clang	bristly	sooty
salty	broken	floppy

EXERCISE 13 Each of the following sentences
lacks words that appeal to the senses. Rewrite each
sentence on a sheet of paper. Add words that appeal
to the senses. Do not change the basic meanings.

EXAMPLE A book lay on the table.

*A battered book, with a torn
and dirty cover, lay on the
scarred table.*

1. The cup sat on the shelf.
2. Marie reached into the refrigerator and took out
   the milk carton.
3. Juan pressed the horn rim on the wheel.
4. Rain came in the open window.
5. The knife fell to the floor.
6. The cap came off the bottle of ammonia.

7i   **Use comparisons to improve your
descriptions.**

When you describe something, you can use
comparisons as well as words that appeal to the

senses. Comparisons relate two things that are similar in certain ways. Comparisons help your reader get a picture of what you are telling about.

EXAMPLES

SIMPLE DESCRIPTION The snow-covered field was bright in the sun.
COMPARISON The snow-covered field looked like a blanket of spun sugar in the sun.

SIMPLE DESCRIPTION The engine made a loud noise.
COMPARISON The engine sounded like the inside of a boiler factory.

By using comparisons in your writing from time to time, you add to the interest of your descriptions.

EXERCISE 14 List A contains objects or features. List B contains comparisons. Number a sheet of paper 1–5. Next to each number, write the item from List A. Then write the best comparison from List B. The first one is done for you as an example.

EXAMPLE an old shoe

an old shoe like some dead animal

LIST A	LIST B
1. An old shoe	as the belly of a kitten
2. Soft	as the blade of a woodfile
3. Distant house lights	as a garbage dump after a rain
4. Rough	like flickering stars
5. Smelly	like some dead animal

EXERCISE 15 The following items need comparisons to make their descriptions easier to understand. Write each item on a sheet of paper. Add your own comparison to each to make the statement come alive.

EXAMPLE **sticky**

> *sticky as a barrelful of honey.*

1. the sidewalk
2. a kiss
3. a river
4. gooey
5. hair

6. a leaf
7. sawdust
8. honey
9. a beam of sunlight
10. a windowpane

EXERCISE 16 Choose one of the following topics. Or choose a topic from Exercise 1 on page 148. On a sheet of paper write a composition of two or three paragraphs describing the topic you have chosen. Be sure to include comparisons in your descriptive composition.

1. A bad dog (or cat)
2. A wonderful friend
3. The funniest person
4. A place to remember
5. A sensational show
6. A bad injury
7. The food I hate the most
8. A noise that annoys me
9. I could have stayed there forever
10. I never want to go back there

7j Be specific by adding details, examples, or reasons.

Too often in writing people use *generalizations* without enough supporting information. A generalization is a broad statement such as *Students need more vacations* or *Parents are too strict.* Generalizations like these mean practically nothing. They have no specific facts to back them up.

When you plan to write a composition about some general statement, make a list of specific details, examples, and reasons you can use to support your statement. Then include them in your writing.

EXERCISE 17 The ideas in the following list are broad statements. They need supporting facts to make them more specific. Choose one of the statements. Write the complete statement on a sheet of paper, filling in whatever words are needed. Then write down at least four details, examples, or reasons to support the statement.

1. (Name of a movie) is the worst movie I have seen.
2. (Name of an athlete) is the best athlete in his/her sport.
3. (Name of a place) is the worst place to go.
4. (Name of a car) is the best car on the road.
5. (Name of a person) is the funniest comedy actor alive.
6. (Name of a food) is the most delicious dessert.

EXERCISE 18 Write a short description (100–200 words) about the topic you chose in Exercise 17.

Use the supporting details, examples, or reasons you listed. Also remember to use words that appeal to the senses. Where you can, make comparisons.

REVISING YOUR WRITING

7k Revise your writing to improve its effectiveness.

Writing good compositions takes care. Part of that care is revising what you have written. To revise well, let a little time go by between your first writing and revising. This way you can come back to your writing with a fresh look. Often you will see a way to improve your composition. You may notice something you would not have seen earlier.

Another way to get a fresh look at your writing is to read it aloud to someone. Or, better still, ask someone else to read it. As both of you listen, you will hear words that do not fit in well or say exactly what you wanted them to say. Writing, after all, is basically speaking on paper.

When you revise your compositions, you will find it helpful to follow the Composition Checklist on page 165.

7l Check the mechanics of your writing.

After you have written what you really mean to say, look over your writing for mechanical errors. Have you written neatly? Is your spelling correct? Do you have capital letters and the right marks of punctuation where they should be? Once again, check your writing against the Composition Checklist.

Composition Checklist

1. Do you know enough about your topic?
2. Have you an audience clearly in your mind?
3. Does your topic suit your audience?
4. Is your topic limited so that you can deal with it?
5. Have you organized the events by time and place?
6. Have you used words and phrases that appeal to the audience?
7. Have you used comparisons?
8. Have you supported general ideas with specific details?
9. Does each paragraph develop an idea or an event?
10. Are your words, phrases, and sentences doing their best work?
11. Have you left any phrases or clauses separated from complete sentences?
12. Have you checked the mechanics to the best of your ability?

REVIEW EXERCISE A Topic and Audience

Read each of the following paragraphs, A through E. Then, on a sheet of paper, answer the following questions about each paragraph. Be prepared to discuss your answers.

A.　　Virgil Rasmussen, chairman of the State Apple Commodity Committee, yesterday said that a record crop of eleven million boxes of apples is expected this year. The crop could gross growers $66 million. In the past five years, growers have averaged a crop of nine million boxes annually.

B.　　Many stores now offer end-of-the-season plums at very low prices. This is a good time to buy a full box of these delicious plums and to make a year's supply of jams and jellies.

C.　　Socko McNutty was a gutty fighter. He could take it and dish it out. He just couldn't beat Kid Gadfly, though, who flattened him with a left to the jaw in the third round.

D.　　I was glad that I had worn my new shoes. They may not make me look taller, but they make me feel taller and older. When I entered the office for the first time, I knew I could do the job. After all, I had on my lucky shoes.

E.　　The crackpots who are supporting the dog-leashing rule on next November's ballot must hate dogs. Why do they fear innocent neighborhood pets walking on the free streets of an American town?

1. Would this paragraph be suitable for publication in your local newspaper? If so, in what section of the newspaper would it appear? Who usually reads that section of the newspaper?
2. Would this paragraph be suitable for publication in the school newspaper?
3. Would this paragraph be suitable for a personal journal?

REVIEW EXERCISE B Broad and Limited Topics

Following are nine topics. Four of these topics are too broad for a short composition; five are limited enough for such a composition. On a sheet of paper, list the five limited topics.

1. The weather in Colorado
2. School sports
3. The football game that I will never forget
4. Trained killer whales
5. American poets
6. A nourishing lunch
7. How to read the school newspaper
8. My favorite comic strip
9. Pioneer life in Texas

REVIEW EXERCISE C Limiting the Topic

Number a sheet of paper 1–5. After each of the broad topics that follows, suggest two specific limited topics that could be developed in a composition.

EXAMPLE television

1. The most annoying advertisement on television
2. The funniest television news report I've seen

1. Prejudices
2. Family
3. Sports
4. Food
5. Music

REVIEW EXERCISE D   Organization

On a sheet of paper, write the following sentences to tell a story of events in the correct order in which they happened.

1. One day a lion lay so still that a mouse ran across its nose.
2. The lion clapped its paw to its face and caught the startled little mouse.
3. The mouse heard the lion's frightened roar.
4. A few days later the lion was caught in a hunter's net.
5. "Spare me, great king," the mouse squeaked out to the lion.
6. "Let me go and some day I will repay you."
7. The lion had to admit it was true.
8. "You see?" the mouse said finally. "A little creature really can help a big one."
9. It ran to the trapped lion and bit away the net with its small, sharp teeth.
10. The lion raised its paw and let the mouse go.

REVIEW EXERCISE E   Organization

Choose a simple incident that has occurred in your school. Perhaps someone has sharpened a pencil; the intercom has buzzed and been answered; a fire drill bell has rung and the class has responded. On a sheet of paper write an account of the incident, organizing the events in the order in which they happened. Be sure, also, to describe the scene of the event.

REVIEW EXERCISE F Cause and Effect

On a sheet of paper, write the three situations listed below. Then state at least two causes for each effect. Finally, write a sentence showing the relationship. Remember to use the words that show relationship between cause and effect: *because, therefore, since, as a result,* and *whenever.*

EXAMPLE Raymond failed math.

> *1. He paid no attention in class.*
> *2. He did not study.*
> *Raymond failed math because he paid no attention in class and did not study.*

1. Harvey arrived in class without the book that he needed that day.
2. Ellie has been elected class president.
3. Hadley has forgotten to go to an appointment with her dentist.

REVIEW EXERCISE G Comparisons

Using a comparison, write a description of each of the following.

EXAMPLE your brother's conversation

> *My brother's conversation is like the sputtering of a popcorn machine.*

1. A row of trash cans at the end of a school lunch hour
2. A slow-moving student
3. A piece of chewed gum stuck under a desk
4. Your own room

8

LETTER WRITING

From time to time you need to write letters. A letter is an expression of yourself. For this reason, you want your letters to show you at your best.

The two main types of letters are *personal letters* and *business letters*. Personal letters are usually written to someone you know well. Business letters often go to people you do not know. In both types of letters, you need to state clearly what you mean.

What a letter tells about is called its *content*. How a letter looks is called its *form*. You make up the content of a letter yourself. The form of a letter should follow a standard pattern. This is most important in the form of a business letter.

This chapter presents the forms of business letters you are likely to need: a letter of request, an order letter, and a letter of complaint or adjustment.

PREPARING THE LETTER

8a Follow the five guides for letter writing.

(1) Think ahead before you write.

Think what your reader would like to learn from your letter. Plan your writing to make it clear to your reader what you have to say.

(2) Choose the best paper and writing equipment.

The stationery you use says something about you. If you write on clean, attractive paper, it makes a good first impression on your reader. If you write on dirty or crumpled paper—or if the pen or typewriter you use writes poorly—the impression is quite different. Avoid using a pencil.

(3) Follow standard form.

In business letters it is especially important to follow standard form. Your envelope should have the address clearly written, with a zip code. It should also have a return address because the United States Postal Service cannot return an undeliverable letter without it. The letter itself should have a date and the name of the person to whom you are writing. Remember to sign your name.

(4) Use standard grammar, spelling, and punctuation.

Letter writing is just like any other writing to be read by others. The standard rules of writing apply.

(5) Read over your letter before you send it.

Errors in a letter can cause more trouble than it takes to correct them before you send the letter. This is particularly true with a business letter. It sometimes helps to find errors by reading your letter aloud. A small error or two can be corrected directly on the letter. However, if you have made several errors, write the letter again.

THE BUSINESS LETTER

8b Use the standard form in a business letter.

The six standard parts of a business letter are shown in the diagram on page 174. Notice also the recommended spacing.

A Request Letter

A request letter asks for something you want or need. Usually what you request is free. Often all you want is information.

BUSINESS LETTER

HEADING	316 Harrison Street Midland, Michigan 48640 June 12, 19—
INSIDE ADDRESS	W.C. Jones Seed Company 12 West Main Street Iowa Falls, Iowa 50126
SALUTATION	Dear Sir or Madam:
BODY	Recently I received an order from you for the Blushing Giant tomatoes that you advertised in your new general catalogue. Although I ordered a dozen plants, I now find I have room for another dozen. If you do not think it is too late in the year to set these plants out, please send me one dozen Blushing Giant tomato plants, at $3.50 a dozen, postpaid.
CLOSING	Sincerely,
SIGNATURE	Lottie Sias

Make sure you have written your return address on the letter and on the outside of the envelope.

You can sometimes assist the process of getting information by enclosing a return envelope with your address and postage.

REQUEST LETTER

1601 Alvarado Drive
Denver, Colorado 80233 } **HEADING**
March 22, 19—

General Mills Company
Minneapolis, Minnesota 55440 } **INSIDE ADDRESS**

To Whom It May Concern: } **SALUTATION**

   For a school project, I am gathering information regarding the amount of bran in breakfast cereals. Would you kindly send me any reports you have about the bran contained in the bran cereals you sell.
   It would also help if you could tell me if you have changed the amount of bran in your cereals in the past ten years. } **BODY**

       Very truly yours, } **CLOSING**

       Joseph Mancini } **SIGNATURE**

EXERCISE 1 Write a letter to an organization requesting information. Look in a magazine or newspaper for the name and address of a company as listed in an advertisement. Ask for any catalogs, brochures, publications, or other printed material. You can also ask for prices of items for sale. Do not send the letter unless you really need the information.

An Order Letter

When writing an order letter, check twice the information about whatever you order. Is the description accurate? Do you have the right identification or catalog number? Are the prices and totals correct? Care about matters like these will save you headaches in the future.

HEADING

> R.D.2
> Millneck Road
> Oyster Bay, NY 11771
> September 25, 19 —

INSIDE ADDRESS

> Solar Supply Company
> 322 Mountain Avenue
> Phoenix, Arizona 85020

SALUTATION

> Order Department:

BODY

> Please send me the following items as advertised in your 1979 catalog:
> 1 "Sunspot" room heating panel, #448-216, $23.50.
> 1 Nonwear connecting water hose, #454-319, $6.00.
> Enclosed is a money order for $31.65 ($29.50 for the cost of the items plus $2.15 postage).

CLOSING

> Sincerely yours,

SIGNATURE

> Margery Waldron

EXERCISE 2 Write a business letter ordering Christmas cards and decorations as follows:

2 dozen red and white cards, #C298, at $2.00 a dozen

1 dozen "Snowfall" window decals, #D144, at $1.50 a dozen

2 boxes of "Stick-on" artificial snow, #S438, at $1.89 a box

The company is Holiday Party Company, 688 Hudson Street, New York, New York 10008. You enclose a money order for the total cost plus $.64 cents for postage.

A Letter of Complaint or Adjustment

If you find something wrong in what an organization has done, you can write a letter of complaint or adjustment. For example, you may think that a company is wasting energy. Or you may have received the wrong merchandise. A letter of complaint or adjustment is needed.

On page 178 is an example of a letter of complaint.

EXERCISE 3 Write a letter of complaint or a letter of adjustment regarding some matter that you believe an organization should correct. Some examples are as follows:

1. The U.S. Olympic Committee should make more money available to athletes on the United States team.

A LETTER OF COMPLAINT OR ADJUSTMENT

HEADING
{
1919 Elm Street
Providence, RI 02903
December 20, 19 —

INSIDE ADDRESS
{
Burton Fuel Company
688 High Street
Providence, RI 02903

SALUTATION
{
To Whom It May Concern:

BODY
{
Last week I passed your offices and noticed that all the lights were burning at 9:30 at night. Yet no one seemed to be in the offices. I could see no reason for the lights being on when we all need to save power in this time of an energy shortage.

Possibly your automatic timer is not working.

I hope you don't think my letter rude, but I am sure you agree that a fuel company should set a good example for us all.

Yours for better use of energy.

CLOSING
{
Sincerely,

SIGNATURE
{
Betsy Winitsky

2. A manufacturing company is making children's toys with sharp edges.
3. You ordered items from a mail-order house and enclosed your money, but you received the wrong items.
4. You mailed in a subscription to a record-of-the-month club three months ago and have heard nothing since.

MAILING YOUR LETTER

8c Use standard form in addressing an envelope.

Following is a model of the front of a business envelope.

Margery Waldron
R.D. 2
Millneck Road
Oyster Bay, NY 11771 } RETURN ADDRESS

ADDRESS { Solar Supply Company
322 Mountain Avenue
Phoenix, Arizona 85020 } ZIP CODE

EXERCISE 4 Set up your paper as though it were the front of an envelope. Write the correct form of an envelope for sending one of the model business letters from Exercise 3.

8d Fold your letter to fit your envelope.

The diagrams show the standard ways of folding and inserting your business letter.

EXERCISE 5   Using a blank sheet of paper as a letter form, practice folding it in the ways shown above. If possible, insert it in envelopes of different sizes.

REVIEW EXERCISE A   The Parts of a Letter

Read the business letter on page 181. On a sheet of paper, write the heading, inside address, salutation, and closing. Identify each part.

REVIEW EXERCISE B   Writing a Reply

Using the information in the sample letter in Exercise A, write a reply, either ordering the boots or cancelling the order.

REVIEW EXERCISE C   Addressing an Envelope

Mark off a large rectangle on a sheet of paper to serve as an envelope. Then address the envelope for the letter in Exercise B.

Olympic Shoe Shop
228 Athens Way
Oakland, California 94002

September 11, 1979

Ms. Marla Freitas
1861 Eucalyptus Drive
San Francisco, California 94121

Dear Ms. Freitas:

Thank you for your order of September 8, 1979, and for the enclosed money order in the amount of $16.81. Unfortunately, the item that you ordered, girls' hiking boots, style #21, is no longer made by the Olympic Shoe Shop. We make a similar boot in tan with hook lacings. I have enclosed a pamphlet showing these comfortable and durable boots, style #22. The additional cost for these boots is $1.87.

If you will enclose a money order for this amount with further instructions, we will be glad to send you style #22 in size 6. If you prefer a refund, we will gladly return your money.

Sincerely yours,

arline Beibel

Arline Beibel
Order Correspondent

REVIEW EXERCISE D   A Letter of Request

Write one of the following letters of request:

1. Write to an important person in your community an invitation to speak to one of your classes at school. Be specific about the time, place, and topic.
2. Write to the nearest state employment office, requesting information about jobs available for students of your age.
3. Write to a person whom you admire, requesting that person's autograph.

REVIEW EXERCISE E   A Letter of Complaint

Write a letter of complaint about one of the following or about some other complaint that you actually have:

1. Write to the telephone company to complain about the large number of wrong-number calls that your family receives late at night.
2. Write a complaint to your newspaper about late delivery or about the paper being thrown in a dangerous or annoying way.
3. Write to a city official complaining about bus service, conditions in city parks, or about the need for more or better traffic signs.

UNIT THREE

USAGE

Using Parts of Speech
Common Confusions

9

USING PARTS OF SPEECH

You already know how to speak and write. In fact, if you are like most people, you began to speak a language when you were about one year old. Why is it, then, you might ask, that you have to study usage in speaking and writing?

You will find the answer if you think of language as a set of tools. You use language tools to do important work in life. The better your tools are and the better you know how to use them, the better off you will be in your work. The study of language usage can help you do a better job in life.

One of the common problems of language usage that are dealt with in this chapter is agreement between subject and verb. Other matters covered are active and passive verbs, the correct use of pronouns, adjectives, and adverbs, and other special problems.

AGREEMENT OF SUBJECTS AND VERBS

9a A verb must agree with its subject in number.

See Verb, p. 387

Nearly all verbs have different forms. The *infinitive* form can be seen in such verbs as *sleep, walk, ride, talk,* and *move.* The infinitive form is used for the present tense for most subjects.

EXAMPLES FIRST PERSON SINGULAR

I ride, talk, run

SECOND PERSON SINGULAR

you ride, talk, run

FIRST PERSON PLURAL

we ride, talk, run

SECOND PERSON PLURAL

you ride, talk, run

THIRD PERSON PLURAL

they ride, talk, run
Juanita and Eric ride, talk, run

Hint: If the plural noun ends in **s**, the verb usually does not end in **s**.

However, a different form of each verb is used in the present tense when the subject is a pronoun in the *third person singular.* The infinitive form of the verb adds **s** or **es**.

EXAMPLES he rid**es**, she talk**s**, it run**s**

The same thing happens when the subject is a noun that is the name of a person or thing.

EXAMPLES Nancy rides, Marc talks, the dog runs

EXERCISE 1 Number a sheet of paper 1–10. Choose the correct verb for each sentence. Write the verb on your paper next to the number of each sentence.

EXAMPLE People (get/gets) around by many kinds of transportation.

get

1. An ambulance driver (hurry/hurries) to the hospital.
2. Airplane pilots (learn/learns) how to fly new jets.
3. A road map (help/helps) tourists find the way.
4. The driver of a bus (stop/stops) at marked curbs for loading and unloading.
5. He (know/knows) the streets of the city.
6. Stagecoaches would stop to (change/changes) horses.
7. To ride a bike, you (pedal/pedals) with the feet.
8. A rider (need/needs) good balance to use a unicycle.
9. Helicopters (fly/flies) in all directions.
10. A train (move/moves) along railroad tracks.

EXERCISE 2 Number a sheet of paper 1–10. Choose the correct verb for each sentence. Write the verb next to the number of each sentence.

EXAMPLE   The customs and manners of people in the United States (has/have) changed during the last two hundred years.

have

1. Women (has/have) taken many roles outside the home.
2. The husband no longer (control/controls) a married couple's property in many states.
3. With the modern convenience of running water, most people (take/takes) a bath every day.
4. Women no longer have to (wear/wears) a hat at the theater.
5. Both boys and girls (go/goes) to school.
6. Women usually (buy/buys) yarn instead of spinning their own to make clothes.
7. A family (travel/travels) by car to go shopping.
8. More people (work/works) in cities than work on farms.
9. Students (study/studies) American history instead of British history.
10. A teacher (give/gives) tests but does not whip students who fail to pay attention.

9b The verb *be* has special forms to agree with its subject.

The verb *be* causes some difficulty in agreement. Its forms in the present and simple past tenses are shown here.

	PRESENT		SIMPLE PAST	
	Singular	Plural	Singular	Plural
FIRST PERSON	I am	we are	I was	we are
SECOND PERSON	you are	you are	you were	you were
THIRD PERSON	he she it } is	they are	he she it } was	they were

If you have trouble using the forms of *be* that agree with their subjects, you will need to study this chart. These forms of *be* are used a great deal in English.

EXERCISE 3 Number a sheet of paper 1–10. Next to each number write the correct form of the verbs in parentheses. Some sentences have two choices for you to make.

EXAMPLE Helen of Troy (is/are) a famous
beauty who (was/were) kidnapped.

is, was

1. The *Iliad* (is/are) a story of the way the Trojan War (was/were) fought thousands of years ago.
2. Troy (was/were) a city in Persia, which (were/was) near ancient Greece.
3. A Greek king (was/were) angry at the Trojans, who he thought (were/was) in the wrong.
4. His wife, Helen, (was/were) kidnapped by a Trojan prince.
5. She (was/were) held prisoner in Troy.
6. Her husband sent a message to other kings: "(Is/Are) you willing to help me?"

7. They (was/were) willing, and so they sailed with their armies to Troy.
8. They and the Trojans (was/were) locked in battle many years, but neither side (was/were) able to beat the other.
9. It (was/were) a stand-off because neither side (were/was) victorious.
10. "(Are/Is) the Greeks ever going to free Helen?" (was/were) the question of the day.

9c **A compound subject joined by *and* usually takes a plural verb.**

EXAMPLES   *Juanita* and *Leonida cook* their breakfast in a hurry.
Dale and *Gary eat* their lunch slowly.
Apples and *oranges are* my favorite snacks.

You can see in each sentence that the verb agrees with a plural subject. Two or more people or things added together require the plural form of a verb.

EXERCISE 4   Some of the following sentences have compound subjects. Some have simple subjects. Number a sheet of paper 1–6. After each number, write the correct choice of the verb in parentheses.

EXAMPLE   A thermometer and a barometer (helps/help) weather watchers predict the weather.

help

1. A pleasant temperature and high pressure (means/mean) clear skies.
2. A changing temperature and low pressure (brings/bring) a storm.
3. Clouds in the northern hemisphere (swirls/swirl) counterclockwise around low pressure areas.
4. Wind and rain (is/are) often found together.
5. When low pressure and high pressure areas (bumps/bump) each other, the wind blows hard.
6. The study of weather systems (has/have) great importance for all of us.

Often two persons or things will be in the compound subject, but they will not be joined by *and*. Look closely to see how they are joined. Look for a connecting word like *or*.

9d **When a compound subject is joined by *or,*** **nor, either . . . or,* or *neither . . . nor,* the** **verb agrees in number with the nearer** **subject.**

EXAMPLES   A ripe *apple* or an *orange tastes* sweet.
[Two things joined by *or* make up the compound subject. However, the nearer subject, *orange,* is singular. The verb *tastes* is in its singular form for the third person.]

Neither *Lysia* nor her *sisters like* sour fruit.
[In this sentence, the nearer subject is plural: *sisters.* The verb must agree in number. Its plural form is used: *like.*]

EXERCISE 5 Look at each pair of verbs in parentheses. Choose the one that agrees with the subject of the sentence. Number a sheet of paper 1–6 and write the correct verb by each number.

> EXAMPLE Both the Louds and Leroy
> (hope/hopes) to become a famous
> musician.
>
> *hope*

1. It seems that both the four Loud sisters and their brother, Leroy, (want/wants) to form a rock group right next door.
2. No matter what time of the day or night it is, Leroy and his sisters (are/is) always practicing.
3. Either the Loud sisters or Leroy (write/writes) all the lyrics and music.
4. Neither Mr. nor Mrs. Loud (cares/care) about the constant noise because they both wear hearing aids, which they can switch off.
5. My parents say that either we or the Louds (has/have) to move.
6. Both my older brother and my sister (plan/plans) to join a music group too, but they have said nothing to my parents yet.

9e When a group of words comes between the subject and the verb, the verb still agrees with the subject.

In some sentences the subject and the verb are not next to each other. Extra words come between them. As you speak and write, pay close attention to the number of the subject. Do not be fooled by the number of other words.

EXAMPLES   The *boxes* piled up in the back
             closet *belong* to Jake.
             [The plural word *boxes* is the
             subject, not *closet*. The verb *belong*
             must agree with *boxes*.]

             The fat *box* with the torn edges
             belongs to me.
             [The singular word *box* is the
             subject, not *edges*. The verb *belongs*
             agrees with the third person
             singular subject.]

EXERCISE 6   In the following sentences, choose
the correct form of the verb in parentheses. Number
a sheet of paper 1–5. Next to each number write the
correct form.

EXAMPLE   People who like special food
           (gives/give) me a difficult time.

           give

1. John Wilk, one of our neighbors, (make/makes)
   me uneasy with his strange appetite.
2. He, with his spades and hoe, (stumble/stumbles)
   all over the garden planting seeds.
3. One of his favorite plants (taste/tastes) to me
   like wet cotton.
4. Can you imagine what two of his favorite plants
   (taste/tastes) like?
5. One of these days one of his neighbors (is/are)
   going to suggest he plant flowers.

9f Certain nouns and phrases that name a quantity may appear to be plural, but they take a singular verb.

EXAMPLES The *news is* not all good.
[*News* seems plural, but its meaning is singular. Therefore, the verb is singular: *is.*]

Ninety cents seems too much to pay for it.
[*Ninety cents* is thought of as a single sum.]

That *crowd is* too noisy.
[*Crowd* names a group of people, but it is thought of as a singular noun.]

EXERCISE 7 Number a sheet of paper 1–5. By each number, write the subject of each of the following sentences and the verb that matches it.

EXAMPLE Fifty dollars (is/are) a high price to pay for a little camera.

Fifty dollars, is

1. A group of creatures often (have/has) its own special name.
2. Sometimes the name sounds like the animals it describes. For example, we say: A *pride* of lions (was/were) photographed by the lake.
3. A group of lions certainly (looks/look) proud.
4. On the other hand, a large collection of fish swimming together (do/does) not look as if it is learning anything—yet it is called a *school.*

5. *Gaggle,* the word for a group of geese, is a funny word—but then, a bunch of geese (is/are) a funny sight.

9g   A collective noun is singular in form but may be singular or plural in meaning.

Whether a *collective noun* is thought of as singular or plural depends on its meaning in a sentence:

EXAMPLES The *group has* made its decision.
[In this example, the group is thought of as a single body of people.]

The *group were* divided in their wishes.
[Here the group is thought of as plural. The members have different wishes.]

Class is dismissed.
[The class is a single group.]

Are you all ready, *class?*
[Here someone is asking if all members of the class are ready.]

EXERCISE 8 Number a sheet of paper 1–5. Write the collective noun in each sentence. After each collective noun write *S* or *P* to show whether it is singular or plural in meaning.

EXAMPLE   The group are still arguing the issue.

group, P

1. The family live in three different states.
2. The team has won four games.
3. The herd were wandering in all directions.
4. The gaggle of geese was honking noisily.
5. Our class come from several countries.

9h Indefinite pronouns that are singular in meaning take the singular form of the verb.

EXAMPLES   *Everyone dreams* of growing up.
           Each of the groups *is* to receive an award.
           Everybody *needs* affection.

Some sentences have words that come between the singular indefinite pronoun and the verb. Be careful not to let the extra words change the agreement of the subject and verb. See Pronouns, pp. 15–16

EXAMPLES   Everyone in the student clubs *is* responsible.
           Nobody in this building *remembers* the fire.

EXERCISE 9   Number a sheet of paper 1–12. Next to each number, write the subject of the sentence and the verb that agrees with it.

EXAMPLE Everyone (knows/know) that strange
things happen to twins.

Everyone, knows

1. I am one of twins, and neither of us (are/is) very happy about it.
2. "It must be fun being a twin," people say, but nobody else really (know/knows).
3. Although Alvin and I look alike, each of us (feel/feels) very different.
4. For instance, neither of us (enjoys/enjoy) the same kind of things.
5. Someone at the front door (is/are) asking for Alvin right now.
6. "One of those twins (have/has) been upsetting my parrot again," we hear the neighbor say.
7. "All right," says Mom, "which one of you (teases/tease) that bird from the window?"
8. Neither Alvin nor I (answers/answer).
9. "Tell us which one of them (does/do) it, Perci-val," the neighbor tells the parrot.
10. "Was it Andy?" Alvin asks quickly. Anyone with any sense (knows/know) that parrots will repeat the last word they hear.
11. "Andy," yells the parrot, and everyone imme-diately (blame/blames) me.
12. As I said, nobody without a twin (understand/understands) how awful having a twin can be, especially when your twin is Alvin.

See Linking
Verb, p. 379 **9i A linking verb agrees with its subject.**

EXAMPLES *Spring is* the months of April, May, and June.
[Note that the subject completer includes several items: *April, May, and June*. The verb does *not* agree with the subject completer.]

The happiest *hours are* Saturday's.

EXERCISE 10 Choose the correct form of the linking verb in each of the following sentences. Write it on your paper.

1. A winner (is/are) someone with more points than the opponent.
2. Good style (is/are) clean strokes and a smooth recovery.
3. Successful efforts (seems/seem) the best way.
4. Practice and performance (makes/make) a winning season.
5. Losses (is/are) the sadder result.

SPECIAL VERB PROBLEMS

Active Verbs and Passive Verbs

9j **An active verb tells of the action done *by* the subject of a sentence. A passive verb tells of action done *to* the subject of a sentence.**

See Verb, p. 387; Subject, p. 386

Examples of action verbs:

Walt *broke* his shoelaces.
[Walt did the breaking.]

Conchita *wrapped* the package.
[Conchita did the wrapping.]

Examples of passive verbs:

The laces *were broken* by Walt.
[The laces had the action done to them.]

The package *was wrapped* by Conchita.
[The package had the action done to it.]

Hint: The passive form of the main verb
takes a helping verb.

EXAMPLES   *were* broken
               was wrapped

EXERCISE 11   Five of the following sentences
have verbs in the active form. The other sentences
have passive verbs. Number a sheet of paper 1–10.
After each number, write the main verb and any
helping verb. Next to the verb, write the word *active* or *passive* to tell its form.

EXAMPLE   The Cherokee Sequoya was
                crippled by a hunting accident.

was crippled, passive

1. Sequoya used his mind, not his body, to help his
   people.
2. The Cherokee nation had no written language
   for its words.
3. Sequoya designed symbols to stand for the
   Cherokee words.

verb
9k

4. Pictures were used by Sequoya for his first symbols.

5. Thousands of pictures were needed for his people's language.

6. Sequoya studied books from a church in a nearby town.

7. Strange symbols were used in these books for the sounds of the white people's language.

8. Sequoya invented two hundred "strange symbols" for his people's language.

9. After twelve years, this number was reduced to eighty-five.

10. Those eight-five symbols were made the official alphabet for the entire Cherokee nation.

Irregular Verbs

Most verbs show simple past time, called *tense*, by adding **ed** or **d** to the infinitive form of the verb. Examples are *walk/walked* and *climb/climbed*.

See Verb, pp. 35–37

Irregular verbs do not add **ed** to form the simple past tense.

9k Irregular verbs form their past tenses in special ways, without adding *ed* or *d.*

EXAMPLES	PRESENT TENSE	SIMPLE PAST
	take	took
	throw	threw
	go	went

Hint: A helpful way to learn the forms of irregular verbs is to practice fitting them into standard sentences:

EXAMPLES   Now we (*take*) . . .
Yesterday we (*took*) . . .

There is another form of irregular verbs that shows past time. This is called the *present perfect*. The present perfect uses the *past participle* form of the main verb and the helping verb *have*.

EXAMPLES

PRESENT	SIMPLE PAST	PRESENT PERFECT
begin	began	have begun
drive	drove	have driven
eat	ate	have eaten
fall	fell	have fallen
give	gave	have given
know	knew	have known
ring	rang	have rung
see	saw	have seen
swim	swam	have swum
write	wrote	have written

The present perfect form tells of action completed in the past.

EXAMPLES   She *has eaten* her dinner.
He *has gone* forever.

The following list shows the basic forms of common irregular verbs. Study the list and refer to it if you have a question about a form.

COMMON IRREGULAR VERBS

Infinitive	Simple Past	Present Perfect
bear	bore	have borne
begin	began	have begun
bind	bound	have bound
blow	blew	have blown
break	broke	have broken
bring	brought	have brought
buy	bought	have bought
catch	caught	have caught
choose	chose	have chosen
come	came	have come
dive	dived, dove	have dived
do	did	have done
draw	drew	have drawn
drink	drank	have drunk
drive	drove	have driven
eat	ate	have eaten
fall	fell	have fallen
flee	fled	have fled
fly	flew	have flown
freeze	froze	have frozen
give	gave	have given
go	went	have gone
grow	grew	have grown
hang	hung	have hung
hang (execute)	hanged	have hanged
keep	kept	have kept
know	knew	have known
lay	laid	have laid
lead	led	have led
lie	lay	have lain
lose	lost	have lost
make	made	have made
mean	meant	have meant

Infinitive	Simple Past	Present Perfect
ride	rode	have ridden
ring	rang	have rung
rise	rose	have risen
run	ran	have run
see	saw	have seen
seek	sought	have sought
send	sent	have sent
shake	shook	have shaken
shine	shone, shined	have shone, have shined
sing	sang	have sung
sleep	slept	have slept
speak	spoke	have spoken
spin	spun	have spun
spread	spread	have spread
steal	stole	have stolen
swear	swore	have sworn
swim	swam	have swum
swing	swung	have swung
take	took	have taken
teach	taught	have taught
tear	tore	have torn
throw	threw	have thrown
wear	wore	have worn
write	wrote	have written

EXERCISE 12 Number a sheet of paper 1–10. Next to each number write the complete subject and the correct form of the verb. If there are two subjects and verbs, write them both.

EXAMPLE   Edgar Allan Poe (wrote/written) many mystery stories.

Edgar Allan Poe wrote

1. He (gave/give) us some good reading.
2. His "The Pit and the Pendulum" (keep/kept) me in suspense.
3. This story has been (maked/made) into a movie.
4. The hero is (keeped/kept) in a dungeon.
5. He (did/done) something wrong, but I never (find/found) out what.
6. He is tied down so he will be (ate/eaten) by big rats.
7. They (creeped/have crept) up close to him.
8. A big pendulum with a sharp blade is (swinged/swung) over him.
9. He thinks he (went/has gone) crazy.
10. He (gave/has given) up hope when he is saved.

SPECIAL PRONOUN PROBLEMS

Personal Pronouns

A personal pronoun may be used as a subject or an object of a sentence. It may also be used as an object of a preposition. Its use, as shown by its form, is called its *case*.

See Pronoun, p. 384

91 Pronouns must agree in number and sex with the nouns or pronouns they replace.

EXAMPLES
INCORRECT AGREEMENT Every *dog* must have *their* shots.
CORRECT AGREEMENT Every *dog* must have *its* shots.

INCORRECT AGREEMENT   Each *girl* needs *their* exercise.

CORRECT AGREEMENT   Each *girl* needs *her* exercise.

9m   A personal pronoun is in the subjective case when used as a subject and in the objective case when used as the object.

EXAMPLES

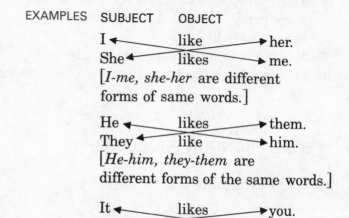

SUBJECT   OBJECT

I ← like → her.
She ← likes → me.
[*I-me, she-her* are different forms of same words.]

He ← likes → them.
They ← like → him.
[*He-him, they-them* are different forms of the same words.]

It ← likes → you.
You ← like → it.
[Notice that *it* and *you* are two personal pronouns that are the same form no matter what position in the sentences they occupy.]

Use the same pronoun forms for objects of prepositions that you use for direct objects of verbs.

EXAMPLES   I left *with her.*
He ran away *from me.*

PERSONAL PRONOUNS

	Subjective Case		Objective Case	
	Singular	Plural	Singular	Plural
First Person	I	we	me	us
Second Person	you	you	you	you
Third Person	he		him	
	she	they	her	them
	it		it	

EXERCISE 13 Number a sheet of paper 1–8. On your paper write the correct form of the pronouns in parentheses in each sentence.

EXAMPLE Ryo Okano said to Dolores Marinas, "Is each mouse in (its/their) cage?"

its

1. Dolores answered (he/him), "(I/Me) don't know."
2. "How can (we/us) make this experiment work," Ryo asked (she/her), "if the mice aren't in (its/their) cages?"
3. (She/Her) answered, "It's up to (we/us) to put (they/them) in."
4. Working together, Ryo and Dolores put every mouse in (its/their) cage.
5. The white mice were supposed to have (its/their) food given to (it/them) only once every two days.
6. All the grey mice could eat (its/their) food whenever it was given to (they/them).
7. Every day (they/them) were weighed to see if any weight was gained by any of (they/them).
8. Ryo admitted (he/him) didn't like not feeding some of (they/them), but Dolores gave (they/them) plenty of food.

Who and *Whom*

Who is a relative pronoun in the subjective case. *Whom* is a relative pronoun in the objective case. Their uses are the same as the uses of *he* and *him* or *she* and *her.*

> EXAMPLES *Who* gave the chewing gum to you?
> [subject of the sentence]
>
> *He* gave it to me.
> [subject of the sentence]
>
> He got it from *whom?*
> [object of the preposition *from*]
>
> He got it from *him.*
> [object of the preposition *from*]

EXERCISE 14 Number a sheet of paper 1–8. On the paper write the correct form of the pronouns in parentheses in each sentence.

> EXAMPLE (Who/Whom) has heard from (he/him)?
>
> *Who, him*

1. (Who/Whom) wrote this editorial?
2. Frank Rostov read the paper given to (he/him).
3. (Who/Whom) gave it to Frank?
4. From (who/whom) did (he/him) get it?
5. He brought it with (he/him) this morning.
6. (Who/Whom) gets to read it next?
7. Well, for (who/whom) did he bring it?
8. He brought the editorial for the one (who/whom) asked for it.

PROBLEMS WITH ADJECTIVES AND ADVERBS

9n **Use an adjective after a linking verb to refer back to the subject.**

See Adjective, p. 366; Linking Verb, p. 379

Do not use an adverb to modify a linking verb.

EXAMPLES

CORRECT   Marion Chun appeared *neat.*
[*Neat* is an adjective. It refers back to *Marion Chun,* the subject.]

WRONG   Marion Chun appeared *neatly.*

CORRECT   She played the piano *smoothly.*
[*Smoothly* is an adverb. It tells how she played.]

CORRECT   Frank Kyle was *sad.*
[*Sad* is an adjective. It refers back to Frank Kyle, the subject.]

WRONG   Frank Kyle was *sadly.*

CORRECT   He played the flute *sadly.*
[*Sadly* is an adverb. It tells how he played.]

Sometimes adjectives and adverbs that follow a verb are confused. This is especially the case with the word *good.* It is used only as an adjective. The word *well,* however, can be used either as an adjective or an adverb.

RIGHT   You write *well.*
WRONG   You write *good.*

EXERCISE 15 In each of the following sentences you have a choice of modifiers. Number a sheet of paper 1–10. Write the correct modifier for each sentence.

> EXAMPLE   My twin, Alvin, and I may look alike, but we do things very (different/differently).
>
> *differently*

1. I swim (good/well), and Alvin hates the water.
2. On the other hand, I'm not the world's best at baseball, and Alvin plays very (well/good).
3. When it comes to basketball, we both play (bad/badly).
4. We practice together (regular/regularly), but I guess we're just too short.
5. Alvin says we should be jockeys when we grow up because short people ride (good/well).
6. I think Alvin should be a chef. Yesterday he made a dessert which tasted really (good/well).
7. Chefs are paid (good/well), too.
8. But Alvin says he wants to be a singer because he cooks too (slow/slowly).
9. That's a laugh, because Alvin doesn't sing as (good/well) as I do.
10. I sound (good/well) compared to him.

THE DOUBLE NEGATIVE

9o Avoid using a double negative.

Usually when two negatives are used in one sentence, they are not both needed. One negative will do. A negative word is *no, not, none, never, nothing, no one,* and *hardly.*

EXAMPLES
WRONG   He said he had not never seen her.
CORRECTED   He said he had never seen her.

EXERCISE 16   Number a sheet of paper 1–5. Re-write each of the following sentences, correcting the double negative error.

EXAMPLE   Carmen never had no cottage cheese.

Carmen never had any cottage cheese.

1. Don't you have none for lunch?
2. I had not eaten hardly any yesterday.
3. The lady said no one never invited her.
4. Hardly none of them came to see me.
5. My friend Angelina had not no one to turn to.

REVIEW EXERCISE A   **Agreement of Subject and Verb**

Number a sheet of paper 1–10. After each number write the verb that agrees with its subject.

EXAMPLE   The chairs that Harry placed around the table (was, were) from the dining room.

were

1. Anyone who studies Greek myths (knows, know) about Pandora.
2. Pandora and her box (is, are) responsible for much of the trouble in the world.

3. The story of Pandora and her troubles (starts, start) when Prometheus fools Zeus.

4. Later, Prometheus's stupid brother (accepts, accept) a gift from Zeus.

5. Neither Prometheus nor his brother (guesses, guess) that the gift is really a punishment from Zeus.

6. The gift (is, are) the first of all women, the beautiful Pandora.

7. According to the story, Pandora (opens, open) her box, which is filled with all of the world's evils.

8. Every one of the diseases that the world knows (is, are) released from the box.

9. Only one thing of all that the box contained (remains, remain) in the box.

10. Of all good things, that one (is, are) the best: hope.

REVIEW EXERCISE B   Agreement of Subject and Verb

Number a sheet of paper 1–15. If the subject and verb agree, write *C* (correct) after the number. If they do not agree, write the correct verb form.

EXAMPLE   A thousand dollars are too much to pay for a pair of shoes.

is

1. The news at our school is that the Spanish class is painting a mural.

2. Anyone who wants may paint with the class.

3. Either Alva Sorres or her sister Jean have done a huge section of the mural already.

4. In this painting a pod of whales is shown swimming in the blue sea.
5. The movement of the whales and of the water around their huge bodies is beautifully painted.
6. Alva and her sister is both talented painters.
7. Neither of the two student body officers in the class are working on the mural.
8. Their job is the writing, typing, and distribution of a pamphlet that describes the mural.
9. The description, which will be about all of the parts of the mural, are in Spanish.
10. Fifty cents seem to them to be a fair price for the pamphlet.
11. Neither the painter nor the students writing the pamphlet is sure about the meaning of one section of the mural.
12. In it, a person with long hair and cupped hands is looking in a mirror.
13. The reflection is a white bird flying.
14. My fifty cents is ready for an explanation of that scene.
15. Neither the principal nor the board of education has seen the mural yet.

REVIEW EXERCISE C Irregular Verbs

Number a sheet of paper 1–25. After each number write the correct form of the irregular verb from the parentheses.

EXAMPLE A Russian czar had (spoken, spoke) to his people about a flying ship.

spoken

1. He promised that whoever (brang, brought) him a flying ship could marry his daughter.

2. The poor and foolish son of a poor and foolish couple (began, begun) to dream of marrying the czar's daughter.

3. After he had (wrote, written) a note to his parents, he set off to find a flying ship.

4. Along the way he met a neighbor who (bore, beared) the foolish boy a grudge.

5. "Stupid boy," the neighbor said, "no ship has ever (flew, flown)."

6. The boy went on and (seeked, sought) the flying ship.

7. He (came, come) upon an old man who greeted him kindly.

8. "Men have (catched, caught) songs in flight; women have (dived, dove) under the sea; children have (swam, swum) oceans," he said.

9. "I believe that ships have (flew, flown)."

10. He (teached, taught) the poor foolish boy how to find a flying ship.

11. The boy, following directions, (went, gone) into the woods.

12. When the boy had (laid, lain) down under a tree and had (fell, fallen) asleep, he dreamed of a flying ship.

13. When he woke up, he (saw, seen) the ship before him.

14. He (run, ran) over to the ship, climbed aboard, and (flew, flown) away to the czar's castle.

15. When he had (drove, driven) the ship to a safe landing, he (rang, rung) the czar's doorbell.

16. The czar, who had (ate, eaten) a good dinner and had (drank, drunk) his golden cup of nectar, was in a mellow mood.

17. He (spoke, spoken) to the boy briefly, (rose, risen) from his chair, and (run, ran) out to see the ship.

18. When he (saw, seen) the ship, he (tear, tore) at his silver shirt in anger and shouted that he had (hanged, hung) other men who wanted to marry his daughter.

19. Although the czar (grew, grown) angry, he (knew, knowed) that he had been fooled by a fool.

20. The daughter was awakened in the tower room where she (slept, sleeped).

21. She had (began, begun) to walk down the stairs when the fool (run, ran) up to meet her.

22. He (lost, losed) no time in introducing himself.

23. He had read stories about royal ladies, and he (know, knew) that anyone who (seeked, sought) the hand of such a lady should fall on his knees.

24. He (did, done) this immediately.

25. As the wedding bells (rang, rung) and the sun (shone, shined) down on the happy couple, they (flew, flown) off in their flying ship.

REVIEW EXERCISE D Pronoun Forms

Number a sheet of paper 1–10. After each number write the correct pronoun form from the parentheses.

1. Huckleberry Finn, one of Mark Twain's most famous characters, was a boy (who, whom) loved freedom.

2. Huck had been a member of Tom Sawyer's gang, but (he, him) and the other members had grown tired of the secret meetings.

3. (He, Him) and Jim, a runaway slave, left home on a raft.
4. Jim's owner had threatened to sell him, which would separate (he, him) and his wife.
5. Jim missed his wife and his little girl, (who, whom) he had once punished unfairly.
6. A close friendship grew between (he, him) and Huck.
7. So many people read about Huck's adventures with Tom Sawyer that Mark Twain, (who, whom) was by then well known, decided to write a third book about the boys.
8. Becky Thatcher, a character (who, whom) appeared in *Tom Sawyer*, would also be in the third book.
9. (She, Her) and the two boys would have adventures in Oklahoma territory.
10. Twain began the book, but stopped working on it before (he/him) finished it.

REVIEW EXERCISE E   Adverbs and Adjectives

Number a sheet of paper 1–10. After each number write the correct word from the parentheses.

1. Last summer my sister, a neighbor, and I performed (hilarious, hilariously) in an play that we wrote ourselves.
2. Gilberto could (easy, easily) write the plot; he just copied the story of Romeo and Juliet.
3. I play the guitar (bad, badly), but I volunteered to accompany the two singers.
4. Since my sister sings (good, well), she was chosen to play Juliet.

5. Gilberto and Inez worked (slow, slowly) and quite hard.
6. We all rehearsed the balcony serenade (careful, carefully).
7. Disguised as Juliet, Inez looked (good, well).
8. The play was a parody of Shakespeare's tragedy, especially with me playing the old nurse very (bad, badly).
9. Hearty applause from our audience, however, made me feel (good, well).
10. Next summer we can (easy, easily) do *Hamlet*.

10

COMMON CONFUSIONS

Too often people confuse simple elements in the English language. The use of one word when another should be used can cause trouble. The forms of words are sometimes confused. Even the spellings of two similar words may get mixed up.

This chapter lists easily confused terms. These terms are arranged in alphabetical order. This order allows you to find a word or term quickly to check how it should be used. By studying this chapter, you can avoid common confusions.

ALPHABETICAL LISTING

Accept/except: *Accept* is a verb that means "to receive."

EXAMPLES We willingly *accept* the honor.
Try to *accept* defeat like a good
sport.

Except is usually a preposition that means "leaving out."

EXAMPLES Everyone *except* Martha caught a
cold.
I like most sports *except* football.

EXERCISE 1 Write the following sentences on a sheet of paper. Fill each blank with either *accept* or *except*.

1. Do we have to _____ the decision?
2. _____ for Luis, all the students voted for the plan.
3. Everybody _____ Sasha finished the work.
4. Please _____ the invitation.

Advice/advise: *Advice* is a noun meaning "an opinion or suggestion."

EXAMPLES The *advice* came too late to do any
good.
What is your *advice?*

Advise is a verb that means "to give an opinion."

EXAMPLES Can you *advise* me in this matter?
A lawyer *advises* a client.

EXERCISE 2 Write the following sentences on a sheet of paper. Fill each blank with a form of either *advice* or *advise*.

1. The president was _____ to stay in bed.
2. Romana took the _____ of her doctor.

3. Dumquist would _____ anyone about anything.
4. Not many followed her _____.

Affect/effect: *Affect* is a verb meaning "to influence."

> EXAMPLES   Did the defeat *affect* you?
> Try not to let the heat *affect* you.

Effect is a noun that means "the result." It is sometimes used as a verb meaning "to bring about."

> EXAMPLES   What *effect* will this have on our district?
> Can you *effect* any change in our system?

All right/alright: *All right* should be written as two words. When you say, "All right," the two words often sound like one word. However, they are really two words.

All together/altogether: *All together* is a term made up of two separate words. They mean "everyone in a group."

> EXAMPLES   Our joys seem to come *all together.*
> Sing *all together.*

Altogether is an adverb meaning "entirely."

> EXAMPLES   Your singing is *altogether* too loud.
> We have had *altogether* too much.

Almost/most: *Almost* means "nearly" or "all but."

> EXAMPLES   Takako and Tae are *almost* ready.
> *Almost* all the food was eaten.

Most can mean "more than anything else."

EXAMPLE Toshima likes the *most* expensive clothing.

Most can also mean "the greatest amount."

EXAMPLE *Most* of the time we work.

Most may sometimes mean "almost all."

EXAMPLE Beth eats *most* foods.

Do not use *most* as a short form of *almost*.

WRITE The hour is *almost* gone
not
The hour is *most* gone.

WRITE The teller had counted *almost* all the money.
not
The teller had counted *most* all the money.

EXERCISE 3 Write the following sentences on a sheet of paper. Put in *almost* where it belongs. Some sentences do not need correcting.

1. Most all the clocks were wrong.
2. Most everyone wore jeans that day.
3. Trinnie likes most colors.
4. Ursula and Angie ate most all the peanuts.
5. Most days are sunny in Arizona.

Already/all ready: *Already* means "before now."

EXAMPLES Maria has finished the book *already*.
We *already* know the schedule.

All ready is two words meaning "completely ready."

EXAMPLES   The team was *all ready* to play.
Each row in the field was *all ready* for the seeds.

Be sure to write the two words *all* and *ready* when you mean something is fully ready.

WRITE   The canvas was *all ready* for painting.
not
The canvas was *already* for painting.

EXERCISE 4   Write the following sentences on a sheet of paper. Fill each blank with either *already* or *all ready.*

1. It is _____ noon.
2. The fried chicken is _____ to eat.
3. Some pieces are _____ getting cold.
4. The salad has _____ been made.
5. Everyone is _____ to go.

Am not, are not, is not/ain't: *Ain't* is a contraction used in casual talk for *am not, are not,* and *is not. Ain't* has been used for at least a hundred years in English, but it is still to be avoided in standard or formal usage.

Among/between: The meanings of these two words is very close. *Among* means "together with others" when you are talking about more than two things.

EXAMPLES   José is *among* his friends.
They say there is no honor *among* thieves.

Between sometimes means "the space or time that separates *two* things."

EXAMPLES The time *between* Christmas and
Easter really seems to drag.
You must stay *between* the two
lines.

Between can also mean "something shared by *two*
people or things."

EXAMPLES *Between* us, Peggy and I have
$25.00.
Just *between* you and me, I don't
believe it.

Use *among* when you are talking about three or
more. Use *between* when you are talking about only
two.

WRITE There's not a loser *among* all of us.
not
There's not a loser *between* all of us.

WRITE What's a dollar *among* four friends?
not
What's a dollar *between* four friends?

EXERCISE 5 Decide whether to fill each blank
with *among* or *between*. Then write the sentences
on a sheet of paper.

1. We don't have a dime _____ all of us.
2. The argument is _____ Willa and me.
3. Just _____ the three of us, I'll say I don't know
for sure.
4. Remember, that secret is just _____ you and
me.

Beside/besides: *Beside* means "next to."

EXAMPLES   The rake is *beside* the shovel.
            The tanker steamed *beside* the
            destroyer.

Besides as a preposition means "in addition to."

EXAMPLES   *Besides* the rain, we had some hail.
            We expect punch *besides* the food.

Besides as an adverb means "as well."

EXAMPLE   You can lose weight. *Besides,* you
            feel better.

EXERCISE 6 Write the following sentences on a
sheet of paper. Put in *beside* or *besides* in each
blank.

1. _____ the high cost, think of the storage problem.
2. Place the lamp _____ the chair.
3. Milt can do without it. _____, he's rich.
4. You can see a tall tree standing _____ the barn.
5. _____ sleep, everyone needs food and exercise.

Burst/bust: *Burst* is the standard verb meaning "to
break open." *Bust* or *busted* is a slang verb and
should not be used in formal speech or writing.

WRITE   The balloon *burst.*
        not
        The balloon *busted.*

Can/may: *Can* means "to be able."

EXAMPLES   Jerry *can* jump over his backyard
            fence.
            This bottle *can* hold enough water.

May means "to have permission."

EXAMPLES Winona *may* stay out until 11:00 o'clock.

You *may* go with her.

Can hardly/can't hardly: *Hardly* means "barely." *Can hardly* means "to be barely able to do something."

EXAMPLE She *can hardly* reach that shelf. [Reaching is hard.]

Do not use *can't hardly*.

WRITE I *can hardly* hear you.

not

I *can't hardly* hear you.

Could have/could of: *Could of* makes no sense. Some people write it by mistake. If you say *could have* quickly, it sounds the same as saying the contraction *could've*. This sounds like *could of,* and so it is sometimes written that way.

WRITE I *could have* gone.

not

I *could of* gone.

Drowned/drownded: *Drown* is the verb meaning "to die in the water." Its past tense adds *ed* only. There is no such word as *drownded*.

WRITE Archie *drowned* at sea.

not

Archie *drownded* at sea.

Good/well: *Good* is an adjective that means "better than usual."

EXAMPLE It was a *good* day for swimming.

Well as an adverb means "in a fine manner."

EXAMPLE Isabelle paints *well*.

WRITE Inez reads *well*.
not
Inez reads *good*.

EXERCISE 7 Write the following sentences on a sheet of paper. Fill the blanks with *good* or *well*.

1. Just give me a _____ bed.
2. I can sleep _____ in it.
3. I look forward to _____ dreams.
4. She did her work _____.

Its/it's: *Its* is one word, a possessive pronoun.

EXAMPLE The horse swished *its* tail.

It's is a contraction for *it is*.

EXAMPLE *It's* late in the day.

EXERCISE 8 Write the following sentences on a sheet of paper. Put *its* or *it's* in each blank.

1. The dog lifted _____ ears.
2. _____ eyes were bright.
3. _____ a happy dog.
4. _____ not my dog.
5. Who is _____ owner?

Lead/led: These two spellings can be *homonyms,* words that are pronounced the same. When they are homonyms, *l-e-a-d* is a word that names a metal.

EXAMPLE They mined the *lead*.

And *l-e-d,* which is said the same way, describes an action that happened in the past.

> EXAMPLE Long ago Harriet Tubman *led* the slaves to safety.

Remember that *l-e-d* always describes an action in the past. *L-e-a-d* is said like *l-e-d* only when it is the name of the metal.

EXERCISE 9 Write the following sentences on a sheet of paper. Fill in the blanks with *led* or *lead.*

1. Rosa's pencil was made out of _____.
2. The mine ran out of _____.
3. Last year the scout _____ the party through the pass.
4. She _____ them home yesterday.
5. The bullet was made of _____.
6. Has she _____ the way before?

Learn/teach: *Learn* is a verb that means "to gain knowledge."

> EXAMPLE Moe *learned* about cars.

Teach is a verb that means "to give knowledge to someone."

> EXAMPLE Ms. Ramie will *teach* French next year.

Leave/let: *Leave* means "to go away."

> EXAMPLE Jeff will *leave* home tomorrow.

Let means "to allow."

> EXAMPLE Please *let* her come with us.

Lend/loan: *Lend* and *loan* mean the same thing when they are used as verbs. Either one is correct. *Loan* is also a noun meaning "the thing given for a while."

See
Intransitive
Verb, p. 29 **Lie/lay:** *Lie* is a verb that does not take an object. It is an intransitive verb. *Lie* means either "to rest in a flat position" or "to tell an untruth." *Lay* is a transitive verb. It means "to put something down."

EXAMPLES   The weary hikers decided to *lie* down in the shade.

To *lie* to anyone is to be false to oneself also.

"*Lay* down your weapons!" commanded the officer.

Like/as: *Like* is a preposition that takes an object.

EXAMPLES   Roberto flew *like* a bird.
His arms flapped *like* wings.

See Clause, p.
368 *As* is a conjunction. It joins a dependent clause to an independent clause.

EXAMPLES   He stumbled *as* he stepped across the rug.
Her arms caught him *as* he fell.

As may also be used as a preposition.

EXAMPLE   Gilberto came dressed *as* a ragpicker.

See
Conjunction,
p. 370 *Like* is sometimes used informally as a conjunction. Its use as a conjunction is not, however, recommended in formal speech or writing.

WRITE Willa uses words *as* she should.
not
Willa uses words *like* she should.

OK, OK., okay/ all right: All of the three spellings of *okay* are common. Usually in writing, it is better to use *all right* instead of *okay*.

Real/really: *Real* is an adjective.

EXAMPLE This is a *real* diamond.

Really is an adverb.

EXAMPLE He looked *really* tired.

Do not use *real* as an adverb in formal speech or writing.

WRITE He drove *really* fast.
not
He drove *real* fast.

Set/sit: *Set* as a verb means "to put something down." It also describes a bird's action on a nest of eggs. It does *not* tell of the action of a person on a chair.

EXAMPLES The waiter *set* the table.
The hen *sets* on the nest nearly all the time.

Sit means "to be seated." People and animals sit.

EXAMPLE The judge *sits* on the bench.

WRITE Let's all *sit* down.
not
Let's all *set* down.

EXERCISE 10 Write the following sentences on a sheet of paper. Fill each blank with the correct form of *set* or *sit*.

1. Natasha, please _____ near me.
2. The bluebird still _____ on the nest.
3. We need to _____ the table for supper.
4. _____ the bag of cement over there.

Shall/will: A tradition began about two hundred years ago in formal English that *shall* should be used in the first person to show simple future and in the second and third person to show serious intention. Tradition also says *will* should be used just the other way around. Most people do not follow the tradition today. Either *shall* or *will* is correct. *Shall* is less common and therefore more formal.

Should have/should of: *Should of* makes no sense. Some people write it by mistake. If you say *should have* quickly, it sounds the same as the contraction *should've*. This sounds like *should of,* and so it is sometimes written that way.

> WRITE We *should have* stayed.
> not
> We *should of* stayed.

Their/there/they're: These three words sound alike in speech. They are *homonyms*. However, they are spelled differently and mean different things. *Their* is a possessive pronoun.

> EXAMPLE *Their* house is on the corner.

There points out a place. It also is used in the subject position in a clause.

EXAMPLES The cat sleeps *there*.
[place]

There are some mice in the barn.
[subject position]

They're is a contraction of the words *they* and *are*.

EXAMPLE *They're* all coming over tonight.

EXERCISE 11 Write the following sentences on a sheet of paper. Put in the correct form *there*, *their*, or *they're*.

1. _____ hurrying to _____ first class.
2. Will they get _____ on time?
3. _____ is no need to run.
4. When does _____ second class begin?

This/this here: Use only *this*. The added word *here* is not needed. The same is true for *that/that there*.

WRITE Do you see *this* mark?
not
Do you see *this here* mark?

It came from *that* knife.
not
It came from *that there* knife.

Those/them (there): *Them* and *them there* are not substitutes for *those*.

WRITE Give me *those* peanuts.
not
Give me *them* peanuts.
or
Give me *them there* peanuts.

To/too/two: These short words get confused in writing. They are homonyms.

To is a preposition.

> EXAMPLE Give the artichokes *to* him.

Too is an adverb. It means "also" or "more than enough."

> EXAMPLES Celeste will eat lunch, *too*.
> Celeste may eat *too* much.

Two means "one plus one."

> EXAMPLE The hen laid *two* eggs.

EXERCISE 12 Write the following sentences on a sheet of paper. Fill each blank with *to, too,* or *two*.

1. In _____ hours we will go _____ the garage.
2. Do you want to come along, _____?
3. The _____ mechanics worked _____ days on the car.
4. We will have to give $194 _____ them.

Try to/try and: You should usually use *try to* in speech and writing.

> WRITE *Try to* open this jar.
> not
> *Try and* open this jar.

Note that it is correct to say or write, "People will *try and* try to do something too hard. Many people *try and* fail."

We/us: Some people make the mistake of saying "*Us* people . . ." in a sentence instead of "*We* people know what's good for us." The pronoun *us* should not be used as part of the subject of a verb.

WRITE   *We* band members need to practice.
        not
        Us band members need to practice.

Who/whom: *Who* and *whom* are different forms of the same word. *Who* is in the subjective case. *Whom* is in the objective case.

EXAMPLES   Who seems happier?
           Who likes swimming?
           Who got the tickets?
           Whom did you see?

Whom should be used after a word like *to, from,* or *for.*

WRITE   to *whom,* for *whom,* from *whom*
        not
        to *who,* for *who,* from *who*

Whose/who's: These two words are *homonyms.* *Whose* is a form of *who* that shows ownership or possession.

EXAMPLES   *Whose* coat is that?
           Can you tell *whose* voice that is?

Who's is a form of *who* and *is.* The apostrophe (') takes the place of the *i* in *is.*

EXAMPLES   *Who's* afraid of Bigfoot?
           We know *who's* coming tomorrow.

Remember to use *who's* only when you mean *who is.*

EXERCISE 13   Rewrite each of the following sentences that has a *whose/who's* error in it.

1. Whose the brightest in the group?
2. Who's brains can we use to solve this?
3. Whose the one whose work will be accepted?

Your/you're: These two words are *homonyms*. *Your* is the possessive form of *you*. It shows ownership.

> EXAMPLES   It's *your* day to do whatever you want.
>
> Let's go to *your* place.

You're means *you* + *are*.

> EXAMPLES   *You're* right.
>
> I think *you're* mean!

EXERCISE 14   Rewrite each sentence that has a *your/you're* error in it.

1. Your the worst liar around.
2. Your too old to expect anyone to believe you're stories.
3. Who's going to think your telling the truth?
4. Your last story is worse than you're first one.

REVIEW EXERCISE A   Homonyms

Number a sheet of paper 1–10. After each number write the correct word from within the parentheses.

> EXAMPLE   The path (led, lead) to a cliff.
>
> *led*

1. (Your, You're) sure to be surprised when I explain why I was late.

2. I was up late last night out of respect to my grandparents, who were celebrating (their, they're) twenty-fifth wedding anniversary.

3. (Their, They're) very good to my whole family.

4. It was (too, to) late for me to do my homework when I got home.

5. I got up at 4:30 this morning to do my (too, two) assignments.

6. (You're, Your) aware of how dark and cold it is at that early hour.

7. Nothing is (too, to) much trouble for me, though, when I am determined to do my work.

8. I started my math when the (lead, led) in my pencil broke.

9. The friend (whose, who's) book I wanted to borrow had given me the wrong book.

10. You should be glad to see me, for (its, it's) a miracle that I have been able to get to school at all.

REVIEW EXERCISE B Usage

Number a sheet of paper 1–16. If the underlined word in the sentence is correct, write *C* (correct). If it is wrong, rewrite the word correctly.

1. A colonel in the army was <u>most</u> ready to retire.

2. He wondered what he could do <u>beside</u> work.

3. He remembered his father from <u>whom</u> he had inherited a large stamp collection.

4. He had to choose <u>among</u> collecting stamps and caring for cats.

5. "Stamp collecting would be <u>all right</u>," he thought.

6. He had saved stamps neatly <u>like</u> his father had taught him.

7. The colonel did not want to <u>set</u> quietly in his old age, however.

8. He wanted to <u>try to</u> make the world a better place.

9. He had <u>already</u> noticed many stray cats in his neighborhood.

10. No one <u>beside</u> him fed those cats.

11. "<u>All right</u>," the colonel thought, "I'll help stray cats."

12. A neighbor came to his door asking, "<u>Can I</u> come in?"

13. The neighbor, <u>whose</u> cat had seven kittens, has a soft gray <u>kitten</u> in her arms.

14. "No one <u>accept</u> you has room for a kitten," she said.

15. "<u>You're</u> looking at a man who collects cats," the colonel replied.

16. "<u>It's</u> just as well that I did not decide to collect elephants," he thought.

REVIEW EXERCISE C Usage

Number a sheet of paper 1–20. After each number, write the correct term from within the parentheses.

> EXAMPLE No one (accept, except) David dared to fight Goliath.
>
> *except*

1. Goliath was the great hero of the Philistines in a battle (between, among) their army and the army of Israel.

2. David was a young shepherd (whose, who's) brothers were in the army of Israel.

3. Goliath armed himself with terrible weapons, (all ready, already) for battle.

4. In his armor he looked as if he (could of, could have) destroyed a whole army by himself.

5. The (affect, effect) of Goliath's great size was frightening.

6. The Israelites were (too, to) terrified to fight.

7. David's flocks were grazing (beside, besides) the battlefield.

8. (Sitting, Setting) by a stream, he dreamed of becoming great.

9. Although he was small, he felt that he was (real, really) large in his courage and good sense.

10. He decided to (try to, try and) defeat Goliath.

11. His brothers gave him the good (advice, advise) to stay safely with his sheep.

12. "(We, Us) shepherds know that the sheep are seldom safe," he answered.

13. "I have killed a bear and a lion while guarding (your, you're) sheep."

14. (Like, As) shepherds did then, he guarded his sheep with a slingshot.

15. David believed that a man who had killed a lion could kill Goliath (too, to, two).

16. The soldiers put David in armor and (led, lead) him to the battlefield.

17. (There, Their, They're) he faced Goliath.

18. He could not fight (like, as) a soldier does.

19. He had to fight (like, as) the shepherd that he was.

20. No one (accept, except) David believed that he could kill a giant with a slingshot.

UNIT FOUR

MECHANICS

Capitalization
Punctuation

11

CAPITALIZATION

Capital letters belong at the beginning of important words. Your name and the names of other persons begin with capital letters. Other special words also begin with capital letters.

Capital letters are used as well in a few standard ways, such as at the beginning of every sentence.

The rules in this chapter will guide you in the use of capital letters.

CAPITAL LETTERS

11a Capitalize the first word in a sentence and the first word in a direct quotation.

EXAMPLES   Small boats drifted back and forth on the calm lake.

From the other side came the call, "Hello, there!"

11b Capitalize the pronoun *I.*

EXAMPLE This is the chance **I** have waited for.

Do not capitalize any other pronoun except when it begins a sentence.

EXAMPLE **Y**ou and *I* can reach the beach if you row harder.

11c Capitalize proper nouns and proper adjectives.

A proper noun names a particular person, place, or thing.

EXAMPLES **E**ngland, **N**ew **Y**ork, **B**aton **R**ouge, **K**ing **K**amehameha

A proper adjective is a form of a proper noun. Like a proper noun, it should be capitalized.

EXAMPLES **E**nglish, **F**rench

(1) Capitalize the names of particular people and animals.

EXAMPLES Call **A**dmiral **O**ldendorf and tell him the men are waiting.
The elephant, **J**umbo, was brought to this country by **B**arnum.

(2) Capitalize the names of particular places.

EXAMPLES

Cities, Towns	Fresno, Portland, Honolulu
States, Counties	South Carolina, Putnam County

Countries	Switzerland, New Zealand
Continents	Africa, North America
Special regions	the Midwest, the Middle East (but not the word *the*)
Bodies of water, Islands, Points of land	the Mediterranean Sea, San Juan Island, Point Mugu
Parks	Yellowstone Park, Hyde Park
Roadways, Waterways	Main Street, the Panama Canal

Do not capitalize directions.

EXAMPLES   "From here, go east about a mile. Then go south," said the ranger in Yosemite.

EXERCISE 1   Number a sheet of paper 1–10. For each proper noun in the following list, write the proper adjective formed from it. For each proper adjective in the list, write the proper noun it comes from.

EXAMPLES   Spain
American

Spanish   America

1. Asian
2. German
3. Poland
4. Greece
5. France
6. Chilean
7. Canada
8. Hawaiian
9. Alaska
10. Vietnamese

EXERCISE 2 Number a sheet of paper 1–10. Next to each number, write the words that need capital letters. Add capitals where they belong.

EXAMPLE   we visited yellowstone to see the geysers and the bears.

We, Yellowstone

1. when i was young, i used to watch birds.
2. what interested me were the birds of the west and southwest.
3. i remember a little roadrunner outside of carson city, nevada.
4. of course, the pacific ocean is a great place to watch birds.
5. gulls and pelicans swoop through the skies along the coast where the salinas river meets the pacific.
6. there are even condors, with wing spans of almost ten feet, in los padres national forest.
7. the condor is the largest bird in the united states.
8. the south american relative of the california condor is even larger.
9. it lives in the andes, a mountain range that stretches through south america.
10. unless we protect them, the condor and other western birds may become extinct in the americas.

(3) Capitalize important words in the names of organizations, institutions, businesses, and branches of government.

EXAMPLES

Organizations	United Nations (**UN**) North Atlantic Treaty Organization (**NATO**)
Institutions	Carnegie Foundation, Torrey High
Businesses and their products	Chrysler, Toyota, Lever Bros., Sweetheart soap
Branches of government	the House of Representa- tives, the Defense Department

(4) Capitalize subjects taught in school when they name particular courses.

EXAMPLE On Fridays, Drama I is offered in the afternoon.

Do not capitalize subjects when they refer to the general subject area.

EXAMPLES Play production and some history of the drama are included.
We study mathematics for two years.

(5) Capitalize the names of nationalities, races, and religions.

EXAMPLES Brazilians, Ugandans, Caucasian, Catholic, Buddhist

EXERCISE 3 Number a sheet of paper 1–6. Next to each number write the following sentences. Put in capital letters where needed.

1. For several years the small cars from toyota, datsun, volkswagen, and fiat sold well in the united states.
2. Students and faculty members at westlake high and hillview college found japanese, german, and italian cars were reliable.
3. Ford, general motors, and chrysler began making small cars to compete.
4. Government agencies, such as the department of labor, buy only american cars.
5. In auto mechanics II, we work on cars from any country.
6. Our teacher had lived with a german family while taking special training in the volkswagen factory.

(6) Capitalize the name of God and other beings worshipped by people.

EXAMPLES Jupiter, Muhammed, Thor

(7) Capitalize important words in the names of historical events, periods of time, or other special events.

EXAMPLES Fourth of July, the War of the Roses, January, Saturday

Do not capitalize the seasons of the year (fall, spring).

(8) Capitalize important words in the titles of people, books, magazines, newspapers, motion pictures, television shows, and other works people produce.

EXAMPLES

People	Senator Proxmire, Corporal Jones, Uncle Tobias
Books, stories	*Black Beauty,* the Bible
Poems	"The Bottle Imp"
Magazines	*People,* the *Readers' Digest*
Newspapers	the *Chicago Tribune,* the *Daily Bugle*
Movies, TV shows	*King Kong,* the "Today Show"
Works in music, art, architecture	London Bridge, *Aida*

EXERCISE 4 Copy the following sentences on a sheet of paper. Put in capitals where they belong.

1. The churches of the middle ages and the renaissance are fine examples of european architecture.
2. Almost everyone is inspired by the great french cathedral, notre dame.
3. It is fortunate that world war II didn't destroy the cathedral.
4. The movie, *the hunchback of notre dame,* takes place in this church.
5. The story for the movie is from a book by victor hugo, a french writer.

EXERCISE 5 Number a sheet of paper 1–5. List the words that should be capitalized in these sentences. Add capital letters.

1. It was general valdez who called the *new york times*.
2. The "wide world of sports" televised the fight.
3. The show, "bicentennial special," celebrated the american revolution.
4. Last night we saw the movie *duck soup* with groucho marx.
5. I would rather visit the taj mahal than the empire state building.

REVIEW EXERCISE A   Capitalization

In each of the following pairs of sentences, one is correctly capitalized and the other is not. Number a sheet of paper 1–10. After each number write the letter of the correctly capitalized sentence.

EXAMPLE   A. Ko-Ko said, "Congratulate me, gentlemen, for I've found a volunteer."
   B. Ko-Ko said, "congratulate me, Gentlemen, for I've found a volunteer."

A

1. A. George M. Cohan was born on the Fourth of July.
   B. George M. Cohan was born on the fourth of July.
2. A. In some English classes in the West, students read *Two Years Before the Mast*.
   B. In some english classes in The West, students read *Two Years Before the Mast*.

3. A. The Eskimo people of the Bering Strait tell of their hero, Raven, who was swallowed by a whale.

   B. The Eskimo people of the Bering Strait tell of their hero, raven, who was swallowed by a whale.

4. A. Richard Henry Dana left Harvard university to be a sailor for two years.

   B. Richard Henry Dana left Harvard University to be a sailor for two years.

5. A. In Paris we saw the eiffel tower.

   B. In Paris we saw the Eiffel Tower.

6. A. With the birthday money that Noreen's Grandfather has given her, she wants to buy a second-hand car.

   B. With the birthday money that Noreen's grandfather has given her, she wants to buy a second-hand car.

7. A. Students at King Junior High School may go to either one of two nearby high schools.

   B. Students at King Junior High School may go to either one of two nearby High Schools.

8. A. James Nakamura took Drama I because he knew that the class would take a field trip to New York to see a play.

   B. James Nakamura took drama I because he knew that the class would take a field trip to New York to see a play.

9. A. Mark Twain's story "The Celebrated Jumping Frog of Calaveras County" is one of his best tall tales from the Old West.

   B. Mark Twain's story "The Celebrated Jumping Frog of Calaveras County" is one of his best tall tales from the old west.

10. A. Twain's story is about the West, but it was first published in Boston and read in the East.

B. Twain's story is about the west, but it was first published in Boston and read in the east.

REVIEW EXERCISE B More Capitalization

All of the capitalization has been left out of the following sentences. On a sheet of paper write the words that should be capitalized. Add capital letters where they are needed.

1. the life of sarah kemble knight showed that even in colonial days a woman could make a career for herself.

2. mrs. knight was born in boston in 1666.

3. she taught in a small school, knight's dame school, which benjamin franklin may have attended as a little boy.

4. she lived in boston until 1713, and then she moved to new london, connecticut, where she lived until her death in 1727.

5. when she traveled through rhode island to new york, she kept a journal of her experiences.

6. in the journal she laughs at the yankee bumpkins who could hardly speak because of the huge wads of chewing tobacco in their mouths.

7. she tells of staying at the hogshead hotel on the connecticut river near the town of essex.

8. because the hotel had only three rooms, she had to share a room with senator bradford, judge hathorne, mrs. whitcomb, and a native american guest whose name is not recorded.

9. the judge told mrs. knight that he had sentenced a young man to a whipping for kissing his girl friend, an action that she thought was only "innocent merriment."

10. some parts of mrs. knight's diary were printed in the spring of 1720 in the boston newspaper.

REVIEW EXERCISE C Still More Capitalization

On a separate sheet of paper rewrite each word in the following paragraphs that should have a capital letter. Capitalize correctly.

The section of the united states covering the present states of wyoming, utah, colorado, and arizona was a big blank on maps made in 1869. This section, 200 miles wide and 500 miles long, was as mysterious to americans in new york then as mars or jupiter.

Of all the mysteries of the region, the most interesting was the colorado river, which had cut a deep gorge, the grand canyon. In their folklore, native americans spoke of the grand canyon as a bottomless place where evil spirits lived.

In may of 1869, a geology professor at illinois wesleyan college decided to explore the colorado river. john wesley powell had been a major in the union army during the civil war. he had lost an arm at the battle of shiloh.

A reporter from a local newspaper, the *journal*, asked mr. powell, "why are you taking this dangerous journey?" He replied that the huge canyon and the powerful river simply amazed him. He wanted to see them and to know their paths.

12

PUNCTUATION

End Punctuation, Commas

The marks of punctuation are small, but their importance in writing is great. The reason is that punctuation marks show how sentences are to be read. For example, if you look at the sentence below, you cannot be sure how to read it.

To Alice Wilson's answer sounded silly.

Could some words be missing from this sentence? No, words are not missing. What is missing is a *comma*. You can read the sentence with a comma.

To Alice, Wilson's answer sounded silly.

Now you can understand that two people are being talked about and that the answer of one sounded silly to the other.

The use of punctuation in sentences can often make the difference between sense and nonsense. Learning the correct way to punctuate your writing will make it possible for you to write clearly. This chapter will give you the basic rules for punctuating sentences.

END PUNCTUATION

A mark of end punctuation comes at the end of every sentence. Either a period (.), a question mark (?), or an exclamation mark (!) comes at the end of a sentence. The end punctuation helps to show how the sentence should be read and what it means.

The Period

12a A period is used to mark the end of a statement or a request.

> EXAMPLES The elevator has been broken for a week.
> Please bring me a pencil.

12b A period is used after some abbreviations.

> EXAMPLES Drexel Ave.   Mr.
> Feb.   B.C.

12c A period is usually used after an initial.

> EXAMPLES The clothes sold at T.C. Bestor's are not new.

Sets of initials used together often do not need periods.

> EXAMPLES USA (United States of America)
> UFO (unidentified flying object)

EXERCISE 1 Write the following sentences on a sheet of paper. Put in periods where they belong and circle them.

EXAMPLE   An early submarine was developed
by D Bushnell

*An early submarine was
developed by D Bushnell.*

1. R Fulton built a submarine in 1800 that was
   about six meters long.
2. The first submarine in the US Navy was J P
   Holland's USS *Holland*
3. Mr Holland lived in Paterson, N J
4. He had come to the USA from Ireland
5. His work for the US Navy was done by the Electric Boat Co in New Jersey

The Question Mark

12d A question mark is used at the end of a sentence that asks a question.

EXAMPLES   How old are you?
When is the next show?

EXERCISE 2   Copy the following sentences on
sheet of paper. Put a period after each statement
request. Put a question mark after each questic

1. Get in and drive
2. Where are the keys
3. Can you see the ignition
4. Start the motor
5. Is another car coming
6. Look over your shoulder
7. The car has gone now
8. Why are you waiting
9. Get out
10. I thought it was your car

The Exclamation Mark

12e An exclamation mark is used at the end of a strong statement.

The statement may show surprise or shock. It may be either a whole sentence or part of one.

EXAMPLES This is amazing!
The clocks are running backward!
Unbelievable!

EXERCISE 3 Number a sheet of paper 1–10. After each number put the mark of end punctuation that goes with each sentence.

1. What kind of music is that
2. A tango is a South American dance
3. That last polka was so fast
4. The jitterbug is like a fast fox trot
5. Mr. Fred Astaire became world famous as a tap dancer
6. Many countries have native dances called folk dances
7. Is dancing one of your favorite pastimes
8. Margot Fonteyn has been called a great ballet dancer
9. May I have this next dance
10. What a dance that was

INSIDE PUNCTUATION

Punctuation marks are used inside sentences to help show how words are related. A *comma* (,) is useful and important to meaning. It is the most widely used mark of inside punctuation. Also useful are the *semicolon* (;), the *colon* (:), the *hyphen* (-), and underlining.

The Comma

12f A comma is used between items in a series.

Three or more items make up a series. The items may be words, phrases, or clauses. They may also be dates or other numbers.

See Phrase, p. 383; Clause, p. 368

EXAMPLES

WORDS   On the walls were hung prints, paintings, and carbings.

PHRASES   The runners surged away from the start, raced across the field, and turned off beyond the trees.

CLAUSES   Maria was near the leaders, Corrine ran a few yards back, but Jason was nowhere in sight.

NUMBERS   The tidal waves hit in 1908, 1924, and 1931.

Some styles of punctuation do not use the comma between the last two items in a series. Follow your teacher's instruction.

EXERCISE 4 The following sentences are missing commas. On a sheet of paper write the words just before and after a missing comma. Put a comma between them.

EXAMPLE   Weather forecasters must study
          temperature air pressure winds and
          other elements.

          temperature, air pressure,
          winds, and

1. The sky at sunset was a combination of pink
   red yellow and orange.
2. The wind howled the rain pelted and lightning
   streaked across the sky.
3. Yesterday was calm in the morning windy in
   the afternoon and rainy in the evening.
4. This drought can cause failing crops loss of
   wildlife increased fires and discomfort to the
   human population.
5. The cloudy sky the barometer and my right
   knee all predicted the rain.
6. Do you use your umbrella rain hat or hooded
   jacket for a walk in the rain.
7. We drove through a dark cold and soaking
   raincloud.
8. When cold, you can wrap in a blanket wear
   more clothes or get some exercise.
9. The temperatures at 8 A.M. 4 P.M. and 8 P.M. were
   Celsius 15° 19° and 14°.
10. During weather like this, I like to play tennis
    ride my bike play with my dog or go for a swim.

12g Commas are used to set off items that interrupt a sentence.

EXAMPLES   Highway 1, *the Boston Post Road,*
           follows the New England shore.

Teddy's sister, *with only a few yards to go*, passed him easily.

Instead of crossing the line ahead of him, *however*, she slowed so that they could cross it together.

(1) Commas are used to set off appositives.

A word or phrase that repeats the meaning of another word or phrase just before it is an *appositive*. Because an appositive interrupts the flow of a sentence, it is set off with commas.

EXAMPLE   Lake Superior, *our country's largest lake*, drains into Lake Huron.

(2) Commas are used to set off words such as yes, no, and well when they interrupt a sentence.

EXAMPLES   *Well*, will you be able to join us?
No, it looks impossible today.
Could you, *perhaps*, get away next week?

(3) Commas are used to set off transitional terms.

Words such as *however* and *nevertheless* show a transition, or carry-over in thought, from one sentence to another. They should be set off with commas from the main part of a sentence.

EXAMPLES   Fifi will lead the way. *However*, I want you to follow right behind. If there is any slowdown, *of course*, I want you to let me know immediately.

(4) **Commas are used to set off names used in direct address.**

EXAMPLES   Do you think we should operate, *Dr. Rivera?*

Certainly we should, *nurse.* Now if you will be kind enough, *my good man*, to give me the scalpel, I can begin.

Hint: A comma usually comes in a sentence where your voice pauses and drops in tone as you read the sentence aloud.

EXERCISE 5 Number a sheet of paper 1–10. The following sentences are lacking commas. Next to each number for each sentence write the words just before and after a missing comma. Put the comma between them.

EXAMPLE Dr. Garcia my friendly dentist has many patients.

Garcia, my dentist, has

1. Dr. Garcia began her practice in 1964 the year of my birth.
2. Her work mostly with young people pays her well.
3. She is an expert of course in psychology.
4. Dr. Garcia offers music for example to soothe her patients.
5. You can have semiclassical or soft rock the kind I like.

6. She asks me about my teeth sometimes a painful subject.
7. She also asks what if anything is new in my life.
8. My mind by that time is empty.
9. She knows so much you see.
10. She finds out all about me from my dad her partner.

EXERCISE 6 Some of the following sentences need commas. Next to each number, write *C* if a sentence needs no comma. Write correctly each sentence that needs a comma.

> EXAMPLE   When she got there however the cupboard was bare.
>
> *When she got there, however, the cupboard was bare.*

1. Therefore you should expect the correct answer from Conchita.
2. My mother is I believe an expert in her field.
3. Good gymnastics coaches generally speaking can perform some of the stunts themselves.
4. However the most important thing is to be able to teach them well.
5. I believe that knowledge of the subject is of utmost importance.
6. As a matter of fact I don't know as much about my job as I would like to.
7. You know your work so well in truth you ought to teach it to others.
8. This is the hardest decision I have had to make in fact.

9. I think Ms. Buckmaster that my job is better than the one you have offered me.

10. Did you know however that many of your people aren't happy with their jobs?

(5) Commas are used to set off nonessential phrases or clauses.

> EXAMPLE Nancy Morton, *the oldest girl in the class*, is the shortest girl in school. [The phrase *the oldest girl in the class* is not essential to the rest of the sentence: *Nancy Morton is the shortest girl in school.*]

Do not put commas around a phrase or clause that is essential to the meaning of a sentence.

> EXAMPLE Girls who are tall often have a good chance to play on the varsity volleyball team. [In this example the clause *who are tall* tells which particular girls have the chance to play on the volleyball team.]

Hint: To tell whether or not to use commas to set off a phrase or clause in a sentence, ask: *Can I tell which person or thing this is among several persons or things?*

If you cannot tell without the phrase or clause, you should not use commas. The phrase or clause is essential to the meaning of the sentence.

Following are some examples of essential and non-essential phrases:

ESSENTIAL PHRASE
The flowers *planted in the hot-house* bloomed early in January. Those outside did not.
[The particular flowers in the hothouse were the only ones that bloomed.]

NONESSENTIAL PHRASE
The flowers, *planted in the hothouse*, bloomed early in January. Those outside did not.
[In this case, the phrase *planted in neat rows* does not tell which flowers had begun to bloom. Therefore, the phrase is not essential to the meaning of the sentence.]

ESSENTIAL PHRASE
Apartment houses *built before 1945* have no washing machines.

NONESSENTIAL PHRASE
These apartment houses, *built one right next to the other*, make for poor living.

EXERCISE 7 Some of the following sentences contain nonessential clauses or phrases. On a sheet of paper, rewrite each sentence that contains a nonessential phrase or clause. Add commas where they belong.

EXAMPLE   The rocket whose flame seemed as bright as the sun made a gigantic roar.

The rocket, whose flame seemed as bright as the sun, made a gigantic roar.

1. The structure that supported the rocket dropped away.
2. The rocket freed from its mooring began to move upward.
3. The flames and smoke that poured from the rocket hid its lower part.
4. The giant cylinder gleaming white in the sun rose free of the tower.
5. Its fuel burning at a fast rate grew lighter.
6. The engine having finished its work was dropped off into space.

12h A comma is used to separate adjectives not joined by the conjunction *and*.

EXAMPLES   Clara gazed at the *still, crumpled* figure.
Then she uttered a *loud, choked* sob.

If the second of two adjectives is closely related in meaning to the noun following, do not use a comma between the adjectives.

EXAMPLE   The *rusty old* hinge squeaked as the door opened.

EXERCISE 8 The following sentences need commas. Number a sheet of paper 1–6. Next to each number, write the word before and after a comma that belongs in the sentence. Put in the missing comma.

EXAMPLE The first submarine was a bulky dangerous object.

bulky, dangerous

1. In 1776 David Bushnell built a clumsy globe-like submarine.
2. Named *Turtle*, it floated along in a slow unsure way.
3. He sat inside in a tight cramped position.
4. He wound a hand crank inside to turn the small awkward propellor outside.
5. His one luckless mission was against a British warship in New York harbor.
6. He failed and came out of it a wet exhausted submariner.

12i **A comma is used to set off a dependent clause at the beginning of a complex sentence.**

See Clause, p. 368; Complex Sentence, p. 370

EXAMPLES *As the night closed in*, Rose could feel the growing cold.
When it was pitch black, she lit the fire.
While the fire burned higher, she looked around for more wood.

EXERCISE 9 Each of the following sentences needs a comma. Number a sheet of paper 1–8. After each number, write the words before and after the place for a comma. Add the comma.

> EXAMPLE   When the American Robert Fulton studied submarines he decided he could build a successful one.
>
> *submarines, he*

1. After Fulton built his submarine in 1800 he tried to interest the French in buying it.
2. Although he blew up a French ship as a demonstration they were not impressed.
3. Even though Napoleon thought Fulton's idea might work the French gave up on Fulton.
4. Because of his lack of success Fulton turned his attention to surface steamships.
5. Although his first steamboat had power it sank on its maiden trip.
6. When he returned to America he built the first successful steamboat.
7. As soon as he proved its success it began regular trips up and down the Hudson River.
8. While others claimed earlier inventions of steamboats Fulton's was the first that proved practical.

See
Conjunction,
p. 370;
Independent
Clause, p. 378;
Compound
Sentence, p.
370
12j A comma is usually used before a coordinating conjunction joining independent clauses in a compound sentence.

> EXAMPLES   Clara Barton decided to devote her life to helping others *but* she never thought she would become a model for all who followed.

It usually takes only one or two leaders like that *and* others know the way is open for them.

Short clauses in a compound sentence may not need a comma before the conjunction. Follow your teacher's direction.

EXAMPLE   One person leads and others follow.

EXERCISE 10   Each of the following sentences needs a comma. Number a sheet of paper 1–6. After each number, write the words before and after the place for a comma. Add the comma.

EXAMPLE   Nations have seen the submarine as a weapon in war but it may have value for peace.

war, but

1. The U.S. Navy needed a submarine and in 1900 the U.S.S. *Holland* became the first submarine in the fleet.
2. It measured 53 feet in length and it displaced 75 tons of water.
3. Underwater it ran on electric power but on the surface it used gasoline for its engine.
4. A torpedo tube was built into it but no one thought to add a periscope.
5. It could not chase surface ships for its speed was too slow.
6. It could slip up on ships at anchor or it could meet them as they steamed toward it.

12k Commas are used in certain standard ways.

Not every use of a comma tells what the meaning should be for a sentence. Some commas are used only to help show divisions in parts of sentences.

(1) A comma is used before the quotation marks around the words of a speaker.

> EXAMPLE Ursula shouted, "Go on," as she fell beside the path.

Commas set off the words of a speaker from the name of the speaker in a quotation. They also set off information about the speaker. Place a comma in front of the quotation marks.

> EXAMPLE Without missing a step in his climb, Greg called back, "We're going, but I'll come back for you."

EXERCISE 11 Write each sentence on a sheet of paper. Insert commas where they belong and circle them.

> EXAMPLE The control center called "T minus 1 minute 35 seconds on Apollo 11 mission to the moon."
>
> *The control center called,*
> *"T minus 1 minute 35*
> *seconds on Apollo 11 mission*
> *to the moon."*

1. Then the center called out "Ignition sequence starts, 6, 5, 4, 3, 2, 1, zero."

2. "Lift-off. We have lift-off" were the next words.
3. Launch control radioed "Good luck and God-speed."
4. "Thank you" answered Armstrong "we know this will be a good flight."
5. Mission control in Houston radioed "You are looking good."
6. At 24,000 miles per hour in orbit Armstrong called back "It was beautiful!"
7. Three days later Houston radioed "You are Go for lunar orbit insertion."
8. In less than twenty-four hours Armstrong called from the moon to earth "The *Eagle* has landed."

(2) **A comma is used to separate items in dates and geographical names.**

EXAMPLE The first travelers to the moon left Cape Canaveral, Florida, on July 16, 1969.

EXERCISE 12 Number a sheet of paper 1–5. Next to each number, write each part of the following items that need commas. Add commas where they belong.

EXAMPLE Elizabeth I was born on Sunday September 7 1533.

Elizabeth I was born on Sunday, September 7, 1533.

1. When her sister Mary died on November 17 1558 Elizabeth became queen of England.
2. She was crowned in Westminster Abbey in London England.

3. In a speech at Tilbury England on August 18 1588, she roused her troops to prepare for an invasion from the Netherlands.

4. As Elizabeth grew older, she named James of Scotland her successor and summoned him from Edinburgh Scotland.

5. Elizabeth's death on March 24 1603, ended the reign of the Tudor family.

(3) A comma is used after the greeting and the closing in a friendly letter.

EXAMPLES   Dear Herb,
Dear Colleague,

Yours sincerely,
Cordially yours,

REVIEW EXERCISES for Punctuation will be found at the end of Chapter 13.

13

PUNCTUATION

Semicolons, Colons, Hyphens, Apostrophes, Italics, Quotation Marks, Parentheses

This chapter continues a presentation of inside punctuation: *semicolons, colons, hyphens,* and *apostrophes.* Several marks of enclosing punctuation— *quotation marks, underlining (italics),* and *parentheses*—are also presented.

INSIDE PUNCTUATION

The Semicolon

13a A semicolon is used between the clauses in a compound sentence that are not joined by a conjunction.

EXAMPLES The houses in this block are small; the houses in the next block are bigger.

> Most of the houses were built by
> one company; a few were built by
> independent contractors.

A semicolon comes between two long, independent clauses. It works like a strong comma.

13b A semicolon is used between the clauses of a compound sentence when either clause has a comma in it.

EXAMPLES   Wanda Cosgrove did not pay for the coat; instead, she took it back for a refund.

It had a high collar, silver buttons, and a belt in the back; yet she felt it looked cheap on her.

13c A semicolon is used to separate items in a series having inside punctuation.

EXAMPLE   He had crossed hot, barren deserts; he had swum icy, roaring rivers; but he had never come across a furious child who had been wronged.

13d A semicolon following a quotation goes outside the quotation marks.

EXAMPLES   Anne yelled, "Climb into the back"; but Jerry, who apparently had not heard her, ran around the side of the truck.

Anne shouted louder, "She's spraying the front"; and just then Jerry was met by a stream of cold water, catching him full in the face and chest.

EXERCISE The following sentences are missing semicolons. Number a sheet of paper 1–12. Next to each number, write the words before and after the place where a semicolon belongs. Put in a semicolon.

EXAMPLE Natalie and Rich went to a party at Georgina's house but Georgina, who got stuck in traffic, was late to her own party.

house; but

1. While waiting for Georgina, Natalie suggested to Rick that they play a magic trick at the party and Rick was willing.
2. "Tell me what to do," said Rick and Natalie explained the trick to him.
3. Other friends began to arrive for the party but, because Georgina was late, they all had to wait outside.
4. Finally someone yelled, "Here comes Georgina" and the hostess let them into her house.
5. Some friends helped Georgina prepare refreshments others set the tables and Natalie and Rick, preparing for their magic, got six cups and a dried bean.
6. "Everyone gather around for the magic," said Natalie and the friends crowded around her table.

7. "Rick is going to leave the room while I place this bean under a cup," she said "however, his spirit will still be here."

8. Rick left the room someone watched to keep him away from the door and Natalie, after waving her arms slowly and saying some mysterious words, put the bean under one of the cups she had set in a row.

9. Rick was called back and Natalie pointed to a cup and asked him, "Is the bean under this one?"

10. "No," he answered and Natalie repeated the question again, this time pointing to a different cup.

11. Again he answered, "No" but when she asked him the third time and pointed to the third cup, he said, "Yes."

12. Their friends could never guess the magic trick but since you were not there, you have a right to know.

[Think of each cup in the row as having a number: 1, 2, 3, 4, 5, 6. If the bean is under cup Number 3, Natalie points to that cup the third time she asks the question. If the bean is under cup Number 5, she points to that cup the fifth time she asks the question.]

The Colon

13e A colon is used to introduce a list of items.

EXAMPLES Here is what we have for sale: shovels, picks, ropes, and buckets.

The prices range as follows: $8.50, $11.20, and $2.49.

13f A colon is used in numerals expressing time.

EXAMPLES 10:20 P.M.

The time is exactly 4:19 in the morning.

13g A colon is used after the greeting in a business letter.

EXAMPLES Dear Mrs. Mayerwheather:
Dear Madam:

EXERCISE 2 Write the following items on a sheet of paper. Put in colons where they belong.

EXAMPLE The lost and found office sold the following a camera, one ski, and an old purse.

The lost and found office sold the following: a camera, one ski, and an old purse.

1. We expect to start the match at 1230 P.M.
2. Our team will have the following members Stankey, Ruffles, and Hopewell.
3. The following equipment will be needed three tables, six chairs, and three playing boards.
4. The scores were as follows 10-2, 10-1, and 10-0.
5. Stankey wrote a letter to the coach afterward. Dear Coach I am sorry we lost. We'll win next time. Stankey

The Hyphen

13h A hyphen is used to connect the parts of certain compound words and word numbers from twenty-one to ninety-nine.

EXAMPLES My *mother-in-law* is *seventy-two* years old today.
He saw the *fifty-first* dragon.

13i A hyphen is used to divide a word between syllables at the end of a line.

EXAMPLES Abraham Weiss told us an in-credible story.

WRONG The cracked and chipped furnit-ure had been advertised as being unbreakable.

RIGHT The cracked and chipped furni-ture had been advertised as being unbreakable.

EXERCISE 3 Number a sheet of paper 1–10. Copy each of the following items. Put in hyphens where they belong. For each single word, write the syllables separately. Put hyphens between the syllables to show how to break each word at the end of a sentence. You may use a dictionary.

EXAMPLE sharpening

sharp - en - ing

1. brother in law
2. develop
3. overcoat
4. Washington
5. primary
6. twenty two

7. communicate   9. automobile
8. fortify   10. apartment

The Apostrophe

13j An apostrophe is used with nouns to show possession or close relationship.

> EXAMPLES Trixie's sister lost her mother's earrings.
> The spoon's handle is bent.
> The bird's wing looked broken.

(1) A singular noun forms the possessive with an apostrophe and an *s*.

> EXAMPLES a dog's bed
> one day's weather
> Roberto's wallet

(2) A plural noun ending in *s* forms the possessive with an apostrophe only.

> EXAMPLES The birds' singing reminds us that spring is here.
> The cannons' roar has frightened the town.

(3) A plural noun not ending in *s* adds an apostrophe and an *s*.

> EXAMPLES The room downstairs was once a men's grill.
> Their children's songs pleased the crowd.

EXERCISE 4 Some of the following sentences are correct. Others have errors in the use of the apostrophe to show possession. Number a sheet of paper 1–8. Write *C* for any sentence that is correct. Copy any incorrect sentence. Write it with the correct use of the apostrophe.

EXAMPLE   The Robinsons lawn began to die.

The Robinsons' lawn began to die.

1. Their childrens vegetable garden dried up.
2. The rose bush's leaves grew smaller.
3. The few roses curled inward.
4. The wells water ran dry.
5. The suns rays seemed everywhere.
6. The earths last moisture was drawn up.
7. The dust of the fields blew through the air.
8. The Robinsons lives were affected by the drought.

13k An apostrophe is used to show that letters have been omitted.

EXAMPLES   didn't (did not)
            would've (would have)
            she'll (she will)
            hasn't (has not)

The above words with apostrophes are *contractions.* Contractions are formed by omitting letters to shorten words. An apostrophe takes the place of the missing letters.

13l An apostrophe is used with the letter *s* to show the plural of letters, numerals, and special symbols.

EXAMPLES   Were the 1920's really roaring?
His typewriter prints *W*'s when he hits the key for *Q*'s.

EXERCISE 5   Rewrite the following items. Put in apostrophes where they belong.

EXAMPLE   Whats his name?

What's his name?

1. dont
2. Whos at home?
3. Its probably mine.
4. hadnt
5. Still in the 1900s.
6. Well take you with us.
7. shouldnt
8. Mind your ps and qs.
9. wasnt
10. Whats on your list?

Italics (the underline)

13m Underlining is used for titles of books, movies, periodicals, ships, letters of the alphabet, and important works. In printed matter, these items are set in italics.

EXAMPLES   A review in *Spotlight* magazine panned the movie *The Great Gatsby*, which was originally a book written by F. Scott Fitzgerald.

Put a *T* after all correct statements in the test.

13n Underlining is used to make special items and foreign words stand out.

EXAMPLES   Please *do not* feed the animals.
This room must be cleaned *every day.*
"Your coat, *s'il vous plaît*," the butler said.

EXERCISE 6 Number a sheet of paper 1–6. Next to each number, write the word or words in the following sentences that need underlining. Underline the words you write.

1. If your card has an H on it, call the director.
2. I have asked you please not to slam the door!
3. Newsspeak magazine offers weekly news.
4. The Queen Mary is now in Long Beach, California.
5. The movie The African Queen stars Bogart and Hepburn.
6. Joanna sneezed and Elena said, "Gesundheit."

ENCLOSING PUNCTUATION

Certain marks of punctuation belong on each side of written words. For example, the exact words of a speaker must have quotation marks (" ") to enclose them. This section points out the special marks of punctuation used to enclose words.

Quotation Marks

13o Quotation marks are used to enclose a speaker's exact words.

EXAMPLES   Timothy asked, "What's under the porch?"

"A litter of kittens," answered Cindy.

Only the exact words of the speaker have quotation marks around them. A speaker's words that are written in a different way do not have quotation marks.

DIRECT
QUOTATION   "What day is it?" asked Pardee.

INDIRECT
QUOTATION   Pardee asked what day it was.

13p Single quotation marks are used to enclose a quotation within a quotation.

EXAMPLES   "Did you say, 'Get a ticket'," asked Pat, "or did you say 'Buy a ticket'?"

"I said 'Get' but you have to come," responded Chris.

EXERCISE 7   Write the following sentences on a sheet of paper. Put quotation marks around the exact words of each speaker.

EXAMPLE   This is going to be a good day, said Maria.

"This is going to be a good day," said Maria.

1. First we'll pack a lunch, she said.
2. José added, Let's not forget to put gas in the car.

3. Of course, continued Maria, we want to get an early start.
4. When you say early start, you must mean before sunrise, José said.
5. Maria said, You are right.
6. Set the alarm tonight, José warned.
7. I will be awake before sunrise, Maria insisted.
8. In case of clouds, said José, we need the alarm.

13q Quotation marks are used to enclose titles of chapters, articles, short stories, poems, songs, and other short pieces of writing.

EXAMPLES The weather seems to be a popular theme for songwriters, as you can tell from "September in the Rain," "Stormy Weather," and "Raindrops Keep Falling on My Head."

Dickens's "A Christmas Carol" is a well-loved story.

13r A period always goes inside the end quotation marks.

A question mark or an exclamation mark goes inside the quotation marks if the quotation is a question or an exclamation. Otherwise, these marks go outside the quotation marks.

EXAMPLES "Where does this big bowl go?" asked Mullins.

"Don't drop that" yelled his sister.

Did she say, "Don't drop that"?

EXERCISE 8 Write the following sentences on a sheet of paper. Put in quotation marks and marks of end punctuation where they belong.

EXAMPLE Good heavens, exclaimed Elsie, I haven't heard that song in years

"Good heavens," exclaimed Elsie, "I haven't heard that song in years!"

1. What's the name of that song asked Carl.
2. Elsie answered slowly Down Lovers' Lane is the name I remember.
3. You don't sound too sure Carl said.
4. I can't be sure she continued.
5. Why not asked Carl.
6. They keep putting in different notes. It's awful she complained.
7. The music is all mixed up she added.
8. Carl commented So are lovers.

Parentheses

13s Parentheses are used to enclose extra items added in a sentence.

EXAMPLE Fill out this form (the one marked *AK*) and then take it to Room 400.

REVIEW EXERCISE A   End Punctuation

Number a sheet of paper 1–9. Copy the last word of each sentence. Add the correct end punctuation.

EXAMPLE   One hot day in August two frogs were hopping along in the dust.

dust.

1. There had been no rain, and the frogs were looking for water
2. They wondered if they would ever find a clear pool or a running stream
3. Finally, they came upon a well
4. How cool and inviting it looked
5. The wiser of the two frogs paused
6. He reasoned that the well must be very deep
7. What would happen to the two frogs if they jumped in and then the well dried up
8. With no water in the well, could they jump out
9. The wiser frog made up his mind to go on and look for a stream

REVIEW EXERCISE B   Commas

The commas have been left out of the following sentences. Copy them on a sheet of paper. Add the commas that are needed. Circle each comma.

EXAMPLE   When Americans turned on their radios on December 7 1941 they heard that Pearl Harbor had been bombed.

When Americans turned on their radios on December 7 1941 they heard that Pearl Harbor had been bombed.

1. On April 9 1940 Hitler's forces began a series of attacks.
2. They overran Denmark Norway the Netherlands Belgium Luxembourg and northern France.
3. Italy sensing that France would fall declared war on France and England.
4. Because the British people felt defenceless the British Prime Minister Winston Churchill encouraged them by radio broadcasts.
5. He promised that Britain would never surrender and he said that Canada and the United States would help the British in their fight.
6. Churchill said to the British "If we can stand up to Hitler all Europe may be free and the life of the world may move forward into broad sunlit highlands."
7. When Hitler's forces tried to destroy the British navy Britain fought back furiously.
8. Although the Royal Air Force was outnumbered it fought successfully.
9. Churchill seeing that Britain was saved said that never before was "so much owed by so many to so few."
10. Meanwhile the American armed forces were also trying to help the small damaged British navy.

REVIEW EXERCISE C Semicolons and Colons

The semicolons and colons have been left out of the following sentences. Copy the words before and after missing punctuation on a sheet of paper. Add the colons and semicolons where they are needed. Circle each colon and semicolon.

1. On a recent excursion into the mountains, my brother took the following items six peanut butter sandwiches, two quarts of milk, a magazine, and some mosquito repellent.
2. Since he was only gone from 230 to 300 o'clock, he probably did not need any food but David does not like to go more than a few minutes without a snack.
3. He likes to read as well as to eat he carries a magazine in his pocket even when he watches television.
4. If the program bores him, he pulls out his magazine for a little reading sometimes he sleeps.
5. If he were shipwrecked on a lonely island, David would want to have the following things with him a stack of books, and a jumbo jar of peanut butter.

REVIEW EXERCISE D Apostrophes, Underlining, Quotation Marks

The apostrophes, underlining, quotation marks, and single quotation marks have been left out of the following sentences. Copy the sentences on a sheet of paper, adding the needed punctuation. Circle each punctuation mark.

1. Its hard to forget any of Edgar Allan Poes chilling stories and poems.
2. Poes poem The Raven, for example, takes place in a dark room at midnight.
3. A man hears a strange tapping at his door; asks, Whos there?; and a raven comes into the room.
4. Someone has taught the raven to say one word: Nevermore.
5. Poe explained the repetition of this word in the poem by saying, The word nevermore is like an echo in the sad heart of the man.
6. When Poe read about a funny raven in a novel called Barnaby Rudge, he decided to write about a terrifying raven.
7. The prisoner in Poes short story The Pit and the Pendulum is strapped to a table while rats climb over his body and a steel blade swings slowly over him.
8. Hes tortured when the steel blade swings slowly down.
9. The Murders in the Rue Morgue, also by Poe, was one of the first detective stories.
10. Would you be surprised to know that Poes horror stories first appeared in Grahams Magazine and in Godeys Ladys Book, both womens magazines?

REVIEW EXERCISE E   Review of All Punctuation

All of the punctuation except the end punctuation has been left out of the following paragraphs. Copy the paragraphs on a sheet of paper, adding the needed punctuation. Circle each punctuation mark.

If Mr. Cleve Backsters experiments are right your plants may be watching you at this very minute. Mr. Backster who runs a lie detection school in New York City has used lie detector tests on philodendrons a type of plant and he has found that plants may have feelings.

One of his experiments used the following two philodendron plants six students and a lie detector. The students names were put into a bowl. The student whose name was drawn then got a secret assignment from the teacher Sneak in at night pull one of the plants out of its pot and tear the plant into little pieces.

When the plant had been secretly murdered Mr. Backster completed his test. He attached a lie detector to the crimes only witness the other philodendron. Each of the five innocent students entered the room but the plant apparently knowing who the real killer was did nothing. When the guilty student came in the lie detector registered excitement in the plant. The plants killer revealed himself and the teacher advised his students, Be nice to your philodendron it too has feelings.

UNIT FIVE

AIDS AND ENRICHMENT

Speaking and Listening
Spelling
Sources of Information
Using Words

14

SPEAKING AND LISTENING

Most people are not aware of the way they speak. Speaking is such an easy, natural process that you may overlook its importance. Yet what you say shows how you think.

Your listening habits also have an effect on your life. If you listen well, you can pick up useful information. People will be willing to spend time talking to you. Learning to listen well is worth an effort.

Good speaking and good listening go together. As you practice to improve these skills, you will find daily rewards. You may find it helpful to follow the rules for speaking and listening that are described in this chapter.

INFORMAL CONVERSATION

14a Think before you speak.

The things you say reveal a good deal of what is going on in your head. Do your words show your mind at its best? Or could you improve both your thinking and your speaking?

Informal conversation, that is, the kind of conversation you use when you meet people casually, may not seem important. However, it needs careful thought just as much as *formal speaking,* which you use when talking to a group of people about a particular subject. Whether speaking informally or formally, you want others to listen to what you have to say. You certainly do not want others to stop listening to you. Some ways of speaking will make your listeners want to listen more. But other ways may make them listen less.

A few simple rules will help your informal conversation. Here are three:

(1) Start with a topic that will interest your listener.

You know that you would rather listen to something of interest to you. Your listener feels the same way about whatever you talk about. Think in advance before speaking. Then talk about what will interest your listener.

(2) Ask questions that will involve your listener.

Sometimes you may not be sure what interests another person. This is the time to ask. Of course,

the way you ask can make a difference. Do not ask
a general question: *"What are you interested in?"*
This kind of question is so broad your listener can
think of many things. Thinking of too many things
can end up with talk about nothing.

Ask a question that mentions something specific. Then your listener can respond directly to
that topic.

> EXAMPLE   "Have you seen the latest (name
> something—for example, a new
> model car, a show, a style of
> clothing)?"

A single opening question may not be enough
to start an informal conversation. Further question-
ing on your part will help others in a conversation
carry the topic along. Of course, you can have your
say about the matter. However, to avoid a one-sided
conversation, ask further questions.

Examples of kinds of questions to keep a conversation going:

"I really like (name of a famous person, a
singer, an actor, a sports figure). Who's your
favorite?"

"I get along best with (name of a person), but I
don't understand (name of a second person).
Can you tell me how there can be such a
difference between the two?"

"The first thing I want to do after school is
(_____). What are you planning to do?"

(3) Listen to and look at the person talking.

The third rule for an informal conversation is to pay attention to others who are talking. You contribute to a good informal conversation just as much through listening as through speaking. Listen to the words of another. Think about the ideas and feelings being expressed. Compare them with your own thoughts and feelings.

Avoid interrupting when another person is talking. If you have something important to say, wait for a pause in the talk. Then offer what you have to say.

14b Speak and listen the way you want others to speak and listen to you.

This is the Golden Rule of speaking and listening. It will help make your conversations more valuable for others and for yourself.

EXERCISE 1 Take the role of the speaker or listener in one of the following situations.

1. You are waiting to see the vice principal (or dean). A classmate you recognize but do not know very well comes in and sits next to you. You both may have several minutes to wait. You begin a conversation.
2. You arrive early at a tryout for a school group (band, club, cheerleaders, or other). Two other students you do not know well are already there. You begin a conversation.

3. You attend a local fair with friends. Going by a booth, you see something that catches your interest. You tell your friends you will meet them at a special place in a few minutes. As you approach the booth, you see that the only one in it is a schoolmate obviously helping to run the booth. You do not know the schoolmate well. You engage in conversation.

4. You are accompanying your parents as they shop for a new car. As your parents are talking with a sales clerk in the auto showroom, you see a classmate who is doing clean-up work there. You know the classmate only slightly, but you start a conversation.

INTRODUCTIONS

The meaning of the word *introduce* is "to lead into." When you introduce other people, you lead them into getting to know each other. The way you introduce people needs a little thoughtfulness and practice.

14c Introduce people who do not know each other.

Saying the right words in the right order makes an introduction successful. There are several statements you can make. Here are some basic ones:

> "Let me introduce (name)."
> "I'd like you to meet (name)."

"May I introduce (name)."
"You may not have met before. This is (name)."

Other introductions are less formal. For an informal situation you may just say the names of the people you are introducing.

In any introduction, be sure everyone hears the names of the people you are introducing. Speak loudly and clearly enough so that no confusion remains about names. Each person's name is important.

Examples of introductions:

You introduce a student to an adult.
"Mr. McCardle, I'd like you to meet Willa Mae Myers. Willa Mae, this is Mr. McCardle."

You introduce two students.
"Nancy, meet Jack Tilden. Jack, this is Nancy Trainer."

When introducing one person to another, speak the name of the person being introduced.

14d When introducing a person who deserves special respect, mention that person's name first.

When you introduce someone to a person who deserves special respect, state the name of the person who deserves special respect first. When introducing persons your age to adults, say the adult's name first.

EXAMPLES   "Dr. Zarb, I'd like to introduce my friend Opal Berg. Opal, this is Dr. Zarb."

"Mrs. Ashcraft, let me introduce Tommy Robb. Tommy, meet Mrs. Ashcraft."

EXERCISE 2 Take a role with classmates in one or more of the following situations.

1. Introduce a school friend to your father.
2. Introduce a school friend to your brother or sister.
3. Introduce an older member of your family to two teachers (Ms. Costano and Mr. Mintz).
4. Introduce a new student in school, whom you have just met, to a teacher, Mr. Abel, and another student.

14e When being introduced, pay close attention to the names of anyone you do not know.

Sometimes in an introduction you may not hear the name of someone being introduced to you. Or you may for a moment forget the name you have heard. If you miss someone's name, you can ask politely that it be repeated. It is important to get names right.

EXAMPLES   "I'm sorry, I didn't hear your name."

"I missed hearing your name. Would you tell me your name again, please."

"Pardon me, but I didn't hear your name."

"Would you repeat your name, please."

If you have trouble remembering someone's name the first time you hear it, make it a point to repeat the person's name after an introduction. You can even say it back to the person as you acknowledge the introduction.

EXAMPLES   "It's a pleasure to meet you, Mr. Carley."

"Hi, Sandra. Nice to meet you."

EXERCISE 3 Take roles with classmates in the following situations.

1. You have just moved into a new neighborhood. A member of the community New Neighbor Welcome Committee comes to call. You answer the door. The person's name is Tetsu Okada.
   A. Introduce yourself.
   B. Invite Okada in to meet members of your family.
   C. Introduce Okada to your mother.
2. Repeat the situation in 1, above. This time introduce Okada to other people, as follows:
   A. Your father and your older sister.
   B. Your aunt and your grandmother, who are visiting.
   C. A neighbor, Mrs. Ramirez, and her daughter, Ruby, about your age.
3. A local lawyer named Ferrer has given an informative talk to your class on "Young Adults and the Law." The next day you and two friends

who did not hear the talk walk by a booth in town where the lawyer and an aide are handing out leaflets. The lawyer is a candidate for public office in a local election and is seeking votes. The lawyer recognizes you and speaks, "Weren't you in the class I talked to at school yesterday? I'd like to meet you and your friends. Tell me your name." You introduce yourself and your two friends.

THE TELEPHONE

Speaking and listening on the telephone require special attention because you and the other person cannot see each other. In a telephone conversation the look of the face and the gestures of hands and body are missing. These visible parts of speaking and listening can be important in a conversation. Their absence requires that you pay special attention to what you say and the way you use your voice.

14f Use the telephone wisely.

Here are some guidelines when using the telephone:

1. Make sure you have the right number and are dialing it correctly.
2. Have a reason for calling and keep it in mind.
3. When the other person answers, state your name immediately.

EXAMPLES

INFORMAL "Hi, Dave. This is (your name)."

FORMAL "Hello, Mrs. Sayers. This is (your name)."

4. If the person who answers is not the one you want, ask, "May I speak with _____?" Or say, "I'd like to speak with _____, please."

5. If the one you are calling is not in or cannot come to the phone, leave your name and number. If you leave any message, keep it short. A long message is hard to take down or keep clear.

When answering the telephone, keep in mind a few basic points:

1. If the call is for you, the person calling may recognize your voice. However, be prepared to identify yourself.

2. Be prepared also to take notes if there is a message for someone else. Having a pencil and notepaper near the phone is a good practice.

3. When the call is for someone else, tell the caller right away that you will get that person. If the person is not in, ask if there is any message. It is helpful, too, to say when that person will be in.

4. Write down the message if there is any. Show the time the call came in, the name of the caller, the number to call in return, and any other basic information.

GIVING DIRECTIONS

Learning to give directions properly takes some thinking and study. Directions are of two main kinds. The first kind is giving directions on how to reach some place. These may be directions that involve only walking or that mean taking some kind of transportation.

The second kind of directions is telling someone how to make something.

14g When directing someone somewhere, put yourself in that person's place.

Think of the position of the person you are directing. Does the person know any of the landmarks in the area? In your own mind, go through each part of the trip from start to finish.

In what direction do you go first? How far do you follow that direction? What landmark do you come to when it is time to change direction?

In what direction do you go next? How far? What do you see along the way? How do you know when you are almost at the destination? What should show that you have gone too far or missed the destination?

By asking yourself these questions, you prepare for the exact directions you would give. If you cannot answer these questions, perhaps you should not try to give directions to the place. Instead, suggest the person seek help from someone else.

If you are sure of the beginning directions, but not certain of the final ones, you should say so. Then let the person decide whether to follow your beginning directions and find help later.

14h When giving directions for making something, think of the necessary materials and the required steps.

The first rule to remember about giving directions for making something is *to keep the directions simple*. If the object being made requires complicated directions, you should write them down. Take the following steps in giving directions:

1. List the objects necessary to make the item.
2. Explain each small step clearly in the correct order.
3. Describe what the item will look like at each step in the process.
4. Warn about things that might go wrong.

EXERCISE 4 Choose either *A* or *B* below. Make notes of the directions you will give. Give the directions orally as your teacher instructs you.

A. Prepare directions that you would give to a stranger in getting from one place in your community to another place at least a mile or more away.
B. Prepare directions that you would give for making or preparing something. Choose an item from the following list or think of one yourself.

    1. a type of seam used in sewing material
    2. a dish of food made of several ingredients
    3. a simple bird feeder
    4. a decoration or ornament
    5. a home aquarium

FORMAL SPEAKING AND LISTENING

The older you grow, the more likely you are to be called upon to speak before a group. Speaking to a group requires more careful preparation, of course, than informal conversation.

14i Use formal language when speaking to a group.

Formal language means using the English language accurately. In a group situation where you are speaking, you will want to use good English. This means choosing the right words and pronouncing them correctly. It also means forming your sentences so that they are complete and clear.

14j Prepare your talk in advance.

Make sure in advance what it is you will say. Choose a main topic and limit that topic so that you can deal with it in the time you have. Look up information about your topic. Organize the information into a *beginning,* or *introduction;* a *middle,* or *body;* and an *ending,* or *conclusion.*

A complete preparation for a successful talk before a group follows basic steps. Here are the steps to guide you:

1. Choose a topic you know about or can find out about.
2. Choose a topic that will interest most of your listeners.
3. Find out more information than you can use in your report.
4. Select the information that will mean the most to your listeners.
5. Organize your information in three main parts: (1) the introduction, (2) the body, and (3) the conclusion.

6. Write out your report. Then write notes. Or follow your teacher's instructions.
7. Practice giving the report by referring only to your notes.

Outlining

It is all right to use notes in giving a formal talk. However, it is not good practice to read the talk word for word. Your notes should be in the form of an *outline*. There are two useful kinds of outlines for notes: one follows a standard form, and the other is a straightforward listing of subtopics.

Here is an example of the standard form of an outline.

I.   (First main point)
     A. (First subpoint)
     B. (Second subpoint)
II. (Second main point)
     A. (First subpoint)
     B. (Second subpoint)
III. (Third main point)
     A. (First subpoint)
     B. (Second subpoint)

For every main point there should be at least two subpoints. If there are other points that come under a subpoint, you can show those by a further indention and the use of numerals 1, 2, and 3. The following example shows this:

The History of Halloween

I.   Ancient superstitions
    A. Irish Jack, the miser
       1. Rejected after death
       2. Walks with lantern until Judgment Day
    B. Druid priests
       1. Ghosts, witches, and elves
       2. Sacred cats and human spirits
II. Holy festivals
    A. Summer's end *(Samhain)*
    B. European harvest festivals
    C. Roman Catholic Church's All Saints' Day (about A.D. 700)
III. Modern customs
    A. Costumes
    B. Pranks

Delivering Your Talk

14k Deliver your talk the way you would want to listen to it.

(1) Speak clearly

A clear speaking voice is one of the basic requirements for giving a good formal talk. People must be able to hear your words. Otherwise there is no point in your talking.

Avoid running your words together or dropping the volume of your voice. Think of speaking loudly and clearly enough so that those who are farthest away from you have no trouble in hearing what you say.

(2) Speak to your audience.

Look at members of your audience while you talk. This will help you keep your chin up and will make your words go out to your listeners. Pick out two or three persons in the back row and two or three on each side. Look at them from time to time as you speak. Do not forget the people in front as well. Look at them on occasion.

(3) Remain still except to make a point.

Do not move unnecessarily. Motion attracts the eyes of your listeners. If, for example, you sway from side to side or shuffle your feet nervously, the motion will catch the attention of people listening. They will be distracted and they will not pay attention to what you are saying.

Use gestures only to underscore a key point in your talk. Otherwise, keep your hands, arms, and body still. If you do not know what to do with your hands, put them behind your back at your waist.

(4) Appear at your best.

Wear a pleasant look and your listeners will feel pleasant about you. Smile once in a while if you can. A smile at the start of your talk and another at the end will help.

Be sure your clothes look neat as well. Sloppy clothing carelessly worn will distract the attention of your listeners.

(5) Avoid useless words and sounds.

You may have heard a speaker start out by saying, "Well," or by clearing his or her throat. Even during a talk, a speaker may now and then add words that have nothing to do with the talk. Or there may be some "um's" and "ah's" sprinkled in the middle. These words and sounds should not be included in a talk. They are not part of it. They distract the audience and can even become annoying after a while.

EXERCISE 5 Select a topic from the list below. Or choose another topic you can speak on. Prepare to give a talk on that topic. Follow the steps in **14i-k** (pages 298–302). Give the talk as your teacher directs.

1. How to find your family history
2. The most frightening character in a movie
3. How to overcome foolish fears
4. How to make an important decision
5. Ways to begin a hobby
6. The special meaning of (a special day)
7. How to win at (name a game)
8. Ways to entertain oneself without money
9. The three most valuable skills for survival in living
10. Important tips for finding and getting a part-time job

14l Listen to another person's talk as you would want others to listen to yours.

As you may know from personal experience, it helps to have people in the audience pay attention during a talk. It does not help to have people in the audience who pay no attention or who carry on other activities during the talk.

To be a good listener, look at the speaker. Avoid turning around, making noises, or rustling books or papers.

If you need to remember what the speaker has said, take notes. Perhaps you will be expected to ask sensible questions after the talk. You may be asked to give a talk on some aspect of the same topic. You can use your notes to help you remember what the speaker has said.

REVIEW EXERCISE A   Introductions

With other members of the class, take part in the following situations that require introductions:

1. You meet your math teacher in a grocery store with your mother. Your mother and your math teacher have not met before.
2. At an informal party of people your own age, you introduce your cousin to your friend. Your friend does not at first hear your cousin's name.
3. You and a friend are leaving a movie theater, discussing the film. You like the film and your friend has disliked it. You meet an adult neighbor and introduce him or her to your friend.
4. Members of your volleyball team are meeting at your home. Your older sister comes in. You introduce her to the team members.
5. You are in a play at school. After the performance you introduce your grandmother and grandfather to your drama teacher.

REVIEW EXERCISE B   Using the Telephone

With other members of the class, act out a telephone conversation in each of the following situations:

1. You are calling a school that you have not attended before to ask when school starts. The switchboard operator answers and then transfers your call to the principal of the school.
2. The football coach calls your brother to tell him of a practice session. Your brother is not at home. You take the message.
3. You call a friend of your own age. His or her uncle, whom you do not know, answers the telephone. Your friend is not at home.
4. You have just passed the test for your driver's license. You call an insurance agent to ask about the need for additional insurance on the family car.
5. You have seen a poster advertising summer camp jobs. You are qualified for one of the jobs and decide to call the organization that is hiring counselors.

REVIEW EXERCISE C   Giving Directions

Prepare and give to the class simple but clear directions about how to do one of the following things. Remember to organize the directions logically and to include all of the needed materials.

1. Give directions on how to prepare a simple food. Soup, pudding, salad, or hamburgers are some possibilities.

2. Give directions on how to start a simple mechanism. A washing machine, motorcycle, or power lawnmower are some possibilities.

3. Give directions on how to use a piece of equipment. Roller skates, a motor scooter, or a food blender are some possibilities.

4. Give directions on how to get from the classroom to some other specific place in the school building.

REVIEW EXERCISE D   Formal and Informal Speech

Number a sheet of paper 1–4. After each number tell whether the sentence is an example of formal or informal speech. Then try to rewrite each sentence, making the formal sentences informal and the informal sentences formal.

EXAMPLE   Bunny Huggins is so out of it that he doesn't know where he's at.

informal

Mr. Huggins is not aware enough to know what is going on around him.

formal

1. In any large bunch there'll probably be one guy who's nutty, one guy who's always broke, and one guy who's a dumbbell.

2. When leaving a social affair, a young person should thank the host or hostess.

3. Charles Dickens's novel *Great Expectations* tells of a boy who learns to value money more than he values goodness of heart.
4. If you want good grades, you'd better crack the books at the beginning of the semester and bone up before exams.

REVIEW EXERCISE E   Listening and Outlining

Listen to a news broadcast on radio or television. Take notes on the program. Then choose one news item from the broadcast. Using your notes, prepare an outline of this topic.

15

SPELLING

Some people find it easy to learn to spell. Not everyone spells well, however. Perhaps you find spelling difficult. Spelling can be made easier if you learn a few basic rules. Practice also helps.

The rules of spelling are not like laws that must be obeyed at all times. Instead, these rules are more like helpful hints. Although not all English words follow these rules, the rules contain useful information for any speller to know. In them, you will find clues to the spelling of many words.

RULES FOR GOOD SPELLING

15a Develop basic spelling habits.

A few basic habits can make your work with spelling pay off for you.

(1) Keep a list of troublesome words.

Some words are spelled wrong again and again. Make a list of words that give you trouble. You might keep this list on pages in a notebook. Be sure to refer to it regularly.

Add new troublesome words to your list as you discover them. When you learn to spell the words correctly, put a check beside each one. See if you can check off all the words on your list.

(2) Study the hard parts of words.

See Master
Spelling List,
pp. 324–327 Often you almost know how to spell the words that cause you trouble. Usually only one part is difficult to remember. You know, for example, that *beauty* begins with **b** and ends with **ty.** But what about its middle? What vowels stand for the sound *yoo*? The **eau** in *beauty* is an example of the difficult part of a word.

Look over your list of difficult words. Draw a line under the troublesome part in each one. Concentrate on learning this part of the word. When you overcome a trouble spot, the rest is easy. You will almost always know how to spell the other parts of the word.

(3) See each syllable. Say each syllable. Write each syllable.

Each word is made of parts called *syllables*. There is one main vowel sound in a syllable. There may also be one or two consonant sounds.

Say one of your difficult words out loud. Listen carefully to the sounds. Can you hear the syllables in the word? Can you see which letters stand for each syllable?

EXAMPLES

SOL-DIER (soldier)	This word has two syllables. Only the last is likely to cause you trouble in spelling. Look hard at the last syllable. Say it and listen to how it sounds in the word. Then write it.
GAS-O-LINE (gasoline)	This word has three syllables. The first two syllables are spelled just as they sound. The last syllable may cause you trouble. The **e** after the **n** in **-line** is silent. But the **i** does not stand for a long **i** sound here. It stands for a long **e** sound instead. Say each syllable. Write each one.

(4) Use a dictionary.

If you know the first letters of a word, you can find its correct spelling in a dictionary. A dictionary divides each word into syllables.

15b Learn basic spelling rules.

Spelling rules can help you spell difficult words. Remember, however, that the rules are only guides. Most of them have exceptions. Learn both the rules and the exceptions. Together, they will help you be a better speller.

See Nouns, pp. 6–7 **(1) Most nouns form their plurals by adding s or es.**

EXAMPLES
NOUNS THAT ADD **S**   door, doors
 ·   plant, plants
      eagle, eagles
NOUNS THAT ADD **ES**   tax, taxes
      dish, dishes
      bench, benches

Add **es** to nouns that end in **ch, s, sh, x,** or **z.** Add **s** to all others.

EXERCISE 1 Number a sheet of paper 1–10. Write the plural of the following nouns:

1. mix
2. truck
3. dress
4. crutch
5. stream

6. coach
7. cycle
8. match
9. quart
10. bush

(2) Nouns ending in y after a consonant change the y to i and add es to form the plural.

EXAMPLES   city, cities
 library, libraries

If a vowel comes before the final **y,** just add **s.**

EXAMPLES   tray, trays
 valley, valleys

EXERCISE 2 Number a sheet of paper 1–8. Next to each number, write the plural of the following nouns.

1. puppy   5. party
2. fly   6. buggy
3. key   7. daisy
4. alley   8. monkey

(3) **Most nouns ending in *f* add *s* to form the plural.**

> EXAMPLES belief, beliefs
> muff, muffs

(4) **Some nouns ending in *f* or *fe* change the *f* to *v* and add *es* or *s*.**

> EXAMPLES life, li**ves**
> thief, thie**ves**

(5) **Most nouns ending in *o* following a vowel add *s* to form the plural.**

> EXAMPLES zoo, zoo**s**
> radio, radios

(6) **Most nouns ending in *o* following a consonant add *es* to form the plural.**

> EXAMPLES hero, hero**es**
> tomato, tomato**es**

(7) **Musical terms ending in *o* add only an *s* to form the plural.**

> EXAMPLES cello, cellos
> piccolo, piccolos

(8) **A few nouns form their plurals without an *s* or an *es*. Some change spelling. Some remain the same.**

EXAMPLES   tooth, teeth
             ox, oxen
             woman, women
             sheep, sheep
             trout, trout
             louse, lice

(9) **Most compound nouns form the plural by adding *s* to the noun part, not the modifier.**

EXAMPLES   daughter-in-law, daughters-in-law
             bookbinder, bookbinders
             onlooker, onlookers

EXERCISE 3   Number a sheet of paper 1–20. Write the plural form of each of the following nouns.

1. tattoo   11. soprano
2. calf   12. window
3. child   13. surprise
4. rodeo   14. potato
5. knife   15. fox
6. branch   16. brush
7. man   17. donkey
8. torpedo   18. handcuff
9. sky   19. piano
10. mouse   20. chief

EXERCISE 4   Number a sheet of paper 1–10. Write the plural form of each of the following nouns.

1. wolf
2. hero
3. radio
4. gash
5. touch

6. solo
7. mother-in-law
8. whiff
9. goose
10. wife

Prefixes

Prefixes are added to the front of words or parts of words to make new words. A word like *heated* can be made into *preheated, reheated,* and *unheated.* In those words the prefixes are *pre-, re-,* and *un-.* The prefixes mean *before, again,* and *the opposite of.* So the new words mean *heated before, heated again,* and *the opposite of heated.*

Many words can be made into new words by adding prefixes. The spelling of the original word remains the same, even after a prefix is added.

(10) A word or root that adds a prefix does not change spelling.

You can use *heated* as a word without prefixes. Most words that add prefixes are words you can use by themselves. A few words, however, are never used without prefixes. *Reduce* is made from the prefix *re-* and the word part *-duce.* The word part *-duce* cannot be used by itself. It is called a *root,* or *stem.* It must be combined with a prefix to become a whole word.

Here are some prefixes, words or roots, and the new words they make.

PREFIX	WORD OR ROOT	NEW WORD
pro-	-ject	project
	-vide	provide
mis-	spell	misspell
	use	misuse
de-	-scend	descend
	-duct	deduct
re-	-vise	revise
	read	reread

EXERCISE 5 Number a sheet of paper 1–10. Following are a list of prefixes and a list of words or roots. Next to each number write a new word that could be formed by adding one of the prefixes to the word or root.

PREFIXES

re-   mis-
de-   pro-

EXAMPLE judge

misjudge

WORDS OR ROOTS

1. -duce
2. -pose
3. -pel
4. understand
5. place
6. tract
7. port
8. treat
9. -ject
10. design

The spelling of a word or root remains the same when a prefix is added. The spelling of the prefix sometimes changes.

(11) Some prefixes change spelling when joined
to a word or root.

PREFIX	WORD OR ROOT	NEW WORD	
in-	mobile	immobile	[The prefix *in-*
	polite	impolite	becomes *im-*]
	legible	illegible	[The prefix *in-*
			becomes *il-*]
	regular	irregular	[The prefix *in-*
			becomes *ir-*]
com-	-spire	conspire	[The prefix *com-*
	-verge	converge	becomes *con-*]

Suffixes

Suffixes are added to the end of words or roots
to make new words. A word like *quick* can be made
into *quickly* and *quickness*. Here, the suffixes are *-ly*
and *-ness*. They mean *in that way* and *the state of
being*. So the new words *quickly* and *quickness*
mean *in a quick way* and *the state of being quick*.

(12) Most words adding the suffixes *-ly* and *-ness*
keep their same spelling.

EXAMPLES   secret, secret**ly**
             good, good**ness**
             nice, nice**ly**
             loud, loud**ness**

(13) Words ending in *y* following a consonant change the *y* to *i* before adding a suffix that does not begin with *i*.

EXAMPLES   crazy, craz**i**ly
happy, happ**i**ness
worry, worr**ied**

(14) Words or roots ending in *ie* usually change the *ie* to *y* when the suffix *-ing* is added.

EXAMPLES   lie, l**ying**
tie, t**ying**

(15) Most words ending in *e* omit the *e* when adding a suffix that begins with a vowel.

EXAMPLES   bake, bak**ing**
drive, driv**ing**

(16) Most words ending in *-ce* or *-ge* keep the *e* when adding a suffix that begins with *a* or *o*.

EXAMPLES   notice, notice**able**
outrage, outrage**ous**

(17) Most words ending in *e* keep the *e* when adding a suffix that begins with a consonant.

EXAMPLES   pale, pale**ness**
move, move**ment**

(18) One-syllable words ending in a single consonant following a single vowel double the consonant when adding the suffixes *-ed, -ing,* or *-er.*

EXAMPLES   dip, dip**ped**, dip**ping**, dip**per**
tan, tan**ned**, tan**ning**, tan**ner**

(19) Double the final consonant when adding *-ed,*
**   *-er,* or *-ing* to words with two or more**
**   syllables ending in a single consonant**
**   following a single vowel if the accent is on**
**   the last syllable.**

EXAMPLES permit, permit**ting**
          prefer, prefer**red**
          [but not *tighten, tightening* because
          the accent is not on the last
          syllable]

EXERCISE 6 Following are words and suffixes.
Number a sheet of paper 1–20. Next to each number, write the new word you can make by joining
the word and its suffix.

EXAMPLE quiz + ing

quizzing

1. empty + ness
2. begin + er
3. change + able
4. alive + ness
5. shovel + ed
6. chop + ed
7. courage + ous
8. die + ing
9. wonder + ing
10. strange + ly

11. squeeze + able
12. aware + ness
13. uneasy + ly
14. lie + ing
15. cancel + ed
16. glory + ous
17. manage + able
18. scrub + ed
19. pace + ing
20. bury + al

SOUNDS OF LETTERS

Listen to the ending sounds as you say these
words: *if, snuff,* and *rough.* Their ending sounds are

all alike. However, that one ending sound is represented by **f**, **ff**, and **gh**. The same sound is inside
the word *telephone,* where it is represented by **ph**.

In English, one sound often has a variety of
spellings.

15c Learn the different ways of spelling sounds.

Some common sounds in the English language
are listed below. Also listed are words that show
various ways that each sound can be spelled.

SOUND	EXAMPLES OF SPELLING PATTERNS
ch (as in *cheese*)	**ch**eese, pit**ch**, ques**ti**on, ven**t**ure
f (as in *full*)	**f**ull, sti**ff**, cou**gh**, ele**ph**ant
g (as in *game*)	**g**ame, **gh**oul
j (as in *jet*)	**j**et, lo**g**ic, fi**dg**et, sol**di**er
k (as in *king*)	**k**ing, **c**attle, a**ch**e, stu**ck**
m (as in *mud*)	**m**ud, bom**b**, ham**m**er, pal**m**
n (as in *now*)	**n**ow, **kn**ee, din**n**er, **gn**ome, **pn**eumonia
sh (as in *shark*)	**sh**ark, pas**si**on, **s**ugar, ra**ti**on, ma**ch**ine
t (as in *toe*)	**t**oe, bark**ed**
z (as in *zoo*)	**z**oo, wa**s**, de**ss**ert
a (as in *cake*)	c**a**ke, **ai**m, b**ay**, st**ea**k, v**ei**n
e (as in *we*)	w**e**, s**ee**m, tr**ea**t, p**eo**ple, gr**ie**f, prot**ei**n, gasol**i**ne, sal**t**y
i (as in *bike*)	b**i**ke, t**ie**, g**uy**, wh**y**, **eye**
i (as in *in*)	**i**n, b**ee**n, b**u**siness, g**ui**lty
o (as in *joke*)	j**o**ke, c**oa**l, h**oe**, bl**ow**, s**ew**
u (as in *cube*)	c**u**be, b**eau**tiful, f**ew**, y**ou**

u (as in *rule*)   rule, fruit, cool, ghoul, move, canoe

Homonyms

The words *cents, sense,* and *scents* all sound the same. Their spellings, however, are quite different. Words like these are called *homonyms*.

Homonyms are words that sound alike but have different spellings. When homonyms are confused, misspellings can happen.

15d Learn which spelling of a homonym belongs with your meaning.

See Chapter 10, pp. 216–235

HOMONYMS	MEANINGS
affect	to influence or to change
effect	the result of a cause
already	earlier, before
all ready	(two words) prepared, completed
capital	city, seat of government
capitol	government building
cents	pennies
scents	odors
sense	perception
cite	to quote, or to name as example
sight	vision; to see
site	place
pair	two of anything
pare	to cut
pear	kind of fruit

| pour | to flow |
| pore | small opening |

rapped	hit
rapt	fascinated
wrapped	covered

their	belonging to them
there	in that place
they're	they are (a contraction)

EXERCISE 7 Each of the following sentences is missing a word in the blank. The missing word is a homonym of the word in parentheses following the sentence. Number a sheet of paper 1–6. Write the missing word(s) next to each number.

EXAMPLE Bessie didn't know what to _____.
(ware)

wear

1. The dinner was _____. (already)
2. She had lost a _____ of shoes. (pare)
3. The box was _____ in foil. (rapped)
4. They are not in _____ usual place. (they're)
5. I didn't have the _____ to look in the box. (cents)
6. What _____ will this have on me? (affect)

REVIEW EXERCISE A Master Spelling List

One of each of the following pairs of words is spelled correctly. Number a sheet of paper 1–16. Next to each number write the correctly spelled

word. Then check your work against the Master
Spelling List, pages 324–327.

1. accommodate
   accomodate
2. acheive
   achieve
3. acquaintance
   acquaintence
4. adolescent
   adolescant
5. amature
   amateur
6. athaletic
   athletic
7. calendar
   calender
8. dependent
   dependant

9. docter
   doctor
10. existence
    existance
11. goverment
    government
12. occurrence
    occurence
13. pleasent
    pleasant
14. privelege
    privilege
15. separate
    seperate
16. succede
    succeed

REVIEW EXERCISE B Plurals

Number a sheet of paper 1–20. Write the plural form of each of the following words. You may
want to check with a dictionary.

1. act
2. alley
3. apology
4. calf
5. cemetery
6. diagnosis
7. grief
8. jealousy
9. banana
10. banjo

11. berry
12. body
13. vertebrate
14. cry
15. embroidery
16. inch
17. scarcity
18. buffalo
19. peach
20. quarry

REVIEW EXERCISE C   Prefixes

Number a sheet of paper 1–10. After each number form a new word by adding a prefix to the word.

PREFIXES   un-   re-
           dis-   non-

EXAMPLE   circulate

recirculate

1. reliable   6. bruised
2. approval   7. acquainted
3. marriage   8. natural
4. appetizing   9. skeptical
5. like   10. sociable

REVIEW EXERCISE D   Suffixes

Number a sheet of paper 1–15. Form fifteen new words by matching suffixes with words or roots. Write each new word next to each number. You may check with a dictionary about the correct spelling of each new word.

SUFFIXES

-ing   -ic
-ly   -ous
-ment   -al
-able

EXAMPLE   hygiene

hygienic

1. ski
2. earnest
3. hysterical
4. embarrass
5. individual
6. like
7. nasal
8. amuse
9. dye
10. exquisite
11. atmosphere
12. brutal
13. courage
14. environment
15. ominous

REVIEW EXERCISE E Homonyms

Number a sheet of paper 1–10. After each number write the correct homonym from within the parentheses.

1. In her book *Silent Spring,* Rachel Carson looks at the (affects, effects) of pollution on nature.
2. She shows how many forms of life really are (affected, effected) when only one form may seem to be.
3. As an example she (cites, sights, sites) chemical pollution in Clear Lake, California.
4. People living (there, their) used DDT to kill annoying mosquitoes and gnats.
5. After a year the chemical had (pared, paired) down the insect population in the area.
6. Clear Lake, however, is also the breeding (cite, sight, site) of the western grebe, a beautiful bird with a long white neck and shining black head.
7. (Pairs, Pears, Pares) of grebes would skim over the lake, carrying a soft gray chick (wrapped, rapped) under one wing.

8. After only one year of using DDT to kill insects, the people of Clear Lake began to notice that dead grebes were (all ready, already) being found on the lake.

9. An examination of (their, there) fatty tissues revealed huge amounts of deadly DDT.

10. (Poor, Pour) planning had led to the poisoning not only of insects, but also of the fish that ate the insects and of the birds that ate the fish.

MASTER SPELLING LIST

The following list includes words that are frequently misspelled. Your study of this list should be by groups of words. Practice spelling ten or twenty at a time. Be sure you also know the meaning of each word. Where necessary, look up words in a dictionary.

From time to time, review words you have misspelled at an earlier time. By doing this you help to keep their spellings clear in your mind.

The difficult parts of words are printed in darker letters. The darkness of the letters will help you pay close attention to the parts of these words that are often misspelled.

absence	acquire	aisle
absolutely	across	allotment
acceptance	actually	altar/alter
accidentally	admittance	amateur
accommodate	adolescent	analyze
accompany	advertisement	annually
accuracy	affectionate	anticipate
achieve	afraid	apology
acquaintance	again	apparatus

apparent
appearance
appreciate
approach
approval
argue
argument
arrangement
athletic
attendance
authority
available

beginning
behavior
believe
benefit
benefited
boundary
breath (e)
buried
business

calendar
campaign
capital/capitol
cemetery
certificate
character
chief
Christian
choice
choose/chose
clothes
color
column
commercial
committee
communist
competitor
completely
conceivable

concentrate
confidential
confusion
conscience
conscious
continuous
controlled
controversial
cooperate
correspondence
courageous
criticism
criticize
cruelly
curiosity
curious
cylinder

debtor
deceive
decision
dependent
describe
despair
desperate
difference
dining
dinner
disappearance
disappoint
discipline
doctor
duplicate

eager
easily
effect
efficient
eighth
eligible
embarrass
emphasize

encouragement
entirely
entrance
environment
equipped
escape
especially
essential
exaggerate
excellent
exciting
exercise
existence
expense
experiment
extremely

fantasy
fascinate
fashionable
fatal
favorite
field
finally
financial
foreign
forty
fortunately
forward
fourth
friend
further

genius
government
gracious
grammar
guarantee
guess
guidance
gymnasium

happened
happiness
hear/here
heavily
height
heroin/heroine
hopeless
hospital
humor
humorous
hungrily
hypocrisy

ignorance
imagine
immediately
incidentally
increase
indefinite
individually
influence
ingredient
innocence
insurance
intelligence
interference
interrupt

jealous

knowledge

laboratory
laborer
laid
leisure
lessen/lesson
license
likely
listener
lively
loneliness

loose/lose/loss
luxury

magazine
magnificent
maintenance
maneuver
manufacturer
marriage
marvelous
meant
mechanic
medical
medicine
melancholy
merchandise
miniature
minimum
minute
mischief
mischievous
moral/morale
muscle
mysterious

narrative
naturally
niece
ninety
noticeable

obstacle
occasionally
occurrence
offensive
official
often
omission
omit
once
operate
opponent

opportunity
optimist
orchestra
organization
originally

paid
parallel
paralyze
particular
passed/past
peace/piece
peaceful
peculiar
performance
permanent
personality
perspiration
persuade
physical
picnicking
pleasant
politician
possession
practically
practice
preferred
prejudice
preparation
presence
pressure
privilege
probably
procedure
proceed
professor
propaganda
psychology
pursuit

quiet
quite

realize
really
receipt
recognize
recommend
referred
relieve
religious
removal
repetition
resistance
resource
responsibility
restaurant
rhythm
ridiculous
roommate

sacrifice
safety
satisfied
scarcity
scene
schedule
scholar

scissors
seize
separate
similar
sincerely
skiing
sophomore
source
specifically
sponsor
straight
strength
stretch
strictly
stubborn
substitute
subtle
succeed
successful
sufficient
summary
surprise
suspense
swimming
synonym

temperamental
tendency
therefore
thorough
though
thoughtful
tragedy
transferred
tremendous
truly

unanimous
unnecessary
useful
useless
usually

vacuum
valuable
various

weather/whether
weird
whole/hole

yield

16

SOURCES OF INFORMATION

Just think of the many sources you can use to find out about your world: books, newspapers, magazines, movies, and television, among others.

At one time people could learn only from their own experiences or from talking to other people. Today there are many more ways to learn.

With so many places to look for information, how can you know where to start? Where is the best place to look for a certain kind of information? This chapter answers these questions and others. It offers you a guide to the sources of information.

TEXTBOOKS

In most textbooks there are special sections that make information easy to find. Here are the sections in a textbook like *Using English*.

The *front cover* usually lists the title, the author, the publisher, and the number of the book in the series. The *back edge,* or "spine," names the publisher and often repeats the information given on the front cover. This information is listed here so that books can be easily identified when they are stacked together on the shelves.

The *inside cover* is sometimes called the "end paper." Many textbooks include space to identify whose property the book is and to whom it has been issued. Some textbooks include additional information on the end papers.

The *title page* repeats the information given on the cover and spine. The *copyright page* is usually the back of the title page. The date of publication is given here, along with the name of the person or company owning the rights to the book. The *introduction* or *preface* explains the importance of the book. It may also tell why particular features have been included. The *table of contents* lists the chapter titles and contents by page numbers.

The *text* contains the major contents of the book. A *glossary* often defines terms used in the book and gives examples. The index lists in alphabetical order, with page numbers, the principal subjects covered by the text. Some books have no glossary, while in other books the index and glossary are combined.

THE DICTIONARY

Words, spoken or written, are the source of much information that is available to you. You have learned the pronunciations and spellings of many words, as well as their meanings. You have also learned the uses of these words in sentences. Whatever you do not know about the spellings, pronunciations, meanings, and uses of words you can find out. All this information is in a good dictionary.

16a Learn to use the dictionary.

A good dictionary is the best single source of information about the English language. Learn to use it wisely.

(1) Words are listed alphabetically.

The words a dictionary defines are called *entry words*. As you know, every dictionary alphabetizes its entry words. Words beginning with the letter **a** come first. Words beginning with the letter **z** come last.

When two or more words begin with the same letter, they are alphabetized according to their second letters. *Accept* follows *about* in the dictionary, but it is listed before *adjective*. *Affect* and *agree* come soon after. Near the end of the letter **a** words, you will find *aye* and *azure*.

Sometimes a group of words shares the same first few letters. In this case, alphabetical order is determined by the first letters that are different.

EXAMPLES **blo**nd   **blo**tter
          bloom   **blo**w
          [The first three letters, **blo**, are
          the same in all these examples.
          The words are alphabetized by
          their fourth letters.]

EXERCISE 1 Number a sheet of paper 1–10. Write the following words in their correct alphabetical order.

medicine   medal
meander   meadow
meddle   meek
medic   medical
medium   mechanic

---

decimal   186   decoy

deciduous leaves; *deciduous* antlers. **2** Shedding leaves every year: *deciduous* trees. ◆ See EVERGREEN.

dec·i·mal [des′ə-məl] **1** *n.* A fraction written using base ten and place values to show 10 or 10 multiplied by itself some number of times as its denominator, as 0.3 ($\frac{3}{10}$), 0.27 ($\frac{27}{100}$), 0.034 ($\frac{34}{1000}$), etc. **2** *adj.* Of or based on the number 10: a *decimal* system; a *decimal* fraction. ◆ *Decimal* comes from a Latin word meaning *tenth.*

decimal point A dot used before a decimal fraction, as in 0.3 ($\frac{3}{10}$) or 3.27 (3 + $\frac{27}{100}$).

dec·i·mate [des′ə-māt] *v.* **dec·i·mat·ed, dec·i·mat·ing** To destroy or kill a large part of: The invaders *decimated* the town. — **dec′i·ma′·tion** *n.*

de·ci·pher [di-sī′fər] *v.* **1** To translate from cipher or code into plain language: decode. **2** To determine the meaning of: to *decipher* a garbled telegram; to *decipher* hieroglyphics.

de·ci·sion [di-sizh′ən] *n.* **1** A making up of one's mind. **2** A conclusion or judgment. **3** Firmness; determination: to act with *decision.*

de·ci·sive [di-sī′siv] *adj.* **1** Putting an end to doubt: a *decisive* victory. **2** Showing decision; firm: a *decisive* statement. — **de·ci′sive·ly** *adv.* — **de·ci′sive·ness** *n.*

deck [dek] **1** *n.* Any floor or platform extending from side to side of a ship. It may be open or roofed over by another deck. **2** *n.* A pack of playing cards. **3** *v.* To dress or adorn: Sh—
col—

de·clen·sion [di-klen′shən] *n.* **1** The changing of the forms or endings of nouns, pronouns, or adjectives according to case. The declension of *they* consists of *they, their* or *theirs, them.* **2** A class of words having similar endings or forms in each case.

de·cli·na·tion [dek′lə-nā′shən] *n.* **1** An inclining or bending downward. **2** The deviation of a compass needle from true north or true south. **3** A polite or formal refusal.

de·cline [di-klīn′] *v.* **de·clined, de·clin·ing,** *n.* **1** *v.* To refuse in a polite way: to *decline* an invitation. **2** *v.* To lessen or fail gradually: His health *declined* over the years. **3** *n.* A gradual lessening or failing: the *decline* of a nation's power. **4** *v.* To slope or bend downward: The land gently *declines* to the sea. **5** *n.* A downward slope. **6** *v.* To give the declension of (a noun, pronoun, or adjective).

de·cliv·i·ty [di-kliv′ə-tē] *n., pl.* **de·cliv·i·ties** **1** A surface, as of a hill, that slopes downward. **2** A sloping downward.

de·code [dē-kōd′] *v.* **de·cod·ed, de·cod·ing** To translate from code into plain language.

de·com·pose [dē′kəm-pōz′] *v.* **de·com·posed, de·com·pos·ing** **1** To decay; rot. **2** To separate into its basic parts or elements: to *decompose* water into hydrogen and oxygen.

de·com·po·si·tion [dē′kom-pə-zish′ən] *n.* **1** The process or result of decay. **2** A separating into basic parts or elements.

de·com·pres·sion [dē′kəm-presh′ən] *n.* The lowering or removing of pressure, especially of air.

dec·o·rate [dek′ə-rāt] *v.* **dec·o·rat·ed, dec·o·rat·ing** **1** To make more fancy, pretty, or —tractive by adding ornaments or frills: to —a street with colored lights. **2** To paint, —new furnishings to (a room, hou— —th a medal or ribbo—

---

(2) **Guide words at the top of each page show which words are on that page.**

At the top of every dictionary page with entry words, two *guide words* are given. These are the same as the first and last entry words on that page. Of course not all dictionaries have the same words on every page. So guide words will not all be the same.

Guide words and alphabetical order will help you find words quickly. Suppose you are looking up the meanings of several words. One word is *valet*. You turn to a page with the guide words *vain* and *vampire*. Will *valet* be listed there? Will you find *vantage* or *vapor* on that page?

The first two letters of all five words are the same, **va**. In *valet,* the third letter is **l**. It comes after **i**, the third letter in the guide word **vain** and before **m**, the third letter in the guide word **vampire**. So you will find *valet* on that page.

The third letters in *vantage* and *vapor* are **n** and **p**. Both these letters follow **m** in the alphabet. You will not find either word on the page with *vain* and *vampire* as guide words. They would be listed on the page with the guide words *vampirism* and *variety.*

EXERCISE 2   Which of the following words would you find on a dictionary page with the guide words *reflex* and *regard*? Write the words on a sheet of paper.

refrigerator	reflector
regatta	region
refuse	reform
reflux	regardless
referee	regal

(3) Words are spelled out by syllables.

The dictionary spells out each entry word by its syllables. *Kangaroo* is spelled out *kan-ga-roo*. *Motorcycle* is *mo-tor-cy-cle*. You may not know the spelling of a difficult word like *quadruped*. If you know it begins with *quad,* however, you can probably find it in the dictionary.

EXERCISE 3 The following pairs of words contain one spelled correctly and one incorrectly. The first syllable of each word is correct. Number a sheet of paper 1–10 and write the correct spellings.

1. gram-mer
   gram-mar
2. def-i-nite
   def-i-nate
3. la-bel
   la-ble
4. sen-sa-tive
   sen-si-tive
5. ig-ne-rant
   ig-no-rant

6. mo-tor
   mo-ter
7. com-it-tee
   com-mit-tee
8. con-grad-u-late
   con-grat-u-late
9. per-ma-nent
   per-ma-nant
10. nec-ces-sary
    nec-es-sary

(4) The pronunciation of every word is given.

Dictionaries also spell each entry word with *diacritical marks.* These are special marks and symbols that show pronunciations. They show the sound each part of a word has in speech.

The system of marks is explained in a key at the bottom of every other dictionary page. A special section at the front of the dictionary usually explains the pronunciation system, too.

Not all dictionaries use the same system. Be sure you are familiar with the system in the dictionary you are using.

de·cline [di·klīn′] *v.* **de·clined, de·clin·ing,** *n.*
1 *v.* To refuse in a polite way: to *decline* an invitation. **2** *v.* To lessen or fail gradually: His health *declined* over the years. **3** *n.* A gradual lessening or failing: the *decline* of a nation's power. **4** *v.* To slope or bend downward: The land gently *declines* to the sea. **5** *n.* A downward slope. **6** *v.* To give the declension of (a noun, pronoun, or adjective).

(5) The part of speech is given for each entry word.

An abbreviation usually signals the part of speech of each entry word. For verbs the abbreviation is *v.* For adverbs it is *adv.* Some words can be used for more than one part of speech. The definitions of these words will list additional abbreviations.

(6) Unusual plural spellings are given.

If a noun has an unusual plural spelling, this spelling will be listed with the entry word. It will be identified as the plural by the abbreviation *pl.*

> EXAMPLE   *ox* (pl. *oxen*)

EXERCISE 4 Look in a dictionary for the plurals of the following words. Write the plurals next to each number on a sheet of paper.

1. index
2. alumna
3. fox
4. apex
5. son-in-law
6. grandchild

See Verbs, pp. 36–37 **(7) Irregular verb forms are given.**

If a verb is irregular, its entry will include spellings for the simple past tense and the past participle. The word *begin* is an example. Its listing will include the forms *began* and *begun.*

(8) Comparative and superlative forms are given for many adjectives and some adverbs.

The comparative and superlative forms are listed for some adjectives. *Simpler* and *simplest,* for example, are given in the entry for the word *simple.*

You will also find comparative and superlative forms given for irregular adverbs like *well. Better* and *best* are both listed in the dictionary entry for the adverb *well.*

(9) Various meanings of words are given.

In a dictionary, each entry word is listed with all its known meanings. Most words have more than one meaning. Some have quite a few.

EXAMPLE

bark (verb)
1. to make the sound a dog makes
2. to speak in anger
3. to advertise with a loud outcry
4. to remove bark from

bark (noun)
1. sound made by a dog
2. sharp, unfriendly tone of speech
3. covering of a tree
4. small sailing ship

The word *bark* can stand for any of these meanings. Its meaning depends upon its use in a sentence, or its *context.* One use would be in the following sentence:

Snapper barked loudly and wagged his tail.

The words surrounding *bark* in this sentence form its context. They offer clues to its meaning. You can tell *barked* is a verb. It is *bark* with the **ed** ending. Because Snapper did it *loudly,* you can tell that it involved making a noise. Using the context, you can tell that *barked* is a verb with meaning #1.

Another context gives *bark* quite a different meaning:

> *Initials were carved deep into the bark of the willow.*

The *bark* in this sentence is a noun. Its context tells you that it means the *covering of a tree:*

> *Initials were carved deep into the covering of the willow tree.*

EXERCISE 5   Each of the words *cast, model,* and *note* has more than one meaning. One of those words belongs with each of the following definitions. Number a sheet of paper 1–11. Next to each number, write the word defined.

cast   model   note

1. a short letter _____
2. a miniature version of something _____
3. to pay special attention to _____
4. actors in a play _____
5. a particular style, plan, or design _____
6. a piece of paper money _____
7. to throw _____
8. a person who displays clothes _____
9. plaster setting for a broken bone _____
10. a single sound in music _____
11. a representation of something to be copied _____

THE LIBRARY

16b Learn how to use the sources of information in a library.

(1) The librarian.

Ask the librarian for directions in the library. The librarian can help you to find the information you need.

However, it is good for you to know the contents of the library yourself. Become aware of the different sources of information. When you know where to look, you can find information quickly and successfully.

(2) Books of fiction.

Books of fiction can be found in one section of the library. Fiction is the opposite of fact. The books and stories in this section are not true. Authors have created them. Many of them make exciting reading.

Fiction shelves are usually open. That means you yourself can take any book off the shelf and read it. Fiction books are arranged in alphabetical order by the authors' last names. If you want a book by E. I. Konigsburg, for example, you would look near the middle of these shelves, since **K** is near the middle of the alphabet. *The Jazz Man* by Mary Hays Weik, on the other hand, will be found closer to the end.

Many authors have more than one book on the shelves. Books by the same author are arranged in alphabetical order by the first main word of their titles. *The Great Brain, The Great Brain Does It Again, The Great Brain Reforms, Me and the Great Brain,* and *Private Eye* were all written by John D. Fitzgerald. They would be found on the shelves in that order.

(3) Books of nonfiction.

Information of all kinds can be found in the nonfiction sections of the library. Some of the books in these sections retell true stories. Others give facts about particular subjects. These books are nonfiction, which is the opposite of fiction.

Nonfiction books in almost all libraries are arranged by *call numbers* on their spines. Each call number has two parts. Its upper part is its Dewey decimal number. These numbers range from 000 to 999, with decimals. Nonfiction books are divided into ten subject areas according to the Dewey decimal system. You use these numbers to locate books in much the same way as you use alphabetical order.

Sometimes, however, two or more books have the same Dewey decimal number. These books are shelved together and arranged alphabetically by the bottom part of their call number. This part of the call number begins with the first letter of the author's last name.

Get to know the basic divisions of the Dewey decimal system. If you do, you can find general subject areas of books quickly. It will be easier to locate the information you need.

THE DEWEY DECIMAL SYSTEM

BOOK NUMBERS	SUBJECTS
000–099	General information (reference sources of information, such as encyclopedias)
100–199	Philosophy (people's beliefs about the meaning of life)
200–299	Religion (religious faiths, mythology)
300–399	Social Sciences (government, economics, history, and more)
400–499	Language (word meanings, word backgrounds, histories of languages)
500–599	Science (chemistry, biology, zoology, and other sciences)
600–699	Technology (agriculture, engineering, inventions, and more)
700–799	The Arts (painting, music, sports, dance, and others)
800–899	Literature (plays, television scripts, poetry, books about literature)
900–999	History (information about the past, biographies, travel books)

Every year thousands of new books are published. Each new nonfiction book is given a number from the Dewey decimal system. In what range would the number be for a book about the art of Michelangelo? It would be in the 700–799 range.

EXERCISE 6 Each of the following titles names a nonfiction book. Number a sheet of paper 1–10. Next to each number, write the Dewey decimal number range for each book.

1. Bulfinch's *Mythology*
2. Fowler's *Dictionary of Modern English Usage*
3. Schweitzer's *Christianity and the Religions of the World*
4. *The Spotted Sphinx* (the story of a cheetah)
5. *Practical Law*
6. *The History of Philosophy*
7. *Blackberry Winter* (an autobiography of Margaret Mead)
8. *The Sea Around Us* (a scientific study of the oceans)
9. *What Is Modern Painting?*
10. *Pepper* (football stories by the coach of Georgia Tech)

(4) The card catalog.

In every library there are cabinets with drawers filled with index cards. These cards contain information about all the books in the library. They form a catalog of what is available.

For each fiction book, there are two cards. One is the *title card*. These cards are alphabetized by the first main word in each title. The other is the *author card*. These cards are alphabetized by each author's last name.

Every nonfiction book has three cards: a *title card,* an *author card,* and a *subject card.* They are arranged alphabetically. Any one of these three cards can lead you to the nonfiction book you want.

Suppose for example, that you are interested in Saint Bernard dogs. By looking in the subject catalog, you can learn what books the library has about these dogs. The cards you want will be filed under D (for dogs) in the subject catalog.

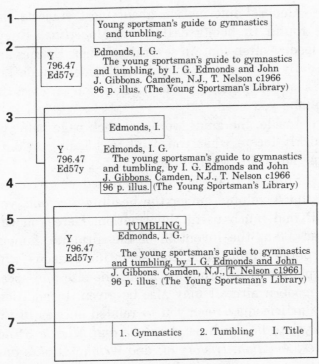

1 Title heading
2 Call number
3 Author
4 Book's physical description
5 Subject heading
6 Publisher, publication date
7 Other headings under which the book is listed

EXERCISE 7 Use the card catalog to find a nonfiction book about three of the following subjects. For each book, write the call number, title, author, date of publication, and number of pages.

1. African mythology   4. Karate
2. Famous women   5. Pigeons
3. Solar heating   6. European travel

(5) Reference works.

General information about most subjects can be found in books called *encyclopedias*. Encyclopedias often contain several volumes. Entries are usually arranged in alphabetical order. Guide letters on the spines of the books help you to select the volume you need.

Inside, the guide words on each page help you quickly locate what you want. A heading in dark type identifies where each entry begins.

Suppose that you are interested in *airplanes*. In the **A** volume, under the heading *airplane,* you will find much useful information. Here you can read about the invention of the airplane, famous airplane flights, and the scientific reasons why airplanes fly. Information about the size and speed of modern aircraft may also be given. In addition, the article may refer you to related entries in the encyclopedia, such as: *Airplane and Missile Structures; Aviation, History of;* and *Wright, Orville and Wilbur.*

Drawings and photographs accompany many of the articles. When helpful, charts or graphs are also included. Some encyclopedias list other books on the subject.

Atlases contain maps and other geographical information. The maps may be of the world or of certain areas only. The information can include facts about population, climate, natural resources, trade, and more.

Almanacs are yearbooks of facts. They contain up-to-date information on a wide variety of subjects. Contents of an almanac can include facts about:

award winners
sports records
important events of the year
population distribution
weather patterns
agricultural production

(6) Periodicals.

The word *periodical* refers to nonbook materials that are printed regularly over short periods of time. Periodicals can be magazines, newspapers, or newsletters. They can be published daily, weekly, bi-weekly, monthly, or quarterly (four times a year).

Periodical magazines can be a valuable source of information. The *Readers' Guide to Periodical Literature* acts like the card catalog. It indexes articles and stories from more than one hundred of the most popular periodical magazines. The *Readers' Guide* publishes twenty-two volumes a year.

Here is a sample of the information contained on a *Reader's Guide* page:

```
PHOTOGRAPHY
  The street. . . M. O'Grady. il Mod Phot 41:84-9
  My '77
  Through the viewfinder. E. H. Ortner. See issues
  of Popular science
    See also
  Ambrotypes
            Apparatus and supplies
  Photo technology: the way we were in 1937.
    B. Schwalberg. Pop Phot 80:80+ My '77
    See also
  Camera bags, cases, etc.
  Electric lamps, Photoflash
            Exhibitions
    See Photography—Exhibitions
```

(7)   Audiovisual materials.

Audiovisual materials are available at some
libraries. Often you can listen to sound recordings
on cassettes or records. Some libraries offer filmstrips and even motion picture film for your use.

Ask your librarian what kinds of audio-visual
materials your library has.

A BASIC LIST OF CONTENTS OF THE LIBRARY

Almanacs: Yearly calendars of facts and events,
especially ones in nature such as weather pre-
dictions, the first day of spring, and the like.

Atlases: Books of maps, often with written information about places shown on the maps.

Audiovisual materials: Audio recordings on disks,
tapes, or cassettes; filmstrips; motion picture
film; prints; microfilm; video recordings.

Bibliographies: Lists of books, usually alphabetized
by titles, by authors, or by subjects, including
information about publishers. An *annotated
bibliography* includes comments about the contents of the listed books.

Books

   Fiction: Novels and long or short stories made up
by authors.

   Nonfiction: Autobiographies, biographies, ac-
counts of instruction such as cookbooks.

Collected works: Plays, poems, songs, musical
pieces, scripts of television or other shows, art
reproductions, and photographs.

Dictionaries: Alphabetical listings of words and
names with definitions, pronunciations, and
related information.

Encyclopedias: Books containing general information about people, places, and things known to mankind, alphabetically arranged.

Indexes: Alphabetical listings of topics, names, or other subject-matter.

Pamphlets: Loosely-bound paper-covered sets of printed sheets containing nonfiction information.

Periodicals: Magazines or journals published regularly such as once a week or every month.

OTHER SOURCES OF INFORMATION

16c Make use of other sources of information.

You may not have realized how many other sources of information there are. You can learn a great deal just from the people around you. Every other person in your community knows at least one thing you do not know.

You might talk to your neighbor about her job. Maybe she works in the paper industry. She may tell you how different kinds of paper are manufactured.

A priest, minister, or rabbi may tell you about religion or philosophy. A newspaper editor may tell you about journalism. Your older brother or sister may tell you how to solve a problem.

Your neighbor, a relative, a newspaper editor, a religious leader—each of these people is an expert at something. You can find local experts on many subjects if you look.

Sometimes it is better to talk to an expert than to search the library for information. A local expert can answer questions and discuss the subject with you—something that library materials cannot do.

Other information is available to you if you know where to find it. Every state publishes information regularly about its people, products, and services. Much of this information is free. You can obtain it by writing to a state government.

The federal government publishes thousands of booklets each year. These booklets cover almost every possible subject having to do with the United States. You can obtain a catalog of current publications by writing the U.S. Government Printing Office in Washington, D.C.

There are many sources of information that can help you become an intelligent shopper. Study advertisements carefully for the information about what you want. When manufacturers claim to have "test results" proving their product to be superior, write for the results. Ask for a copy of the information. Compare the information it gives you with what consumer publications have to say about the product.

Always keep your eyes open for publications and people from whom you can learn. Be aware of the many sources of information that are available.

REVIEW EXERCISE A   The Dictionary

Number a sheet of paper 1–10. Then put the following words in the alphabetical order in which you would find them in a dictionary.

1. obsolete   6. oasis
2. occasion   7. oyster
3. opal   8. ominous

4. overseer
5. obsession

9. ogre
10. orientation

REVIEW EXERCISE B Guide Words

On a sheet of paper write the words from the following list that you would find on a dictionary page between the guide words *hindmost* and *history*.

1. heritage
2. hilarious
3. hint
4. hiss
5. hindrance

6. hinge
7. hireling
8. hippodrome
9. historical
10. hippopotamus

REVIEW EXERCISE C Meanings

The answers to the following questions are all in the following sample dictionary entries. Number a sheet of paper 1–6 and answer the questions.

hint (hĭnt) *n.* a remote allusion, a hidden suggestion Syn. see *suggest*

hip[1] (hĭp) *n.* The ripened fruit of a rosebush

hip[2] *n.* A. The projecting region of each side of the body below the waist B. at a disadvantage—as "on the hip"—a phrase derived from wrestling

hip[3] *interj.* A call to attention, as in the beginning of a cheer

hip·po·pot·a·mus (hĭp-ō-pŏt-o-mŭs) *n.* pl. hippopotamuses, hippopotami. A huge, thick-skinned aquatic mammal, next to the elephant the largest existing four-footed animal

1. What part of speech is hint?
2. What part of speech is hip in its third meaning?
3. What is a synonym for hint?
4. How many syllables are in hippopotamus?
5. What are the two plural forms of hippopotamus?
6. Using the sample entries, write the number for the meaning of the underlined word as used in the following sentences:
   A. Cooks in Norway make a delicious soup with hips.
   B. Edmond broke a hip in a skiing accident.
   C. The cheerleaders shouted, "Hip, hip, hooray!" for the victorious soccer team.
   D. Sally had her tennis opponent on the hip and took advantage of this to win the match.

REVIEW EXERCISE D   The Library

Number a sheet of paper 1–10. Organize the following list of fictional books in the alphabetical order in which you would find them on the fiction shelves of a library.

1. Jules Verne: *Mysterious Island*
2. Kate Seredy: *The Good Master*
3. Laura I. Wilder: *Little House on the Prairie*
4. Mark Twain: *A Connecticut Yankee in King Arthur's Court*
5. Mark Twain: *Pudd'nhead Wilson*

6. Pamela Travers: *Mary Poppins*
7. Jean C. George: *Julie of the Wolves*
8. William Saroyan: *The Human Comedy*
9. Marguerite Henry: *King of the Wind*
10. Rudyard Kipling: *Kim*

REVIEW EXERCISE E Card Catalog

Number a sheet of paper 1–7. Answer the questions about this sample card from the card catalog:

```
525
An


   Angrist, Stanley W.

   How our world came to be, by Stanley W.
   Angrist. Drawings by Enrico Arno.
   New York, Crowell (1969)



   75 p.    illus

   1. Earth   2. Creation   3. Title
```

1. What is the title of the book?
2. Who is the author?
3. What is the call number of the book?
4. Why is the book listed in the 500's of the Dewey decimal system?
5. How many pages is the book?
6. How can you be sure that the book includes pictures?
7. Where else is this book to be found in the card catalog?

REVIEW EXERCISE F Reference Books

Number a sheet of paper 1–10. Tell in what reference book you would first look for information on the following topics. You will be considering a dictionary, an encyclopedia, an atlas, and an almanac.

EXAMPLE What river runs through Hannibal, Missouri?

atlas

1. What is the plural form of *bear*?
2. Is *lorry* a slang word?
3. What is the difference between the synonyms *tyrannical* and *domineering*?
4. What is the capital of Michigan?
5. What is the meaning of the prefix *mis-*?
6. How many games did your favorite professional basketball team win in 1978?
7. How could Huckleberry Finn have landed in Louisiana when he set off by raft from Missouri to go to Illinois?
8. Who was Thomas Dewey?
9. What were some of the problems of building the Panama Canal?
10. At approximately what date did Aesop tell his stories?

17

USING WORDS

Words can be slippery to use. For example, they may stand for more than one meaning. In time some words may change their meanings, their pronunciation, or their spelling.

What makes words and meanings so hard to pin down? This chapter presents a few basic facts about words.

THE MEANING OF WORDS

17a A word may stand for more than one meaning.

An example is seen in the word *race*.

1. She won the *race* to the finish line.
2. She is a member of the Mongoloid *race*.

In Sentence #1 the word *race* means "a contest to see who is the fastest." In Sentence #2 *race* means one of the major divisions of the world's people. *Race* is the same word in both sentences. Yet its meanings are not the same. Many words have more than one meaning.

EXERCISE 1 Write the following ten words on a sheet of paper. Next to each word write another word or group of words to show its meaning.

> EXAMPLE   hand
>
> *hand- to give something to someone*

fast	trunks
base	net
light	box
ring	jar
top	well

EXERCISE 2 Write the ten words from Exercise 1 on a sheet of paper. Next to each word write a meaning different from the one you used in Exercise 1.

17b More than one word may be used to stand for a single meaning.

Most people know what a frying pan is. The term *frying pan* is used widely. However, other words are used to stand for a frying pan. One of these is *skillet.* Another is *spider.* Different words that mean the same are called *synonyms.*

> EXAMPLES scales—balances
> anger—fury
> bucket—pail
> confession—admission

EXERCISE 3 The following two columns contain synonyms. Number a sheet of paper 1–15. After each number write the word from column A. Next to each word write a synonym from column B.

> EXAMPLE **sorrow**
>
> *sorrow – grief*

	A	B
1.	tired	hurt
2.	answer	commence
3.	ache	mug
4.	pardon	collect
5.	begin	help
6.	accept	steed
7.	lift	progress
8.	gather	sofa
9.	advance	reply
10.	aid	volume
11.	mount	weary
12.	book	forgive
13.	cup	chest
14.	trunk	adopt
15.	sofa	raise

17c The meaning of a word is often shown by its context.

The meaning that a word carries becomes clear from its *context*, the surrounding words. You can very often learn new meanings for words by studying the context.

For example, what does the word *set* mean to you? The dictionary gives several meanings for the word *set*. Its exact meaning is known only when it is used in a sentence surrounded by several other words.

EXAMPLES   She *set* the table.
[This sentence means she "prepared the table before a meal."]

She *set* the clock.
[This sentence means she "put the clock at the right time."]

The doctor *set* her leg.
[This sentence means the doctor "put straight" a broken leg.]

These are only a few of the meanings for *set*. The context for each reveals its meaning.

In English you use words whose meanings may be unclear. Make sure the context gives the meaning of the word.

EXERCISE 4   Choose one of the meanings for each underlined word. Number a sheet of paper 1–4. Write the word and its meaning next to each number.

EXAMPLE When Cynthia decided to <u>abstain</u> from smoking, she threw away her cigarettes.

    smear   do without   pay for

ab abstain - do without

1. If she <u>desists</u>, she will save money by not having to buy cigarettes.

    starts again   stops   gets sick

2. By stopping, she gets rid of an unnecessary <u>vice</u>.

    suggestion   grip   bad habit

3. The air she breathes will be less <u>polluted</u>.

    expensive   dirty   colorful

4. She will be less <u>inclined</u> to become ill.

    likely   tipped   aged

EXERCISE 5 Each of the following words stands for more than one meaning. First think about the different meanings each word can have. Then choose one meaning for each word. On a sheet of paper write a sentence using the word with the meaning you have chosen. Underline the word. Following each sentence write the short definition you have chosen.

EXAMPLE **compose**

She remained calm and <u>composed</u> in the angry crowd.

undisturbed

1. prime   4. default
2. lapse   5. novel
3. chord   6. balance

17d Many words change in many ways.

The English language has changed a great deal during its history. The changes in certain words show this. For example, the meanings people give to words change over a period of time. Words also change in their forms and the ways they are pronounced.

(1) Words change in their meanings.

Several hundred years ago the word *clown* did not refer to an entertainer in a circus. Instead, *clown* referred to a country peasant who had bad manners. The word *circus* originally meant only "a circle." Both these words have changed as time has passed.

Here are more examples:

WORD	PRESENT MEANING	OLDER MEANING
clock	a timepiece	a bell
holiday	a vacation	a holy day
journey	a trip	one day's work
wrong	incorrect	twisted

EXERCISE 6 Write each of the following words in a column on a sheet of paper. After it, write its present meaning. After that, write an older, different meaning. Use a dictionary that lists this information.

EXAMPLE starve

starve - go hungry - die

1. pay
2. lady
3. husband

4. harvest
5. janitor
6. curious

(2) Words change in their forms and pronunciations.

Over long periods of time many words change in their spellings. A simple word like *be* was once spelled *bee*. *Show* was spelled *shew*. *Kind* was spelled *kinde*.

Many other examples can be seen in the following picture of a page from a schoolbook used in the sixteenth century in England.

W.

The duble w, is a letter that hath accompanied our *vv.*
tung frō the originall Germane, and is vsed somtime as
a vowell, somtime as a consonant. It is neuer vowell but *vv, the vowell.*
in the diphthongs as, *draw, knew, throw,* neither is it to
enter the midle syllab of anie word, sauing in thré cases.
The first whereof is, with the deriuatiues of those finall ₁.
diphthongs, as of *know, knowing, knowledge, vnknown.*
The second is, when *custom* will frame another primitiue ₂.
after the proportion of one of these, as *ówn,* like *vnknówn.*
The third is som manifest difference, where the single *u,* ₃.
might easilie be mistaken, and ioyned to the vowell following, as in *vouell, couard,* like *houell, couert,* and therefor,
2006   **K**   theie

Pronunciations of words have also changed with time. Even today, some of the very old pronunciations are used in certain regions among groups of people.

17e Different groups of people who speak the same language may use different words, word forms, or pronunciations to mean the same things.

The name for a form of a language used by a group is a *dialect*. There are many different dialects in English. Some include a few different words or word forms. Most dialects have slightly different ways of pronouncing certain words.

EXAMPLES

DIFFERENT   hello, howdy, aloha
WORDS   peanuts, goobers

DIFFERENT   idea, idear
PRONUNCIATIONS   window, winda, winder
                        Missouri, Missourah

As long as a dialect communicates ideas between speakers and listeners, it serves its purpose. One dialect is no better than another dialect unless one communicates better than the other.

The *standard dialect* in the United States is the one used by professional people who must communicate clearly to a large number of people. Speakers of standard dialect, therefore, are most likely to be national broadcasters on television and radio, editors of national publications, and leaders of national organizations.

Speakers of a nonstandard dialect do not speak a bad dialect, however. Theirs is only a *different* dialect. Many people who come from homes where another language or dialect is spoken may speak English with a nonstandard dialect. This is true for children from homes where a language from Asia, Mexico, or Europe is spoken. It is true for children who come from homes in which English is spoken with a Black dialect, an Irish dialect, an Australian dialect, or any other form of English that uses special words or pronunciations.

EXERCISE 7 Number a sheet of paper 1–5. Write the standard spelling that shows the standard word form or pronunciation of the following dialect terms.

    EXAMPLE **taters**

         potatoes

1. Ioway (a state)
2. crick (a stream)
3. pop (a soft drink)
4. two bits (money)
5. buck (money)

REVIEW EXERCISE A One Word, Several Meanings

In the following exercise more than one definition is given for the defined word. Then the word is used in a series of sentences.

On a sheet of paper, write the defined word, followed by the numbers 1–3. After each number, tell which of the defined meanings of the word is used in the sentence.

    EXAMPLE **run** A. To move swiftly or with quick action; B. to go back and forth; C. to compete in an election.

1. Juanita Gomez will <u>run</u> for class office.
2. The new bus will <u>run</u> between Deep River and <u>Essex</u>.
3. If there is an explosion, <u>run</u> for cover.

run 1. C   2. B   3. A

root A. the part of a plant that grows beneath the ground; B. an ancestor; C. the lowest place or the essential part; D. an element of a word without prefix or suffix.

1. The <u>root</u> of *philosophy* is *philo-,* which means "love."
2. The <u>roots</u> of the fern were killed by hot weather.
3. Finally, Andrew and his father got to the <u>root</u> of the problem.

nice A. good, well-mannered; B. able to make fine distinctions.

1. The gourmet's sense of taste was so <u>nice</u> that he could tell the difference between chicken that had been cooked when fresh and chicken that had been frozen first.
2. It is not <u>nice</u> to wipe your muddy feet on the rug, Agnes.
3. Because of the <u>niceness</u> of his taste in cars, Gilbert has been <u>hired</u> to write automobile advertising.

conceit A. an exaggeratedly good opinion of oneself; B. a clever or witty wording or idea.

1. Burns uses an exaggerated conceit when he says he will love a lady "until the ricks melt in the sun."
2. Allan is so conceited that his best friend is the person he sees in his mirror.
3. Conceit led Dr. Li to describe himself as "the best dentist west of the Mississippi River."

redeem A. to regain possession of by buying again; B. to rescue or deliver as from kidnapping by paying ransom; C. to make amends for or to atone for

1. Although Howard got a low grade in math, he redeemed himself by doing well in all his other subjects.
2. The highjackers said that only a million dollars could redeem the carload of diamonds.
3. Gladys is slothful, but her humor and kindness redeem her.

pocket A. to steal; B. small; able to fit in a pocket; C. in mining, a small cavity filled with ore

1. The thief simply pocketed the jewelry and ran.
2. Why are you trying to use a pocket handkerchief as a tent?
3. Even a small pocket of silver in the Comstock lode could make a miner rich.

REVIEW EXERCISE B Using Context

See Chapter 2, pp. 52–53

Number a sheet of paper 1–10. Identify the part of speech of the underlined word in each sentence.

EXAMPLE A play may have a long <u>run</u> on Broadway.

noun

If you catch the football, <u>run</u>.

verb

1. <u>Blue</u> was the only color that appeared in some of Picasso's paintings.
2. These are the paintings from Picasso's <u>blue</u> period.
3. Billie Jean King has been a champion at playing <u>tennis</u>.
4. A <u>tennis</u> racquet has been named for Billie Jean King.
5. The manufacturer guarantees that the <u>work</u> pants will never tear.
6. The people who <u>worked</u> on the building of the Golden Gate Bridge took some terrible risks.
7. Do not <u>experiment</u> with explosives in your own home.
8. Thomas Edison's <u>experiments</u> did not always work.
9. Jenny's driving <u>rivals</u> a stuntman's.
10. The <u>rivals</u> fought over the golden apple.

REVIEW EXERCISE C Synonyms

Number a sheet of paper 1–10. Choose the better synonym for each blank and write your choice on the paper. You may use a dictionary.

EXAMPLE   As she reached for the fly ball, Annie felt a sudden sharp _____ in her arm. (pain, ache)

pain

1. The governor's _____ came just in time to save the convict from execution. (pardon, excuse)
2. Because the rest of his family was away for the evening, Mr. Johnson just fixed himself a small _____ of leftovers. (banquet, dinner)
3. Mario's grandmother is ninety; she is an _____ and respected lady. (old, antique)
4. Carter's hand _____ with the cold as he tried to open the car door in the icy wind. (shook, shuddered)
5. Thoreau learned to respect the _____ when he quietly observed the changing seasons, the growing plants, and the droning insects. (earth, world)
6. Karen wanted to see the _____ ruins on the Acropolis in Athens. (old, ancient)
7. Marian Muir finally grew angry with the weeds that were destroying her flowers. She bought a weak poison to _____ them. (kill, assassinate)
8. Thomas Alva Edison _____ the electric light bulb. (discovered, invented)
9. My sister has a _____ ability in sports. (native, natural)
10. Kate is not a glutton, but she finds _____ in having a good lunch in the middle of the day. (pleasure, happiness)

REVIEW EXERCISE D Changes in Meaning

There are four ways in which words tend to change in meaning:

1. A pleasant word becomes less pleasant.
2. An unpleasant word becomes more pleasant.
3. A general word becomes more specific.
4. A specific word becomes more general.

Write the kind of change that is described in each of the following items.

EXAMPLE   A underline{butcher} was once a person who killed only goats and sold goat meat. Today a butcher sells all kinds of meat.

A specific word has become more general.

1. An undertaker was once a general repairer. An undertaker undertook many kinds of small jobs. Today an undertaker undertakes the arrangement of funerals.
2. Corn was once the name of any grain. Today corn is the name of a particular grain.
3. Fond once meant stupid. Today it means affectionate or loving.
4. Pretty once meant sly or clever in a sneaky way. Today it means attractive.
5. Sly once meant skillful or good at a craft. Today it means sneaky or clever in an underhanded way.
6. Nice once meant ignorant or foolish. Today it means pleasant or not offensive.

7. To <u>arrive</u> once meant to come to the end of a sea voyage. Today we arrive at the end of any kind of journey.

8. <u>Immoral</u> once meant unusual. Today it means evil or wrong.

9. <u>Reek</u> once described any odor, whether pleasant or unpleasant. Today only a very unpleasant odor reeks.

10. A <u>deer</u> was once any animal that was hunted by people. Today, in America, a deer is a particular kind of animal.

REVIEW EXERCISE E   Dialects

Each word in the first column has a synonym in the second column. The words in the second column are peculiar to certain American dialects. On a sheet of paper, try to match the words in the first column with their synonyms in the second column. You may use a dictionary.

A	B
bucket	piazza
porch	pail
frying pan	spider
peanut	flapjack
cottage cheese	cayuse
cornbread	pot cheese
angleworm	johnnycake
pony	woodchuck
ground hog	goober
pancake	earthworm

GLOSSARY

This glossary lists special terms that appear in the text. Most terms are defined here. Terms not defined are cross-referenced to other terms with definitions. Wherever examples will help, they are provided.

References to parts of the text appear with many terms in this glossary. The text treats these terms more fully.

adjective A word that describes a noun. (See also **article**.) See **1f**.

A *strong* wind blew from the north.

It toppled *tall* trees.

An adjective helps *compare things*. Most adjectives change form to show comparison.

A *small* glass is on the bench.

A *smaller* glass sits on the table.

The *smallest* glass is on the shelf.

adverb A word that *describes* sentence *actions*. An adverb tells *where, when,* or *how* something happens. It usually does this by describing the verb in the sentence. An adverb can also describe some other part of speech. See **2e**.

These adverbs tell *where* the action happens.

The dog just lies *there*.

Can it sit *up?*

These adverbs tell *when* the action happens.

Salvador left *yesterday*.

We should leave *now*.

These adverbs tell *how* the action happens.

We climbed *quickly*.

The snow melted *slowly*.

agreement The forms of words that show the same number. See **9a**.

A single *bump hurts*.
Many *bumps hurt* worse.

antecedent The word or group of words referred to by a following pronoun.

The *athletes who* train hard can win.

antonym A word that means the opposite of another word.

small/big   quiet/noisy

apostrophe A mark that looks like a comma above the line to show possession, missing letters, or the plural of numbers. See **13j (1)-(3), 13k, 13l**.

Walt's shoe, won't, 6's

appositive A word or group of words placed next to another to explain a meaning or idea.

She explained her philosophy, *her feeling about life.*

We whistled for Eric, *the mammoth dog,* but heard no answer.

article   The words *a, an,* and *the.* An article is a kind of adjective.

auxiliary verb   (See **helping verb**.)

case   The form of a pronoun that shows its relation to other parts of the sentence. See **1e (1)-(3).**

SUBJECTIVE CASE usually serves as the subject of a sentence.

I run two miles a day.

OBJECTIVE CASE usually serves as the object of the sentence or the object of a preposition.

It is easy for *me.*

POSSESSIVE CASE shows ownership.

My goal is to run five miles a day.

clause   A group of words with both a subject and a predicate. A clause can be a sentence or part of a sentence. See **4a, 4b,** and **4c.**

INDEPENDENT CLAUSE   A clause that can stand alone as a complete thought.

A light floated near and *the bystanders pointed at it.*

A light floated near. The bystanders pointed at it.

DEPENDENT CLAUSE   A clause that depends upon an independent clause to complete its thought.

As a light floated near, the bystanders pointed at it.

colloquial   Acceptable words or forms in informal conversation, but usually not acceptable in formal speech or writing.

Get *in the spirit.*
You don't seem to be *with it.*

comparison   The forms of an adjective or adverb that show more or less about the words they describe. (See also **modifiers**.) See **1g** and **2f**.

POSITIVE   *old, sad*

COMPARATIVE   *older, sadder*

SUPERLATIVE   *oldest, saddest*

completer   A word or words that complete a statement about the subject of a sentence. A completer comes after the verb. It is part of the predicate. (See also **predicate**.) See **5j–5k**.

Completers are words or phrases that can fit in sentence blanks like these:

Alphonso hit _____.
He seemed _____.

NOUNS AND NOUN WORD GROUP COMPLETERS
Alphonso hit *the fender.*

ADJECTIVE COMPLETER
Alissa was *weary.*

ADVERB COMPLETER
You are *there*.

complex sentence   A sentence with an independent clause and a dependent clause. (See also **clause**.) See **5e**.

Marta stopped laughing although she still saw the humor.

compound   A word or group of words made up of two or more parts that could stand alone.

COMPOUND WORD   *basketball, maid-of-honor*

COMPOUND SUBJECT   *Old wagons* and *new cars* rolled in the parade.

COMPOUND OBJECT   He scooped *rice* and *barley*.

COMPOUND PREDICATE   Kangaroos *sit in the shade* or *hop across an open area*.

compound sentence   A sentence made up of two or more independent clauses. See **5d**.

Amadeo Ramirez likes to watch car races, but he is too young to drive.

compound verb   Two or more verbs in a clause or sentence. See **5b (4)**.

Elsina *cleaned* and *stacked* the bricks.

conjunction   A word that connects words, phrases, or clauses. Two kinds of conjunctions are *coordinating conjunctions* and *subordinating conjunctions*. See **2i**.

COORDINATING CONJUNCTIONS connect parts of words, phrases, or clauses. The most common coordinating conjunctions are *and, but,* and *or.*

ham *and* eggs
Climb in *or* get out.

SUBORDINATING CONJUNCTIONS connect ideas not equal to each other. Some examples are *after, although, as, because, before, like, since, though, unless, until, when, where, while.*

She folds the paper *after* she has read it.
You can hear the waves *when* the wind dies.

connectors Words used to connect other words or groups of words. Some examples are conjunctions, such as *and, but, after;* and connecting adverbs, such as *then, therefore,* and *afterward.*

consonants All alphabet letters that are not vowels (*B, C, D,* for example). Consonant sounds are made in speaking by closing or bringing together parts of the throat, mouth, teeth, tongue, or lips.

context The words surrounding a word that help define it.

contractions A word form using an apostrophe to show missing letters.

can't, don't, could've

dangling modifier A modifying word or word group without a subject to modify.

Pushing and shoving, the boat finally floated off the sandbar. [The sentence seems to say that the boat did the pushing and shoving.]

CORRECTED Pushing and shoving, the people finally floated the boat off the sandbar.

dependent clause   (See **clause.**)

determiner   (See also **article.**) Determiners are words like *a, an, the, one, some, their.* A determiner is a kind of adjective that always is followed by a noun.

a rock, *an* arm

Determiners help tell whether a noun is singular or plural.

one cat, *several* cats

diacritical marks   Marks used with letters to show how they are pronounced.

Examples are **ā** [as in *say*], **ē** [as in *set*], **ä** [as in *father*].

diagraming   A way of showing how parts of a sentence relate to one another. Two main types of diagraming are sometimes used. One type is a traditional diagram. The other is a tree diagram.

Any diagram of a sentence is only one way of showing the relationships among its parts.

TRADITIONAL DIAGRAMING Six sentences are diagramed below. Each diagram shows how added parts of a sentence fit together.

(1) A farmer lifted the plow

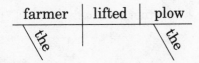

[The simple subject belongs first on the horizontal line. Under it on a slanted line belongs its modifier. The verb follows the simple subject, separated by a vertical line through the horizontal line. The direct object follows the verb, separated by a vertical line resting on the horizontal line.]

(2) The strong farmer lifted the plow.

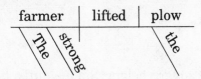

[Additional modifiers of the subject belong on additional slanted lines.]

(3) The strong farmer in the field lifted the plow.

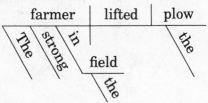

[A prepositional phrase modifying the subject belongs on slanted and horizontal lines as shown in (3) above.]

(4) The farmer had lifted the plow.

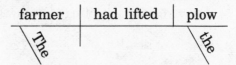

[Helping verbs belong with the main verb on the horizontal line.]

(5) The farmer lifted the plow carefully.

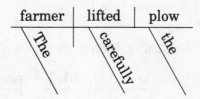

[An adverb belongs on a slanted line under the verb it modifies.]

(6) The strong farmer in the field lifted the bent plow carefully.

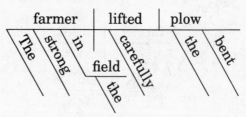

[The completed diagram is shown in (6) above.]

(7)

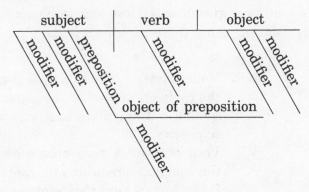

[All parts of the sentence are shown in (7) above.]

TREE DIAGRAMING

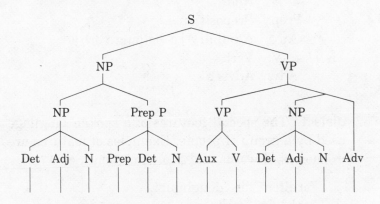

The strong farmer in the field lifted the bent plow carefully.

A tree diagram gets its name from its shape. Turn it upside down and it looks a little like a tree. The abbreviations used in the tree diagram have the following meanings. These meanings are not all the same as those in traditional grammar. Follow your teacher's direction in using these meanings.

S:	Sentence
NP:	Noun phrase A noun phrase is often the complete subject or the object of a sentence. It may have another, smaller phrase in it.
VP:	Verb phrase A verb phrase can be the complete predicate of a sentence. It can have a verb phrase and a noun phrase in it.
Prep P:	Prepositional phrase
Det:	Determiner
Adj:	Adjective
N:	Noun
Prep:	Preposition
Aux:	Auxiliary [a helping verb]
V:	Verb
Adv:	Adverb

dialect   The special features of a spoken language used by a group of people. Examples of features are in choices of words and pronunciation. See **17e.**

"cruller" for "doughnut"
"cah" for "car"

double negative   The incorrect use of two words that mean "no" in the same sentence. The most common negatives are *no* and *not*. Other negatives are *none (no + one), nothing (no + thing), never (not + ever),* and *neither (not + either).* See **9o.**

Here are examples of double negatives:

1. She didn't see nothing.
2. They can't hardly run.

CORRECTIONS
1. She didn't see anything.
2. They can hardly run.

expletive A word without meaning used as the subject of a sentence.

It is hailing.
There are no eggs left.

Also, an expletive is an interjection that expresses strong feeling.

How *in the heck* can they do that?

exposition Writing that expresses, explains, or "exposes" one's ideas, for example, a newspaper editorial, an essay, or a research paper.

fragment An incomplete sentence, one without either the necessary subject or predicate. See **51.**

Fixed with glue. [What is fixed with glue?]

CORRECTED The handle is fixed with glue.

helping verb Words that are used with main verbs. The most common helping verbs are listed here. See **2a (5).**

be: am, are, is, was, were, being, been
do: do, does, did, done
have: have, has, had

Here are some other common helping verbs:

can, could, may, shall
will, would, might

Helping verbs help the verbs express their actions.

Elda *was* surfing near the beach.
She *had* stayed up on several waves.

Helping verbs also help show time.

Her skill *will* improve. [action in the future]
She *has* practiced a long time. [action completed in the past]

idiom   A word or phrase used in a special way.

She *did herself proud.*

independent clause   A group of words having a subject and predicate able to stand by itself without need of other words to finish its meaning. [See also **clause.**] See **4b.**

indirect object   The secondary receiver of sentence action.

Dave bought *her* a bracelet. [For whom did Dave buy the bracelet? Answer: *her.*]

infinitive   The standard or base form of a verb, often with *to.*

to sleep, to dream

The infinitive is sometimes used as a noun.

To sleep would be a blessing.

inflection   The change in the form of a word to show a change in meaning or grammatical use.

> *dog* [singular], *dogs* [plural], *dogs'* [plural possessive]
> sing [present], sang [past], sung [past participle]

interjection   A part of speech showing strong feeling. An interjection is not grammatically related to the sentence. See **2j.**

> *Deuce it all!* Why can't they fix this?

irregular verb   A verb that does not add **ed** to form the past tense. (See also **verb.**) See **2d.**

italics   Slanted letters printed to draw special attention. See **13m–13n.**

linking verb   A verb that links the subject to the subject completer. See **2a (4).**

> *appear, become, feel, look,* and forms of the verb *be.*

main clause   An independent clause.

metaphor   A figure of speech in which one item is compared to another.

> The wave with a *mountain of water*

modal auxiliary   A verb used as a verb helper that does not change form.

> *can, could, might, ought*

modifiers   Words used to describe someone, something, or some action. [See also **adjective** and **adverb**.]

mood   The purpose of the speaker as shown in the form and use of the verb. The three moods are (1) to state something, (2) to order or request something, and (3) to show a condition that is not true or is desirable.

    (1) INDICATIVE MOOD   The sun warms the soil.

    (2) IMPERATIVE MOOD   Dig in the ground.

    (3) SUBJUNCTIVE MOOD   If only I were older, I could go.

nominative   The subjective case. (See also **case**.)

nonrestrictive clause or **phrase**   A group of words that tells something more about someone or something in the same sentence. A nonrestrictive clause or phrase is not necessary to make the sentence complete, but it adds to its meaning.

    A little bird, *singing cheerily,* flitted from branch to branch. [phrase]

    A little bird, *which was singing cheerily,* flitted from branch to branch. [clause]

noun   A word or group of words used to name a person, place, thing, or idea. See **1a.**

    Names of persons: Jody Schwartz, Gilberto Ramos
    [proper nouns]

Names of places: Atlantic Seaboard, Times Square
[proper nouns]
Names of things: hail, iron, hair
[common nouns]
Names of ideas: democracy, leadership
[common nouns]

number   One or more than one person or thing. In English, singular or plural number is shown in most nouns by the addition of **s** or **es.**

map/maps, dish/dishes

A few nouns change their spellings in special ways.

woman/women, mouse/mice

Number is shown in most pronouns by a change in form.

this/these, that/those
he, she/they   her, him/them
hers, his/theirs

object   The result of action or the receiver of the action in a sentence. See **5j.**

DIRECT OBJECT Paula Ortiz bought a *purse.*

INDIRECT OBJECT The clerk gave *her* some change.

The object of a preposition is a noun or pronoun which is related to another word by the preposition.

He gave the change to *her.*

objective case Pronouns show the objective case when they serve as the objects of a sentence or of a preposition. (See also **case**.) See **1e (2)**.

> Jack met *her* and *us* after school. [*Her* and *us* are in the objective case.]

paragraph A paragraph is a group of sentences beginning with an indention. The sentences should all be about one idea. There should be enough sentences to make the idea clear to the reader. See **6a–6c**.

The topic of a paragraph is often written in a topic sentence. The topic sentence usually comes at the beginning of a paragraph.

> *The duck-billed platypus is a strange animal.* It looks like a mixture of a mole, a duck, and a beaver. It lives in a mudhole near water. It eats worms and other such creatures. Its babies are born in eggs. However, the hatched babies drink milk from the mother just as mammals do.

participle The **ing** or the **ed** form of a verb that can be used as an adjective. A few irregular verbs form their participles in irregular ways. (See also **phrase**.)

> happening [present participle]
> happened [past participle]
> broken [past participle of irregular verb *break*]

parts of speech English sentences can have eight main kinds of words in them. These eight kinds of words are called parts of speech. These words do the work of the sentence. They help show meaning.

The eight parts of speech are *noun, pronoun, verb, adjective, adverb, preposition, conjunction,* and *interjection.* (See separate listings.)

phrase A group of words belonging together, but not making a complete statement. See **3a.**

> PREPOSITIONAL PHRASE under the box
>
> VERB PHRASE having started
>
> NOUN PHRASE a terrible storm

plural More than one. The plural is shown by words that mean more than one *(many, ten)*. It is also shown in the forms of nouns *(man/men),* pronouns *(her/them),* and verbs (she *runs*/they *run*).

possessive A form of a noun or pronoun showing that someone owns something or that things belong close together. See **1c; 1e (3).**

> the *girl's* slipper [possessive noun]
> *his* plan [possessive pronoun]

predicate The part of a sentence that tells about the subject. See **5b (2).**

> S P
> Joe strapped the brace to his arm.
>
> S P
> She is an auto mechanic.

prefix A prefix is one or more syllables added to the front of a word or root to affect its meaning. See **15b (10)–(11).**

indecent, **un**told, **de**tract, **im**possible

preposition A part of speech that points out how two words are related. Most prepositions show time or place or direction. See **2g.**

under the floor, *after* hours, *up* the ladder

prepositional phrases (See **phrase.**)

pronoun A word that can stand for a noun. Usually, a pronoun stands for a group of words in which the noun is the main word. See **1d.**

The pilot of the airplane flipped a switch.
She flipped a switch. [*She* stands for *the pilot of the airplane.*]

The switch made a light go on.
It made a light go on. [*It* stands for *the switch.*]

There are three cases of pronouns. The first is the *subjective case.* It usually shows the doer of the action in a sentence.

She flipped a switch.
She then started the engine.

The second case of the pronoun is the *objective case.*

She looked at *them.*

The third case of a pronoun is the *possessive case.*

It was *her* airplane.

punctuation The marks used with words to show how they relate and how they are to be read. See Chapters 12–13.

root The basic part of a word. Parts are added to it to change its meaning. (See also **prefix** and **suffix**.)

> in*direct,* re*trace, trace*able

run-on sentence Two or more sentences run together without correct punctuation or connecting words. See **5m.**

> The large fish did not see Maryl she was able to approach very close.
>
> CORRECTED The large fish did not see Maryl. She was able to approach very close.

sentence A group of related words needing no other words to complete its thought. A sentence has a subject and a predicate. See **5a.**

> SENTENCE Bits of chocolate fell across the table and to the floor.
>
> NO SENTENCE Fell across the table and to the floor. (See also **fragment**.)

singular Only one of anything. (See **plural** for a comparison.)

slang A word or phrase not yet accepted for general use by most educated people.

> *"Stash the loot!"* shouted the robber.

subject   A noun (or its equal) that the rest of its sentence says or asks something about. The subject of a sentence is the *who* or *what* that belongs with the predicate. See **5b (1)**.

> A *helicopter* swooped low.
> *People* ducked low to the ground.

subject completer   (See **completer**.)

subordinate clause   A dependent clause. (See also **clause**.)

subordinating conjunction   (See **conjunction**.)

suffix   One or more syllables that add meaning to a word or root. A suffix is added to the end of a word or a root. See **15b (12)–(19)**

> play*able*, quick*ly*, care*ful*, young*est*

syllable   A letter or group of letters containing a vowel that is pronounced as one unit. A syllable may be a single vowel.

> ab-surd, el-e-gant, hu-mor-ous

Most syllables contain a vowel sound plus a consonant sound or sounds.

> re-peat, de-pend [2 syllables]
> con-sti-tute, ad-ver-tise [3 syllables]
> con-sti-tu-tion, ad-ver-tise-ment [4 syllables]

synonym   A word that means the same as another.

> biscuit/bun, new/fresh, old/aged

syntax The arrangement of words and parts of a sentence.

> The plumber gave them a new sink.
> The plumber gave a new sink to them.
> They were given a new sink by the plumber.
> [All three sentences mean the same. However, the syntax, or order of words, is different in each.]

tense Time as shown by the form of a verb. See **2b.**

> PRESENT he *falls,* they *fall*
>
> PAST he *fell,* they *fell*
>
> FUTURE he *will fall,* they *are going to fall*

topic sentence (See **paragraph.**)

transformation The changes in form that can be made in sentences and word groups.

unity In composition, making sentences refer to the same topic or subject.

verb A part of speech that shows action *(run),* states something *(is),* or shows condition *(seems).* Most verbs change their form to show time *(run—ran).* (See **tense.**) Other changes show number (One woman *was* there. More *were* not). See **2a.**

A verb tells the action in a sentence. Or it tells that something exists. Exists means "is" or "to be."

> *action:* chops, cuts, fixes
> *existence:* am, is, are, was, were

verbal   A form of a verb used as another part of speech. (See **infinitive**.)

vocabulary   The words and their meanings used in a language.

voice   The form of a verb that shows who or what is doing something.

ACTIVE VOICE   The animal *grabbed* the glove.

PASSIVE VOICE   The glove *was grabbed* by the animal.

vowel   The letters *A, E, I, O, U,* and sometimes the letters *Y* and *W*.

INDEX

A

Abbreviations, periods after, 250
Accept/except, 216, 217
Action verbs, 28–30
in phrase, 61, 62
Active verbs, 197–199
Addresses, 179, 180
Adjective clause, 79–81
Adjectives, 16–21, 366
adverb clauses with, 82
commas for separation of, 260, 261
prepositional phrase as, 64, 65
problems with, 207, 208
Adjustment, letter of, 177–179
Adverb clause, 81–83
Adverbs, 37–43, 366, 367
as connectors, 157
prepositional phrase as, 65–68
problems with, 207, 208
Advertisements, 346
Advice/advise, 217, 218
Affect/effect, 218
Agreements, 185–197, 367, 203–205
Ain't, 220
All right, 218, 227
All together/altogether, 218
Almost/most, 218, 219
Already/all ready, 219, 220

Am not/ain't, 220
Among/between, 220, 221
And
commas in place of, 260, 261
with compound subject, 189, 190
Animal names, 239
Antecedent, 367
Antonym, 367
Apostrophes, 273–275, 367
for possessive case, 7, 8
Appositives, 367, 368
commas setting off, 255
Are not/ain't, 220
Articles, 17, 268
As/like, 226, 227
Auxiliary verb. *See* Helping verbs

B

Be, 187–189
Beside/besides, 221, 222
Between/among, 220, 221
Books, 329, 338
capitalization in titles of, 243, 244
underlining titles of, 275
Burst/bust, 222
Business letters, 172–179
colons in, 271
Business names, 241, 242

C

Can/may, 222, 223
Can hardly/can't hardly, 223
Capitalization, 238–248
  of proper nouns, 5
Card catalog, 340–342
Case, 11–14, 368
Clause, 73–88, 368, 369
  commas in, 258–260
  as fragments, 113
  semicolons with, 267, 268
Collective nouns, agreement
  with, 194, 195
Colloquial phrase, 369
Colons, 270, 271
Commas, 253–266
  with independent clauses,
    99
  with interjections, 52
  with run-on sentence, 116
Comparisons, 369
  of adjectives, 18–20
  with adverbs, 41–43
  in compositions, 160–162
  in dictionary, 334, 335
  in paragraph, 134, 135
Complaint letter, 177–179
Complete predicate, 93, 94
Complete subject, 92
Complete verb, 61
Completers, 18, 104–107,
    369, 370
Complex sentence, 370
  commas in, 261, 262
  dependent clauses in,
    100–102
Composition, 147–182
Compound nouns, 9, 312
Compound prepositions, 44,
    45
Compound sentence, 370
  commas with, 262, 263
  independent clause in, 99,
    100

semicolons in, 267, 268
Compound subject, 95, 96,
    189–191
Compound verb, 370
Compound words, 272
Compounds, 95, 96, 370
Conjunctions, 48–52, 370,
    372
  commas in place of, 260,
    261
  as connectors, 157
  semicolons in absence of,
    267, 268
  subordinating conjunctions,
    50–52, 371
  see also Coordinating
    conjunctions
Connectors, 371
  in composition, 139, 156,
    157
Consonants, 371
Coordinating conjunctions,
    48–50, 371
  commas with, 262, 263
  with compound predicates,
    96
  with compound subject, 95
  with independent clauses,
    99
  with run-on sentence, 116
Copyright page, 329
Correlative conjunctions, 49
Could have/could of, 223

D

Dangling modifier, 371, 372
Dates, commas in, 265, 266
Declarative sentences, 102
Deity names, 243
Dependent clause, 76, 77,
    368, 369
  commas setting off, 261,
    262

in complex sentence,
100–102
as fragments, 113, 114

Dewey Decimal System,
338–340
Diacritical marks, 333, 372
Dialects, 358, 359, 376
Dictionary
as resource, 329–336
for spelling, 309
Direct objects, 104, 105
pattern of, 109, 110
Directions, 240, 295–297
Double negative, 208, 209,
376, 377
Drowned/drownded, 223

E

Effect/affect, 218
Either/or, 190, 191
Enclosing punctuation,
275–279
Encyclopedias, 342
End punctuation, 250–252
Envelopes, 179, 180
Except/accept, 216, 217
Exclamation marks, 252
with exclamatory sentence,
103
with interjections, 52
Expletives, 377
Exposition, 377

F

Foreign words, 275
Formal speaking, 297–303
delivery of speech, 300–302
Fragments of sentences,
113–115, 377
Future tense, 35

G

Geographical names. *See*
Place names
Glossary, 329
God, 243
Good/well, 207, 223, 224
Government, as information
source, 346
Groups of words
adverbs modifying, 40, 41
agreement with, 185–197
and conjunctions, 48
Guide words, 331, 332, 342

H

Helping verbs, 32, 33, 377,
378
with passive verbs, 198
in phrases, 61, 62
in present perfect tense, 35,
200
and tense, 34, 35, 200
Homonyms, 319, 320
Homophones, 224, 225,
228–232
Hyphens, 272, 273

I

Idiom, 378
Imperative sentence, 103
Indefinite pronouns, 15, 195,
196
Independent clause, 75, 76,
368, 369, 378
commas with, 262, 263
in complex sentence,
100–102

in compound sentence, 99,
    100
in simple sentence, 98
Index, 329
Indirect object, 378
pattern of, 109, 110
Infinitives, 34, 35, 378, 379
and prepositional phrases,
    63
of regular verbs, 35, 36
Information sources,
    328–350
Initials, periods after, 250,
    251
Interjections, 52, 379
Interrogative pronouns, 15
Interrogative sentence, 102,
    103
Intransitive verbs, 29, 30
Introduction of people,
    290–294
Irregular adjectives, 20, 21
Irregular nouns, 7
Irregular verbs, 36, 37,
    199–203, 379
    be as, 187–189
    in dictionary, 334
Is not/ain't, 220
Italics, 275, 276, 379
Its/it's, 224

Librarians, 337, 338
Library, use of, 337–346
Lie/lay, 226
Like/as, 226, 227
Linking verb, 30–32, 379
    adjectives with, 207, 208
    agreement with, 197
    patterns with, 111, 112
    in phrase, 61, 62
    and subject completer,
        105–107
Linking words. *See*
    Connectors
Listening
    in informal conversation,
        289, 290
    to introductions, 292, 293
    to speech, 302, 303
Loan/lend, 226

M

Magazines
    capitalization of titles, 243,
        244
    in library, 343
    underlining titles of, 275
Master spelling list,
    324–327
May/can, 222, 223
Metaphor, 379
Modal auxiliary, 379
Modifiers, 380
More/most
    with adverbs, 41, 42
    for comparisons, 20
Most/almost, 218, 219
Movies
    capitalization of, 243, 244
    underlining titles of, 275
Musical terms, plurals of,
    311

J

Lay/lie, 226
Lead/led, 224, 225
Learn/teach, 225
Leave/let, 225
Lend/loan, 226
Let/leave, 225
Letters, 171–182
    colons in, 271
    commas in, 266

N

Names. *See* Proper nouns
Negatives, 208, 209, 376, 377
Neither/nor, 190, 191
Never, as adverb, 41
Newspaper titles, 243, 244
Nominative. *See* Subjective case
Nonfiction books, 338
Nonrestrictive clause, 380
Nonstandard dialect, 358, 359
Noun clauses, 77–79
Nouns, 3–9, 380, 382
  and adjectives, 16–21
  agreement with, 193–195
  phrases, 60, 61
  in prepositional phrase, 63–65
  and prepositions, 43, 44
  and pronouns, 10–16
  spelling plurals of, 310–313
Number, 381
Numbers
  hyphens in, 272
  apostrophes with, 275
  colons with, 271

O

Objects, 29, 381
  patterns of, 108–112
  of personal pronoun, 204, 205
  of preposition, 45–48, 63
  see also Direct objects; Indirect objects
Objective case, 382
  of personal pronoun, 12, 13, 204, 205
  whom as, 206

OK/all right, 227
Order letter, 176, 177
Organization of composition, 150–158
Outlining speech, 299, 300

P

Paragraphs, 126–146, 382
  for subtopics, 151, 152
Parentheses, 279
Participle, 382
Passive verbs, 197–199
Past participle, 35, 200
Past tense, 35
  and irregular verbs, 199–203
Periodicals. *See* Magazines
Periods, 102, 103, 250, 251
Personal pronouns, 11
  agreement with, 203–205
Phrases, 59–72, 383
  agreement with, 191–193
  commas in, 258–260
  as fragments, 113
Place names
  capitalization of, 239, 240
  commas in, 265, 266
Plurals, 6, 7, 383
  agreement, 185, 189, 193, 194
  apostrophes for, 273–275
  in dictionary, 334
  spelling of, 310–313
Possessive, 383
  apostrophes showing, 273
  nouns, 7–9
  of personal pronouns, 13
Predicate, 383, 384
  of clause, 73, 74
  completer with, 104
  compound predicate, 96–98
  of sentence, 93–95

Prefix, 313–315, 384
Prepositional phrases, 63–68
Prepositions, 43–48, 384
  as connectors, 157
  pronouns as object of, 204
Present participle, 34
Present perfect tense, 35, 36,
  200–203
Present tense, 34
  agreement in, 185, 186
Pronouns, 10–16, 384
  agreement with, 195, 196
  with noun phrases, 60
  in prepositional phrase, 63
  and prepositions, 43, 44
  problems with, 203–206
Pronunciation
  changes in, 357
  and dialects, 357, 358
  in dictionary, 333
Proper nouns, 3–6
  capitalization of, 238–248
Punctuation, 249–284, 385
  in letter, 173
  with run-on sentence, 116

Q

Question marks, 251
  in interrogative sentence,
  103
Questions, 15, 287, 288
Quotation marks, 276–279
  commas with, 264, 265
Quotations, 238, 277
  semicolons with, 268, 269

R

Race names, 242
Reference books, 328–350

Relative clause, 79–81
Relative pronouns, 15, 206
Request letter, 173–175
Root, 385
Run-on sentences, 115–117,
  385

S

Semicolons, 99, 267–270
Sentences, 89–123, 385
  capitalization in, 238
  diagramming of, 372–376
  independent clause as, 75,
  76
  in paragraph, 126
  topic sentence, 128–130
Series, 8, 253, 254, 268
Set/sit, 227
Shall/will, 228
Should have/should of, 228
Simple predicate, 93, 94
Simple sentence, 98
Simple subject, 92
Singulars, 6, 7, 385
  agreement with, 185–197
  apostrophes with, 273
Sit/set, 227
Slang, 385
Sources of information,
  328–350
Spelling, 307–327
  of homonyms, 319, 320
  in letter, 173
Subject, 386
  and adjective, 207, 208
  agreement with, 185–197
  of clause, 73, 74
  of compound subject, 95, 96
  in imperative sentence, 103
  in interrogative sentence,
  103

patterns of, 107–112
in sentence, 91–93
Subject completers, 31, 32,
   105–107
in sentence pattern, 111,
   112
Subject-linking verb-subject
   completer pattern, 111,
   112
Subject-verb pattern, 107,
   108
Subject-verb-indirect
   object-direct object
   pattern, 109, 110
Subject-verb-object pattern,
   108, 109
Subjective case
of personal pronoun, 12,
   204, 205
who as, 206
Subordinate clause, 386
Subordinating conjunctions,
   50–52, 371
Suffix, 316, 317, 386
Superlative form, 18–20
in dictionary, 334, 335
Syllables, 386
in dictionary, 332, 333
hyphens dividing words
   into, 272
in spelling, 308, 309
and suffixes, 316, 317
Synonyms, 352, 353, 386
Syntax, 387

T

Table of contents, 329
Teach/learn, 225
Telephones, use of, 294, 295
Tense, 33–35, 387
Their/there/they're, 228, 229

Them/those, 229
This/this here, 229
Those/them/them there, 229
Title page, 329
To/too/two, 230
Topic sentence, 128–130
Topics, 148–152
of informal conversation,
   287
of paragraph, 131, 132
sentence, 128–130
Transitional terms, commas
   with, 255
Try to/try and, 230

U

Underlining, 275, 276, 379
Us/we, 230, 231

V

Verbs, 27–37, 387
active verbs, 197–199
and adverbs, 37–43
agreement of, 185–197
in interrogative sentence,
   103
passive verbs, 197–199
patterns of, 107–112
phrases, 61, 62
predicates, 73, 74
problems with, 197–203
tense of, 33–35
Verbal, 388
Vocabulary, 72, 388
Voice, 388
Vowel, 388

W

We/us, 230, 231
Well, commas setting off,
    255
Well/good, 207, 223, 224
Who/whom, 206, 231

Whose/who's, 231, 232
Will/shall, 228

Y

Yes, commas setting off, 255
Your/you're, 232

TAB KEY INDEX

CORRECTION

SYMBOL	DEFINITION	CHAPTER
ad	adjectives and adverbs	9
adj	adjective	1
adv	adverb	2
agr	agreement of subjects and verbs	9
ap	apostrophe	13
cap	capital letter	11
cl	clause	4
comp	incomplete or false comparison	5
conj	conjunction	2
cxt	context	2
dm	dangling or misplaced modifier	
dn	double negative	9
frag	fragment	5
g	good use	17
glos	glossary	
info	sources of information	16
inj	interjection	2
ital	italics	13
k	awkward sentence	
let	letter writing	8
n	noun	1
nc	not clear	
p	error in punctuation	12, 13
paral	parallelism	
phr	phrase	3

TAB KEY INDEX
(Continued)

CORRECTION SYMBOL	DEFINITION	CHAPTER
plan	planning and writing a composition	7
prep	preposition	2
pro	pronoun	1
ref	reference of pronouns	9
ro	run-on sentence	5
sp	spelling	15
spk	speaking and listening	14
ss	sentence structure	5
verb	verb	2
ww	wrong word	10
¶	paragraph	6
./	period	12
?	question mark	12
!	exclamation mark	12
,/	comma	12
;/	semicolon	13
:/	colon	13
-/	hyphen	13
"/	quotation marks	13
( )	parentheses	13
[ ]	brackets	
—	dash	

GERMANIC
English
Norwegian
Swedish
Danish
Dutch
German

ALBANIAN
Modern Albanian

GREEK
Modern Greek

BALTO-SLAVIC
Polish
Czech
Slovak
Russian

INDO-EUROPEAN
LANGUAGES

INDO-IRANIAN
Modern Persian
Sanskrit
Modern Indian

LATIN
Italian
French
Spanish
Portuguese

CELTIC
Irish
Welsh
Scots
Gaelic

ARMENIAN
Modern Armenian